THE AGE OF INE

THE AGE OF INEQUALITY

Corporate America's War on Working People

A FORTY-YEAR INVESTIGATION
BY *IN THESE TIMES*

VERSO
London • New York

First published by Verso 2017
© *In These Times* 2017
Editor's Introduction © Jeremy Gantz 2017
Contributions © The contributors 2017

1 3 5 7 9 10 8 6 4 2

Verso
UK: 6 Meard Street, London W1F 0EG
US: 20 Jay Street, Suite 1010, Brooklyn, NY 11201
versobooks.com

Verso is the imprint of New Left Books

ISBN-13: 978-1-78663-114-5
ISBN-13: 978-1-78663-115-2 (UK EBK)
ISBN-13: 978-1-78663-116-9 (US EBK)

British Library Cataloguing in Publication Data
A catalogue record for this book is available from the British Library

Library of Congress Cataloging-in-Publication Data
A catalog record for this book is available from the Library of Congress

Typeset in Minion Pro by MJ&N Gavan, Truro, Cornwall
Printed in the US by Maple Press

Contents

Acknowledgments   xiii
Editor's Introduction by Jeremy Gantz   1

PART ONE: GROWING APART

1 Trading Away the Working Class
  Introduction by Kari Lydersen   7
  "Youngstown Steel Plant Deliberately Abandoned"   10
    Daniel Marschall (1977)
  "U.S. Multinationals Make Labor Put on Its Fighting Shoes"   12
    John Judis (1977)
  "Fear and Loathing on the Chrysler Assembly Line"   15
    W. P. Norton (1988)
  "Run for the Border"   17
    David Moberg (1993)
  "Train in Vain"   19
    John Judis (1994)
  "Factory Collapse in Bangladesh Exposes Cracks in the System"   20
    Michelle Chen (2013)
  *"This Small Town Shows Why the Trans-Pacific Partnership Could
    Be a Disaster for American Workers"*   22
    Peter Cole (2015)
  *"Our Choices Aren't Only Xenophobic Nationalism or Neoliberal
    Globalization"*   24
    Leon Fink (2016)

2 The Rich Change the Rules
  Introduction by Rick Perlstein   27
  "The Business of the U.S. Is..."   29
    John Judis (1978)
  "Dems Are Becoming Governing Wing of the GOP"   30
    Manning Marable (1979)
  "Whose Side Are Tax Cutters On?"   31
    John Judis (1981)
  "Reaganomics: One Down, Three to Go"   33
    Richard B. Du Boff (1982)

"The Poor Still Getting Poorer"   34
David Moberg (1984)
"Women's Common Ground"   35
Frances Fox Piven (1984)
"Stuck in the Middle With You"   37
David Futrelle (1993)
"Welcome to New Orleans"   39
David Sirota (2005)
"We Are All Waiters Now"   43
Thomas Geoghegan (2006)
"The Failed Prophet"   45
Sen. Bernie Sanders (2009)
"Oligarchy in the U.S.A."   48
Jeffrey A. Winters (2012)
"Who Is John Galt? Now We Know!"   50
Slavoj Žižek (2013)

3 Busted: The Decline of Unions
Introduction by Nelson Lichtenstein   53
"Labor Movement: Stuck but Stirring"   56
David Moberg (1976)
"Equal Time for Union-Busting Firms"   58
Richard Kazis (1980)
"As PATCO Goes, So Go the Unions"   59
David Moberg (1981)
"Labor's Problems Are the Nation's Problems"   61
Nicholas von Hoffman (1981)
"To Concede or Not to Concede"   62
David Moberg (1982)
"Striking People in a Sticky Situation"   64
David Moberg (1986)
"Working It Out"   66
David Moberg (1993)
"Lexus and the Right to Pee"   67
Barbara Ehrenreich (1999)
"Southern Bellwether"   69
Ian Urbina (2002)
"All Apart Now"   70
David Moberg (2005)
"Symbol of the System"   71
Christopher Hayes (2005)

"Not Your Parents' Labor Movement"   74
David Moberg (2009)
"Capitol Offensive"   76
David Moberg (2011)

4 Blowing Bubbles: The Rise of Finance

Introduction by Dean Baker   79
"Bank Deregulation Threatens Stability"   81
David M. Kotz (1986)
"Bush's S&L Plan Would Make Us Pay Twice"   83
James Weinstein (1989)
"Easy Money"   83
Ralph Nader (1996)
"Easy Money and the Rest of Us"   85
Juan González (1998)
"Enronomics 101"   87
David Moberg (2002)
"Bursting Bubbles: Why the Economy Will Go From Bad to Worse"   88
Dean Baker (2003)
"The Subprime Bait and Switch"   90
Alexander Gourse (2007)
"Killer Credit"   91
Adam Doster (2008)
"The Only Road Out of Crisis"   94
Joseph M. Schwartz (2009)
"A New Strategy to Make the Banks Pay"   95
Laura Gottesdiener (2014)

5 Public Goods, Private Hands

Introduction by Thomas Geoghegan   99
"Central American Refugees for Profit"   101
Dennis Bernstein and Connie Blitt (1986)
"Corporate Caseworkers"   103
Adam Fifield (1997)
"War Profiteering and You"   105
Christopher Hayes (2004)
"Publicopoly Exposed"   107
Beau Hodai (2011)
"Privatizing Government Services Doesn't Only Hurt Public Workers" 110
David Moberg (2014)
"How to Sell Off a City"   112
Rick Perlstein (2015)

6 Welcome to the Precariat
Introduction by Rebecca Burns   115
"Cab Companies Use Leasing to Boost Profits"   117
   David Moberg (1976)
"Marginal Work Is on the Rise as Traditional Jobs Evaporate"   119
   Robert B. Carson (1977)
"Immigrants Sweat It Out in Illegal Garment Factories"   120
   Doug Turetsky (1990)
"Life of Leisure Evading the American Worker?"   121
   David Moberg (1992)
"Temp Slave Revolt"   123
   David Moberg (2000)
"Hey Millennials, Debt Becomes You"   125
   Mischa Gaus (2006)
*"For Disgruntled Young Workers, Lawsuits May Spark Intern
   Insurrection"*   127
   Michelle Chen (2013)
"The Wage-Theft Epidemic"   128
   Spencer Woodman (2013)
"Forever Temp?"   131
   Sarah Jaffe (2014)
"An Udderly Bad Job"   134
   Joseph Sorrentino (2014)
"Domestic Workers Emerging From the Shadows"   136
   Stephen Franklin (2014)
"The Adjunct's Lament"   137
   Rebecca Burns (2014)

INTERLUDE
"In Search of Solidarity"   141
   Christopher Hayes (2006)

PART TWO: PUSHBACK

7 Solidarity Without Borders
Introduction by Michelle Chen   147
"Time Bombs"   150
   Noam Chomsky (1994)
"Making History"   151
   David Bacon (2000)
"Wall Done"   153
   David Graeber (2001)

"Take It to the Streets" 154
Naomi Klein (2001)
"Another World Is Possible" 156
Ben Ehrenreich (2003)
"People vs. Empire" 157
Arundhati Roy (2005)
"Freedom of Movement" 159
Michelle Chen (2009)
"This Land Is Our Land" 160
Micah Uetricht (2010)
"All Over the World, Migrants Demand the Right to Stay at Home" 162
David Bacon (2013)
"No Papers, No Fear" 165
Michelle Chen (2013)
"The Immigration Movement's Left Turn" 166
Michelle Chen (2014)
"Are Open Borders the Solution to the Refugee Crisis?" 167
Michelle Chen (2015)

8 The Black Freedom Struggle, at the Ballot and Beyond
   Introduction by Salim Muwakkil 171
   "Washington Still Has a Hard Row to Hoe" 173
   David Moberg (1983)
   "Jackson's Ascent and the Dynamic of Racism" 175
   Salim Muwakkil (1988)
   *"Advocating Drug Decriminalization a Tough Stand in Black
   Community"* 177
   Salim Muwakkil (1990)
   "Being Black in America: The Quiet Riot Continues" 178
   Donell Alexander (1992)
   "Proud of Obama ... for Now" 180
   Salim Muwakkil (2008)
   "The 'Post-Racial' President" 182
   Salim Muwakkil (2009)
   "From Hope to Disposability" 184
   Martha Biondi (2013)
   *"In Baltimore and Across the Country, Black Faces in High Places
   Haven't Helped Average Black People"* 187
   Keeanga-Yamahtta Taylor (2015)

9 Labor's Fate: New Solutions to Old Problems,
   Old Solutions to New Problems
      Introduction by Micah Uetrich   189
      "Cleaning House"   191
         Zack Nauth (1995)
      "Face-off at UPS"   193
         Jane Slaughter (1997)
      "Too Cruel for School"   194
         David Moberg (2002)
      "Doing It for Themselves"   196
         Mischa Gaus (2007)
      "Democratic to the CORE"   197
         Micah Uetrich and Jasson Perez (2012)
      "Even Without Unions, Walmart Warehouse Employees
         Win Change"   201
         David Moberg (2013)
      "Is Fight for 15 for Real?"   202
         Micah Uetrich (2013)
      "Big Business Aims to Crush Worker Centers"   205
         Micah Uetrich (2013)
      "A Co-op State of Mind"   207
         Ajowa Nzinga Ifateyo (2014)
      "Bringing Back the Strike May Be Our Only Hope"   209
         Shaun Richman (2016)

10 After the Crash: Searching for Alternatives
      Introduction by Frances Fox Piven   211
      "Take the Fight to the Streets"   213
         Stephen Lerner (2011)
      "An Occupy Road Trip"   215
         Arun Gupta (2011)
      "Voices From the Occupation"   217
         Jeremy Gantz (2011)
      "The Violent Silence of a New Beginning"   219
         Slavoj Žižek (2011)
      "No Vacancies: Squatters Move In"   220
         Rebecca Burns (2012)
      "Anti-Foreclosure Activists Put BlackRock in a Hard Place"   222
         Sarah Jaffe (2013)
      "Can Socialists Win Elections in the U.S.?"   223
         Bhaskar Sunkara and Micah Uetrich (2013)

"Bringing Socialism Back"
   Joseph M. Schwartz (2015)
"From Hashtag to Strategy: The Growing Pains of Black Lives M
   Bill Fletcher, Jr. (2015)
"Black Lives Matter Puts Prosecutors on Trial"   229
   Jennifer Ball (2016)
"The Radicalism of Black Lives Matter"   230
   Martha Biondi (2016)

Contributors   235
Index   241

Acknowledgments

This book started as an idea I proposed to *In These Times* editor and publisher Joel Bleifuss during an issue release party in January 2015. That he immediately expressed interest and subsequently allowed me to pass forty years of archives through the filter of my own interests is a testament to his generous spirit.

One of the most satisfying things about editing this book has been how the process reconnected me to *In These Times*, where I once worked as associate editor. Exploring the archives in depth confirmed what I had long assumed: the magazine's coverage was unusually perceptive (and prescient) from the beginning, and money to keep the enterprise going has always been scarce. Seeing founder James Weinstein's full-throated fundraising appeals in so much faded newsprint reminded me that *In These Times* has always been more of a mission than a business. Its relative longevity—most political magazines don't make it to middle age—is proof of its uniquely valuable role on the American Left.

Despite many hours reading the archives, editing this book has hardly been a solitary experience. Many thanks to Diana Finch, *In These Times*' book agent, for helping me turn my ideas into a coherent proposal and then, of course, finding a publisher. Thanks to Rebecca Burns, Micah Uetricht, and especially *In These Times* executive editor Jessica Stites for helping to improve the book's structure, suggesting pieces to include and never ignoring my various requests. Thanks to the other *In These Times* staff members who provided input and feedback: Christopher Hass, Miles Kampf-Lassin, and Ketseeyah Yosef. And thanks to Andy Hsiao at Verso for gently telling me what was missing.

Many thanks to all the *In These Times* interns who collectively helped gather the archival material: Princess-India Alexander, Parker Asmann, Jennifer Ball, Caroline Beck, Tom Burnett, Julia Clark-Riddell, Marc Daalder, Lauren Gaynor, Karen Gwee, Lorenzo Gudino, Rachelle Hampton, Colin Hanner, Dayton Martindale (now an assistant editor at the magazine), Eli Massey, Regina Tanner, and Katie Way. And thanks to

Ron Unz, who generously digitized most of the magazine archives back in 2005.

To all of the magazine's writers, whether in this book or not: thank you for telling stories that matter.

Finally, to Caitlin. Your unwavering support (often in the form of solo parenting) throughout this book's long gestation leaves me without words.

Happy fortieth anniversary, *In These Times*.

Editor's Introduction

JEREMY GANTZ

Inequality is timeless; the danger it poses to any society varies by degree. The title of this book therefore could, I suppose, refer to almost any period of time. A central tension courses throughout the history of the United States, between the promise of equal opportunity—we were all created equal, right?—and the reality of inequality. The great struggles of U.S. history, from the Civil War to the civil rights movement, have at their core been fights over the gap between this promise and reality.

Yet since the late 1970s, as the economy globalized and the rich grew much richer, this gap has widened dramatically. More and more Americans admit this and are refusing to tolerate growing divides as the inevitable cost of globalization. But thirty-five years before the Occupy movement drew the public's attention to a broken system, and forty years before presidential candidates across the political spectrum acknowledged inequality as a problem, *In These Times* was on the case. Launching an "independent socialist weekly," founding editor and publisher James Weinstein looked forward to covering a growing left movement buoyed by the election of Jimmy Carter. Instead, his magazine would chronicle a faltering movement, a newly conservative political era, and the emergence of the country's new gilded age. With a mission to expose the struggles of the powerless, *In These Times* was well positioned to report on a government and economy more and more tilted toward the powerful.

U.S. incomes began growing more unequal in 1979, and money has been flowing upward ever since. Fast-forward nearly forty years, and:

- The richest 1 percent of Americans now own more wealth than the bottom 90 percent.
- The richest .01 percent of Americans controls 22 percent of the wealth, up from 7 percent in the late 1970s.
- The country's median household income (adjusted for inflation) is less today than it was in 1989.

More and more Americans are aware of the wealth disparity that now characterizes the country. But while these numbers make clear who has been winning the class war—as Warren Buffet has said, it's his side—they don't show us how inequality grew since the 1970s and what it felt like to be left behind. They don't show us the lives of striking workers permanently replaced by union-busting companies. They don't show us fast-food workers impoverished by a stagnant minimum wage or the migrant farm laborers making less than that wage. They don't show us the army of "permatemps" and "independent contractors" that corporations have raised to avoid providing the benefits that middle-class Americans once expected as their birthright.

Many books about the growth of inequality illuminate the problem through historical data and research. This book takes a different approach, collecting *In These Times* articles from the last forty years to show why the country became so unequal so quickly—and how people pushed back against this trend. Think of it as a real-time narrative of a still-unfolding man-made disaster: a history of the present. In the introductions to each chapter, longtime contributors and current editors reflect on the view from 2017.

Part One examines the causes and effects of growing inequality. These include a globalizing economy and free trade agreements, which have decimated U.S. manufacturing jobs (Chapter 1); a government increasingly tilted toward the wealthy (Chapter 2); and the decline of the labor movement, a singular bulwark of the middle class (Chapter 3). The rise of the financial industry and deregulation are the subject of Chapter 4, while Chapter 5 looks at privatization, an often-overlooked culprit abetted by the same free market fetishization on display in preceding chapters. Finally, Chapter 6 captures what all this has meant for many U.S. workers: precarity.

"In Search of Solidarity," Christopher Hayes' interlude following Part One, underscores that movements for change are built upon a sense of shared struggle. While the idea of solidarity has become increasingly anachronistic in recent decades, many people have refused to accept inequality. In Part Two, we focus on those who have pushed for change—struggles that *In These Times* has reported from the front lines, providing an inside take on movements as they unfolded.

Intensifying globalization has both undermined and heightened the power of borders, sparking transnational solidarity and protest. Chapter 7 focuses on the global justice (antiglobalization) and migrant rights movements. In the United States, as elsewhere, race and class are inescapably intertwined. African Americans, hamstrung by the legacies of slavery and the Jim Crow era, have long borne the brunt of growing economic inequality. Their struggles against uniquely violent oppression prompt Chapter 8, which focuses on the course of the black freedom movement since the early 1980s. We look at the mixed record of that movement's electoral focus, along with how black leaders have responded to the pernicious effects of the "war on drugs." Chapter 9 looks at strategies and tactics for building worker power that have emerged in recent decades—some of them novel, others a return to the militancy that defined the labor movement's early history. Finally, Chapter 10 focuses on movements and political campaigns that have challenged our unequal order since the recent financial crash exposed the economy for what it is: broken. From Occupy to Black Lives Matter to Bernie Sanders, radical change is starting to look more attractive to many.

Although more than one hundred articles are collected here—virtually all condensed from their original versions—this book is by no means a greatest hits collection. The breadth and depth of *In These Times* coverage has always extended far beyond ground covered here, which is just one path through rich archives comprising the news of the day.

If reversing inequality is the great challenge of our time, then the great mystery of our time is why so many people for so long seemed to accept a new reality that demands more work for less money. James Weinstein offered a big clue in the magazine's inaugural issue in 1976. "Capitalism is the unspoken reality of American politics," he wrote. "That is the one thing the major parties agree upon: Praise capitalism (not too often and preferably by another name) but don't discuss it. Preclude serious discussion of the central reality of our times."

In recent years the reality of American politics and inequality is being articulated more and more. The Occupy and Black Lives Matter movements and the surreal ruptures of the 2016 presidential election season are signs that our age of inequality has, in a sense, come of age. In very different ways, and with tragically different outcomes, the campaigns of Bernie Sanders and Donald Trump served notice that the status quo is untenable. Both exposed growing divides for what they are: not the natural order of things, but rather the result of how we choose to create and regulate markets, and how we choose to treat those living within them. The toxic rise of Trump, who with stunning success articulated the anger felt by many Americans left behind by a changing economy, cannot be separated from obscene levels of inequality. His victory will likely compound a great tragedy of our time, that growing disaffection with a ruling elite can be weaponized to maim the very thing most able to spread prosperity: the government. But action is the antidote to despair—and as the second half of this book shows, people across the country are working to build egalitarian movements. Change is coming—the question is what kind.

PART ONE

GROWING APART

CHAPTER ONE

Trading Away the Working Class

INTRODUCTION

By Kari Lydersen

On Chicago's Southeast Side, there sits a huge, mostly empty expanse on the shores of Lake Michigan. The only structures rising amid the tall grass and trees are a small brick former union hall and a pair of crumbling "ore walls" stretching toward the lake. But this land was once teeming with people and pulsing with sound and light. It was U.S. Steel's South Works plant, employing 30,000 people at its height and supporting countless families in the once-thriving surrounding neighborhoods.

Today those neighborhoods are depopulated. After hemorrhaging jobs in the 1970s and 1980s, the plant had effectively closed by 1992. Ambitious plans for a sprawling residential and commercial development on the site were canceled in 2016 for lack of investment. For the foreseeable future it will likely remain a forlorn monument to the loss of good-paying unionized manufacturing jobs, and the economic and social devastation that follows. Similar sites exist across the country, in places like Bethlehem, Pennsylvania; Youngstown, Ohio; and Galesburg, Illinois. The latter two towns are spotlighted in this chapter's opening and penultimate pieces, respectively.

The sharp decline of the U.S. steel industry was triggered by the appearance of cheaper imports in the 1970s. This dynamic, which had been gutting other manufacturing sectors like apparel and electronics for years, accelerated as markets continued globalizing and politicians failed to erect trade barriers. The country's auto industry also struggled to compete with imports; "Fear and Loathing on the Chrysler Assembly Line" shows what a plant closing looked like on the ground. In 1970, manufacturing made up about 25 percent of total U.S. employment; in 2013, it was 8.8 percent.

Of course, the implementation of the North American Free Trade Agreement (NAFTA) in 1994 didn't help, as David Moberg notes in "Run for the Border." More agreements followed, such as the Central American

Free Trade Agreement and the (unratified as of late 2016) Trans-Pacific Partnership, even as NAFTA's disastrous impacts became clear. U.S. manufacturers automated plants or just moved operations abroad. Even when plants didn't move overseas, the threat that they might gave employers the upper hand over unions and workers. Strikes were replaced by concessions. For most laid-off workers, federally-backed Trade Adjustment Assistance and retraining programs were too little, too late, as John Judis explains in "Train in Vain."

It is impossible to quantify the economic and social impact on American society of the loss of manufacturing jobs. Far more than union locals have disappeared. So has the idea that an average young person—even one with only a high-school education—can confidently look forward to a stable career that supports a family and funds retirement.

But something deeper and more pernicious has occurred with the country's industrial decline during the last forty years. The idea that an American is entitled to a clear path to stable, decent-paid work has been gutted. The climate of instability, fear, and transience that has arisen in the wake of the manufacturing crash has meant not only plummeting rates of union membership; it has also eroded the culture of collective struggle, replacing it with individual desperation and competition.

The recent economic crisis shredded the last vestiges of economic stability and opportunity for many families and communities already squeezed by the collapse of the manufacturing economy. It caused more closures and layoffs among the manufacturers still in business, but it also provided convenient cover for employers already planning to slash their workforces or move operations. More than 2 million manufacturing jobs were lost during the recession starting in 2008. During the tail end of President Barack Obama's first term, there was hopeful talk of "reshoring"—companies like Nike, Target, and Master Lock bringing jobs back to the United States. Thousands of manufacturing jobs were reportedly "reshored" in 2014, driven by rising wages and currency values in China and quality concerns about products made there. The movement was also, ironically, bolstered by the increasingly "competitive" nature of U.S. labor—meaning lower wages and benefits than in years past (in inflation-adjusted dollars), and less need for people altogether due to automation.

In recent years, President Obama, regional leaders, and manufacturing employers have touted high-tech manufacturing as the future, pointing to the promise of 3D printing, clean energy, and flexible hybrid electronics, among others. But it's doubtful that these hyped sectors can generate positions equal to the number of downwardly mobile former "low-tech" manufacturing workers.

So can there ever be a real renaissance of manufacturing in the United States, tapping new technology and offering stable, decently paid union jobs? It's an open question. The aforementioned bright spots pale beside the continued loss of manufacturing jobs due to free trade, automation, and other factors. The country lost a net 5 million manufacturing jobs between 2000 and 2014. Multinational corporations are freer than ever to search abroad for the cheapest wages, a dynamic *In These Times* highlighted back in 1977 in "U.S. Multinationals Make Labor Put on Its Fighting Shoes." When rising Chinese wages cut into profits, companies head to places like Bangladesh. The results can be fatal, as Michelle Chen makes clear in "Factory Collapse in Bangladesh Exposes Cracks in the System."

What is clear is that as manufacturing has declined, exacerbating inequality, American workers have grown alienated and angry. Watch the YouTube video of the president of Carrier Corporation informing employees at an Indianapolis plant in February 2016 that they would all lose their jobs because the company was moving operations to Mexico. Amid boos and jeers, one terse response can be heard: "Fuck you."

Versions of this scene have occurred in thousands of U.S. factories during the last 20 years; we can expect to see the scene replay again and again. This is why, last year, the issue of trade took on a prominence not seen since the 1992 presidential campaign; it's a large part of what powered the unexpected success of Bernie Sanders and Donald Trump. The GOP nominee's anti-free trade stance was laced with xenophobic nationalism—which needn't be the only alternative to the dominant neoliberal trade regime, as Leon Fink notes in his contribution to this chapter. But whether or not the trade status quo changes, in the years ahead we're likely to see more politicians appealing to the wounded psyches of millions of Americans left abandoned by a shifting economy to fend for themselves.

Donald Gorobegko is one of those Americans. A fifty-eight-year-old veteran and machinist who once made $45 an hour at union jobs, he now struggles to find temporary work paying $10 an hour. He often spends his days in the Chicago Public Library filling out job applications. Gorobegko is among the many people who live in a makeshift encampment of the dispossessed on the Near South Side of Chicago, between the river and the railroads that once transported manufactured goods across the land.

"If we could organize, we could take this country back," Gorobegko said one cold winter day beside his tent. "This is supposed to be the greatest country in the world. What happened to that?"

"YOUNGSTOWN STEEL PLANT DELIBERATELY ABANDONED"

By Daniel Marschall (1977)

Youngstown, Ohio—At the heart of the Mahoning River Valley in Ohio lies the Campbell Works of Youngstown Sheet and Tube Co., a reddish, pulsating mass of blast furnaces, coke ovens, open hearths, and rolling mills that occupies over one hundred acres along the river.

For factory workers here, producing steel is not just a nine-to-five job, but a source of pride and a way of life that begins at the mill and extends into the neighborhood bar, the corner church, and the local union hall.

Despite warning signs, few expected that it could perish so abruptly.

The fatal announcement came on September 19, 1977—"Black Monday" —when the Lykes Corp., a shipping/mining/manufacturing conglomerate based in New Orleans, decided to close most of its steelmaking facilities around Youngstown, dumping 5,000 out of 8,500 workers.

The corporation charged that foreign steel imports and environmental controls necessitated the shutdown. But conversations with steelworkers, local political figures, and lower-level union officials reveal that their decision was actually the last step in a series of moves by Lykes that had steadily drained profits and investment from the Youngstown operations to other parts of their business.

"The day after the announcement, there was a blood donors drive in Campbell," says Duane Irving, a young grievanceman in United Steel Workers Local 1418. "People said they wished Lykes were here now so they could draw blood from them like they took it from us."

Two weeks after the company's sudden decree, the residents of Campbell and Struthers—the two towns surrounding the mill—were still stunned and discouraged. The term "ghost town" was used to describe the region's economic future.

TOTAL HATRED

Shirley Richards had heard it all. A stocky, blond-haired woman, she operates "Shirley's Place," a tiny tavern up the hill from the main entrance of the Campbell Works and across the street from the split-level union hall of United Steelworkers (USW) Local 2163.

She blames both union and management for the problem and resents the callous refusal of the Carter administration to help. "People had an inkling something like this was coming, but still thought that it would be years before it all went to hell. Their first reaction was shock, then bewilderment, and then anger. Their attitude towards Lykes: total hatred," she explains.

Mismanagement at the "upper echelons" of Lykes is primarily responsible, according to Andy Ragan, a first helper in an open-hearth furnace. "They just let the place go to hell. They took all the money and put in nothing for improvements."

Middle-aged men like Ragan will be particularly hard hit; they're too old to readily find another job, too young to qualify for a pension, and usually have a family to support and a home mortgage to pay. He worked in the mill for twenty-nine years, nine months, and twenty-two days and thus may not even be eligible for his thirty-year pension.

Wilford Brown, a twenty-five-year-old black man, had labored there for seven years as an electrician in open-hearth maintenance. Unlike many of his fellow workers, he has been promised a chemical plant job in Headline, Alabama, and is happy at the chance to leave the area. "There's no future here and we all knew it. You could see it coming," he says.

"The first five years, we were working steady. Then we were off all the time and things began to fall apart. In the last few years they've cut expenses in every department by scrapping machines and offing people. It was like the difference between night and day.

"They drained this place to the extent that everything needs to be worked on. I've seen breakdowns where foremen told me to go make the parts myself. They stopped keeping the machines clean—there was oil and grease all over the place. The company just ran it until it fell apart, and now they're throwing it away. This place is dead—everything but the casket."

The union, in close cooperation with the steel industry, is pushing for higher import quotas. At one press conference, Youngstown's mayor wondered whether the United States had really won the Second World War, and a local union officer proposed a campaign to encourage local housewives to wear buttons with the slogan: "I'm shopping for American products."

Not all officials are satisfied with the union's current efforts, however. Russell Baxter, president of Local 2163, is infuriated at the lies of company representatives, the inaction of international officers, and the empty rhetoric of the governor and other politicians. "Lloyd McBride [USW president] cares no more for 5,000 people than the man in the moon," he declares. Two-thirds of his local will be wiped out by the layoffs.

Weeks before the announcement, Baxter and other union officials were assured by the company that rumors of a shutdown were "categorically false."

Campbell Mayor Mike Katula, whose father and grandfather worked in the mills, hopes to compel Lykes to fulfill its obligation to local residents by at least tearing down the vacant plants and donating the property to the town for new industry.

"What we're dealing with is a multifaceted corporation," he says. "They don't care about people. All they're looking for is profits. They deal with industries like pieces on a checker board. Lykes milked this plant dry and put the profits elsewhere. Now they're getting rid of the cow."

"U.S. MULTINATIONALS MAKE LABOR PUT ON ITS FIGHTING SHOES"

By John Judis (1977)

Next to the extension of slavery, it was the main issue that divided the North and the South before the Civil War. In the last decade of the twentieth century, it may be the main issue that divides capital and labor.

In 1978, it will probably be the main issue that divides President Jimmy Carter and labor.

The issue is that of free trade versus protectionism: in present terms, whether the United States should make the elimination of all trade barriers its first priority, or whether it should pass tariffs or impose quotas to protect the jobs of American workers that might be lost from rising foreign imports.

In April 1977, thousands of garment workers demonstrated around the country to demand import controls on foreign garments and textiles, whose share of the American market has risen from 4 to 35 percent in the last ten years. According to union officials, these rising imports have cost American workers 145,000 jobs.

Prior to that, labor leaders had vigorously protested President Carter's refusal to go along with the International Trade Commission's recommendation that import quotas and tariffs be imposed on rising shoe imports.

In the months to come, Carter will be faced with demands for import controls on color TVs, steel, and rubber products. Indications suggest that he will go to great lengths to avoid acceding to these demands.

PREVENTING ECONOMIC CHAOS

In the past, American labor and industry usually agreed on trade questions. Beginning in the early nineteenth century, they united in support of tariffs that they saw as necessary to protect infant American industries from foreign competition. Then, after the Second World War, with American industry the most advanced in the world, they turned to free trade as essential for American growth.

Both capital and labor believed that postwar policy must aim to prevent trading blocs and to eliminate all tariffs and quotas. Within such a "free" world market, American goods would hold a competitive edge, and exports would rise.

Rising exports would provide needed security against another depression. "Foreign trade," as a United Auto Workers statement put it, "can be the margin between a drop into economic chaos and a steadily expanding economy."

But between 1962 and 1970, a sharp turnabout occurred. While labor has by no means abandoned its support for free trade, it has come to insist on protection for industries jeopardized by free trade policies rather than simply on compensation for workers whose jobs were lost.

Three things have shaken labor's confidence in free trade. The first is the ability, largely unforeseen in 1962, of European and Japanese firms to compete successfully with American firms in such highly touted American fields as steel, auto, and electronics.

The second is the rise of the multinational corporations. American firms have gone multinational largely in search of lower wage costs. The president of Zenith, the last American electronics firm to go overseas for its component production, explained that the same TV that costs $56 in labor to build in the United States costs $4.50 in Taiwan. A shoe manufacturer who moved his plant to Europe gave the House Ways and Means Committee a similar explanation: "The labor where I am now making shoes is 50 cents an hour as compared to the $3 I was paying."

The American Federation of Labor and Congress of Industrial Organizations (AFL-CIO) estimates that as many as 900,000 American workers lost their jobs between 1966 and 1971 as a result of multinational expansion. These multinationals end up competing, on favorable terms, with domestically produced products.

From labor's standpoint, this role of the multinational subverts the function of free trade. No longer is it possible to argue that free trade merely weeds out the less efficient firms that cannot compete with the better organized and more technologically advanced ones. With multinationals, free trade tends to weed out organized workers who have won higher standards of living.

As a result, labor has moved both to place restrictions in the path of American corporations that want to relocate overseas and to put import controls against goods produced by American and foreign multinationals.

Finally, the third factor that changed labor's view has been the world recession. With unemployment in the United States over 8 percent, the special compensation given to workers displaced by imports becomes, in many cases, merely a prelude to welfare.

FEAR OF A TRADE WAR

But the same circumstances that have impelled American labor to oppose unlimited free trade have made corporate leaders and their political allies all the more adamant in its defense.

This is clearly the case with the growth of multinationals. The multinationals have a stake in preventing any import restrictions on their products. With Japanese and German investors vying for favors, they also are concerned that American trade policies not alienate their host countries.

The world recession, combined with growing competition from West Germany and Japan, has meanwhile raised among corporate leaders the specter of a new trade war. They see the threat of a return to the 1930s in the recently successful attempt to get the U.S. Customs Court to declare countervailing duties against Japanese TV imports that owe their low price to government tax rebates.

Corporate leaders see any step toward tariffs or formal quotas as a dangerous precedent that could justify further action. Therefore, they advocate private agreements, where necessary, between the United States and other countries, and increased technical and financial aid to embattled American industries.

In this respect, as in others, Carter is the representative of America's most class-conscious corporate leadership rather than of the labor or minority voters who elected him. In his decision to reject quotas and a tariff on shoe imports, Carter spelled out his position: "I'm very reluctant to restrict international trade in any way. For forty years, the United States has worked for the reduction of trade barriers around the world, and we are continuing to pursue this goal because it's the surest long-range way to create jobs here and abroad."

Carter did promise to attempt to reach private agreements with Taiwan and South Korea to limit their exports. But he insisted that "over the long haul" the only solution to the American shoe industry's difficulties lay in the modernization of its factories.

That, and the reintroduction of child labor.

"Fear and Loathing on the Chrysler Assembly Line"

By W. P. Norton (1988)

Kenosha, Wisconsin—Thick in the air outside Freddy's bar is that stinging industrial smell common to company towns. Inside, the bar is decorated with all the usual paraphernalia of working-class taverns: ceremonial swords and rifles on the walls, illustrations of muskie and walleye pike on the mirrors.

Also hanging on display is a T-shirt that expresses many patrons' sentiments about the Chrysler Corporation's imminent pullout from its auto plant here: "[Chrysler CEO] Lee Iacocca says we're #"—and instead of the numeral one is an extended middle finger.

The bartender, Fran, has been serving beer and food at Freddy's for more than nineteen years. She speaks of the auto plant's scheduled December 19 closing, when Chrysler shuts its doors to all but 1,000 of the 6,500 men and women who work there now. "I don't know what all them people are gonna do," she says between puffs of a Marlboro Light. "There's gonna be a lot of depression around here."

Plant Gate 15 faces the bar, and a handful of workers begin to straggle over at about 2:30 a.m., when the first shift gets off. The talk inside is mostly centered on one subject—what will happen after the plant shuts down.

Kenosha boasts the oldest auto-manufacturing plant in the United States. Cars first rolled off the lines at the Nash Motors plant in 1903. By 1954, when the American Motors Corporation (AMC) was created out of a series of mergers, the auto plant had become an economic magnet. The popular Rambler model was made there, as well as the Jeep.

But when AMC threatened a shutdown in 1987, it was feared the plant's 6,500 employees would lose their jobs. Then the Chrysler Corporation bought AMC and promised to keep the plant at full strength through 1992. But in January 1988—just months after its initial promise—Chrysler announced that it was prepared to pull out of most of its Kenosha facilities by September. A negotiated agreement later delayed the pullout until December 19.

The End of a Story

Robert Petsin is fifty-three years old. He mechanically recites the date he was hired at the American Motors auto plant here—October 10, 1960. He still wears a small red-white-and-blue AMC patch on the left shoulder of his beat-up denim jacket. It is a remnant of the good years.

The oft-repeated story of American life during the postwar boom years was acted out again and again in this company town: high school graduation, maybe a hitch in the military, and then a job at the plant, where the pay was good; you could raise a family.

Like many who come to Freddy's, Petsin has lived that story for most of his life. He married, raised three children, put two of them through college, made the mortgage and car payments. In many ways, he is a typical figure in this slice of Americana: union man, Republican during the Reagan era's glory days in the early '80s, drinker of Old Style beer.

He will quit work in two years and draw more than $300 a week for the rest of his life, in addition to health benefits and insurance. He is among the lucky ones who, by virtue of age and seniority, will not be forced into the unemployment line or a job at the local fast-food franchise come December 19.

Still he is angry, and he is not alone. "There's a lot of bitter people here," he says. "It's gonna have a very devastating effect on the city of Kenosha, which is hanging by the skin of its teeth anyway."

Petsin blasts city and county officials and Governor Tommy G. Thompson for refusing to press a lawsuit against Chrysler this past September. The unprecedented suit would have sought to keep the corporation from closing the plant.

"You can't blame us people for being bitter at Iacocca," Petsin, an inspector, says. "This city could have expanded. We're gonna be left out in no man's land with the rest of the world passing us by. I feel sorry for the younger generation that has devoted ten or twenty years of their lives to this town. What the hell are they gonna do? A lot of people are gonna either have to take welfare or move on. I'm bitter but mostly for the people who are gonna suffer. I'll survive."

THE PULLOUT'S PRICE

What isn't commonly known or even agreed on is the precise scope of the damage the pullout will cause to the local economy. But there are some estimates, most of them grim. According to a union-commissioned report issued this spring by the Chicago-based Midwest Center for Labor Research, the settlement package will do little to offset the disastrous social and economic costs Kenosha will pay long after the plant shuts down. The report says that for each Chrysler worker who loses a job, an additional 1.78 workers in associated jobs will eventually be let go.

Moreover, the closing will cost government $209 million—or $38,000 for each unemployed Chrysler worker—in welfare and unemployment benefits, along with lost taxes, for the first two years after the shutdown. Rates are predicted to surge in the areas of crime, suicide, spouse and child abuse, drug and alcohol addiction, and murder. Also predicted to rise are stress-related diseases such as ulcers, high blood pressure, heart attacks, insomnia, and mental disorders.

Next door to Freddy's is Freddy's East. Inside sits a man who just got off the first shift. "I think they sold us down the river," he says about the United Auto Workers leadership. A number of union officers will indeed remain on the job for the full five years of remaining production, "They were looking out for their interests long before they were looking out for us. It's just politics."

Longtime plant worker Jesse Sewell agrees. "The union ain't worth two cents," he says. "They gave us a dirty deal all along." Such grim talk about the organization that fought to bring average wages to the $14 an hour level is not all that surprising. It is human nature to lay blame in times of frustration, and Lee Iacocca does not make it down to Kenosha often enough to take any of the flak for the corporation's imminent move.

At Freddy's, the T-shirt with its symbolic hand gesture is another way for the displaced workers to deal with that frustration. A bit of humor helps to make the best of things when hard times come. A man tells the story of how the governor came to the bar not too long ago.

"I gave Tommy Thompson that shirt," the man says. "I told him to wear it the next time he negotiates with Chrysler. He just laughed."

"Run for the border"

By David Moberg (1993)

President Bill Clinton's choice of a salesman for the North American Free Trade Agreement (NAFTA) gives a clue as to why the Democrats are in trouble. It also demonstrates why Clinton embraces an agreement hurriedly negotiated for former President George H. W. Bush's re-election campaign.

Lawyer William Daley is the Chicago mayor's brother, but above all he is a high-stakes fundraiser for the Democratic Party. Implicitly or explicitly, Daley will convey the message to wavering members of Congress: big corporate political money is behind NAFTA; ignore it at your peril.

Nonetheless, both the core of the Democratic Party and much of the country as a whole oppose the Canadian–Mexican–U.S. trade pact. On most trade issues, only the Washington lobbyists and corporate money are relevant, but "this is an issue where members of Congress are listening to what people have to say at home," argues former Representative Jim Jontz, head of the anti-NAFTA Citizens Trade Campaign.

To placate core Democrats, Clinton had promised during the campaign to deal with shortcomings in NAFTA by negotiating labor, environment, and agricultural "side" agreements to supplement the original pact. Farmers were soon dropped altogether. Now the labor and environment side agreements have been revealed to have no teeth. They barely have gums. The labor agreements even retreat from protections under current trade law.

The side agreements are important because there is widespread fear that U.S. firms will take advantage of NAFTA to shift investment south of the border, exploiting workers and ravaging the environment in Mexico while leaving U.S. workers without jobs. The record of U.S. firms along the border in the *maquiladora* factories, where workers typically make $1.60 an hour and the environment has become what the American Medical Association describes as a "cesspool," gives ample grounds for concern.

More ominously, the corporate threat of moving jobs, as well as NAFTA's rules prohibiting trade barriers, may be used to drive down wages and weaken environmental protection in the United States.

The labor side agreement is even weaker than the environmental accord. The preamble commits all three parties to uphold the right to form unions, to bargain, and to strike. Yet the weak enforcement mechanism applies only to persistent failure to enforce laws on health and safety, child labor, and minimum wages. This leaves out the heart of labor rights, which have been suppressed as a matter of national economic policy in Mexico and, to a lesser extent, in the United States.

Through this labor side agreement, Clinton "has given the U.S. government imprimatur of approval to a Mexican labor relations system that continues the abuse of worker rights in Mexico," argues Jerome Levinson, former general counsel to the Inter-American Development Bank.

Indeed, the side agreements take precedence over existing trade laws, all of which permit punitive trade and investment sanctions when international labor rights are violated. "Instead of being an historic step forward, it's a substantial step backward from the enforcement power currently available," argues American Federation of Labor and Congress of Industrial Organizations (AFL-CIO) trade economist Mark Anderson.

The weak labor enforcement—and total avoidance of key labor rights issues—stand in dramatic contrast to the protection of intellectual property rights, such as patents and copyrights. NAFTA sets new international standards of protection and does not rely on enforcement of domestic law. And rather than show a persistent pattern of failed enforcement, a

U.S. multinational only needs to show one infraction by a Mexican company. "If a company hires children or dumps toxic wastes," Economic Policy Institute economist Thea Lee notes, "I have to show it happened many times and that it hurt my ability to compete." But if there is a single copyright violation of a videocassette, for example, NAFTA can be invoked to stop goods at the border, confiscate the tapes and even the factory without compensation, force compensation for lost profits, and get reimbursement of legal fees.

Clinton had a chance to refashion NAFTA into an agreement that would have strengthened rights and raised incomes for workers and set new standards for environmental protection across the continent. Over the long term, that would have also improved prospects for jobs in all three countries. NAFTA, even with the new side accords, remains a triumph for corporate interests. If U.S. job growth remains weak, NAFTA will politically haunt Clinton and the Democrats who support it for years to come.

"Train in vain"

By John Judis (1994)

Washington, D.C.—Retraining for dislocated workers has become the clarion call of the Clinton administration's program on jobs and wages. It's the answer to workers who feel the White House doesn't care about runaway factories or about the growing disparity between economic classes. It's also the answer to liberal critics who charge that the administration has betrayed its promise of public investment.

According to Secretary of Labor Robert Reich, retraining is designed to accomplish two important objectives. First, it is supposed to provide better, higher-wage jobs for workers who lose their jobs because of imports, the North American Free Trade Agreement, automation, or corporate downsizing. Second, it is expected to generally reduce unemployment by allowing workers to satisfy the rising demand for highly skilled employees.

But the administration may be vastly overstating the importance of retraining—both in its ability to increase the wages of dislocated workers and to mute the threat of structural unemployment.

Reich says, "All of the studies show that if you get long-term training, a year or more, you're going to affect your future incomes by increasing that future income by an average of 5 to 6 percent."

In fact, most studies show exactly the opposite of what the labor secretary claims: they demonstrate that retraining has little effect in raising wages.

THE SKILLS GAP FALLACY

Reich and the administration's argument is also based on a broader fallacy about the relation between wages and training. Reich argues that the growing wage gap between workers with only high school educations and workers with college diplomas is caused by a mismatch of skills: too many semi-skilled workers are seeking too few jobs, while too few college-educated workers are available for positions that require advanced training.

But the theory doesn't fit the reality of jobs and wages. It's a gross oversimplification to deduce that the growing salary gap between high school- and college-educated workers means that a laid-off forty-five-year-old worker can substantially raise his or her salary by taking one year of intensive training. In reality, that middle-aged worker will be competing in the job market against twenty-year-olds who require fewer benefits, are subject to fewer illnesses and disabilities, and are likely to be capable of working longer shifts and more days.

Even on a more general level, Reich's argument doesn't fit the facts. First, there has not been—and will not be—a surplus of high-skill jobs awaiting workers who undergo training.

Retraining is far from futile, and there are many reasons to go to college besides vocational education. But by imputing miracles to education and retraining, the administration is avoiding its responsibility to create jobs for workers and not merely to create workers for jobs.

"FACTORY COLLAPSE IN BANGLADESH EXPOSES CRACKS IN THE SYSTEM"

By Michelle Chen (2013)

There are few ways to make a decent living in Bangladesh, but many ways to die trying. The cruel weight of that reality bore down on a Dhaka factory complex on April 24 as it crashed to the ground and instantly extinguished hundreds of lives and livelihoods. The final body count at Rana Plaza: 1,130.

While families struggle to identify the dead, activists have begun to investigate the aftermath. They've uncovered a slew of multinational labels associated with Rana: U.S.-based The Children's Place and Walmart, France's Tex (Carrefour brand), Benetton, Spain's Mango, and Canada's Joe Fresh, Germany's NKD, and others.

Some workers had reported a crack in the building's edifice shortly before the incident, but their warnings went ignored. Some were told to report to work anyway or risk losing a month's wages. With minimum pay set below $40 per month (about the retail price of a typical sweater they might produce), workers could ill afford to be concerned about their safety. So they followed orders and reported to what would be for many their last day of work.

Family members scoured for any sign of loved ones amid the rubble, while rescue workers used a strip of fabric as a makeshift "slide" for bodies. The scene of carnage captured the peculiarly dehumanizing nature of the global manufacturing system.

Workers and their communities are reduced to anonymous bodies while profit continues to flow smoothly to Benetton, The Children's Place, and Joe Fresh. Catastrophes like the building collapse or factory fires or the everyday, low-grade disasters of poverty—all that suffering is welded to the profit structure, occasionally papered over with token "corporate social responsibility" and "ethical sourcing" programs.

Perhaps the most tragic aspect of the building collapse is that the factory workers could have been heroes had they had the power to act on the warning signs they had spotted earlier on. If they had the support of a union, they might have collectively refused to report to work until the hazard was addressed. But since Bangladesh's garment sector has virulently blockaded and squelched union organizing, their vigilance could not protect against, but merely portend, their fate.

The anti-union environment girds the brutal manufacturing structure that imposes a feverish pace of production on workers, many of them impoverished young women. The production chain is further lubricated by the geographic distance of the companies placing the order, which gives U.S.- and Europe-based brands "plausible deniability" when these man-made accidents erupt in the global South.

While companies feign ignorance and puzzlement over "what went wrong" at Rana, they've already proven that they're well aware of the root problem. They shipped their manufacturing overseas specifically to avoid protective regulations and thus keep overhead and labor costs unfathomably cheap. Conversely, corporations could reverse this vicious trade-off between rights and profits by investing heavily to improve working conditions and strengthen safety enforcement, as well as monitoring under a program like the Bangladesh safety agreement. But that would mean expending the very same resources that they'd worked so hard to hoard by contracting with the cheapest and most dangerous workplaces in the world.

The cracks in the manufacturing system are showing. As workers grimly await the next tragedy, the world will ignore their warnings at its peril.

"THIS SMALL TOWN SHOWS WHY THE TRANS-PACIFIC PARTNERSHIP COULD BE A DISASTER FOR AMERICAN WORKERS"

By Peter Cole (2015)

Every time politicians look to pass a new free trade agreement like the Trans-Pacific Partnership (TPP), they reassure the American people that this time around, workers will be protected. But the experience of a small industrial town in Illinois reveals that "free trade" has been a nightmare for most of the American people. Galesburg, Illinois—which happens to have a long connection to President Barack Obama—is a poster child for why free trade deals are a problem rather than a solution to the precarious reality experienced by most working- and middle-class Americans.

In 1994, President Bill Clinton worked largely with Republicans in Congress to pass the North American Free Trade Agreement (NAFTA) that drastically reduced tariffs and other "trade barriers" intended to spur greater cross-border trade and investment. However, as billionaire-turned-presidential candidate Ross Perot famously said at the time, "If this agreement is signed as it is currently drafted, the next thing you will hear will be a giant sucking sound as the remainder of our manufacturing jobs—what's left after the two million that went to Asia in the 1980s—get pulled across our southern border."

Sadly for American workers, Perot—and the Democratic congressional majority who voted against the treaty—were right. President Obama has admitted that NAFTA resulted in massive job losses for American workers when corporations made the economically rational choice and moved production to Mexico.

Now, for the past few years and almost entirely in secret, the Obama administration has been negotiating with a dozen other Pacific Rim nations to create a mammoth new "free trade" zone. The administration asserts that the TPP will "expand opportunity for American workers, farmers, ranchers, and businesses." Of course, Obama claims the TPP will be different than NAFTA: that all the corporations that could benefit from lower wages in another nation have already left and that this treaty's labor and environmental provisions will be better enforced.

Galesburg's post-NAFTA decline suggests cause for alarm. Shortly after the deal's passage, Maytag announced it would move its plant there to Mexico. Though it took the company another decade to completely shut down its Galesburg facility, Maytag's announcement sent shock waves through the town. As Maytag worker Carol Marshall told me in 2005, "Both my parents worked at Maytag, my grandfather, my aunt, my uncle. I used to joke that it kept our family off the welfare rolls."

Understandably, the nearly 2,000 workers employed there suspected they would never find as good of a job. The rest of the community also feared the worst as those good-paying Maytag jobs helped the economy of the entire community, county, and surrounding areas.

The effects of Maytag's departure were immediate. Unemployment increased drastically. House construction dropped to nearly zero and the real estate market froze. Erin Nelson, another Maytag worker, lamented that she immediately lost her health insurance. "Who can afford antibiotics that are $70 for twenty-eight pills?" Ten years on, Galesburg's poverty level has increased to 19 percent.

At the 2004 Democratic National Convention, Obama famously declared that Americans have "more work to do for the workers I met in Galesburg, Illinois, who are losing their union jobs at the Maytag plant that's moving to Mexico, and now they're having to compete with their own children for jobs that pay seven bucks an hour." He had visited the town some months earlier, not long before the last refrigerator rolled off the assembly line.

Less than a year later, he gave a speech at Knox College and said something similar: "Here in Galesburg, you know what this new challenge is. You've seen it. You see it when you drive by the old Maytag plant around lunchtime and no one walks out anymore. I saw it during the campaign when I met the union guys who used to work at the plant and now wonder what they're gonna do at fifty-five-years-old without a pension or health care; when I met the man whose son needs a new liver but doesn't know if he can afford when the kid gets to the top of the transplant list."

Even then, Obama gave hints that his "solution" would be more of what Clinton had to offer: embracing corporate-driven globalization. Technology had changed the world, he said: "Today, accounting firms are emailing your tax returns to workers in India who will figure them out and send them back as fast as any worker in Illinois or Indiana could."

Fast forward to 2013, when Obama returned to Galesburg to champion another of his efforts to renew America's middle class. He acknowledged that the town had suffered: "What had swept through a lot of towns throughout the Midwest and Northeast had happened in Galesburg, where people were left high and dry." As a result, the "tax base had declined, unemployment had soared, a lot of folks out of work; the jobs that replaced them generally were jobs that paid a much lower wage."

All true. Alas, it was not clear what Obama's solution was to their plight—the plight of millions of other Americans, too.

Now, in 2015, it seems Obama's solution doesn't differ much from Clinton's and his Republican allies: just substitute TPP for NAFTA. How

TPP will help Galesburg residents find good-paying jobs with benefits is not clear. What is clear is that Obama still thinks the U.S. government must make it even easier for corporations to move production and capital around the world while American workers drop further and further behind.

"OUR CHOICES AREN'T ONLY XENOPHOBIC NATIONALISM OR NEOLIBERAL GLOBALISM"

By Leon Fink (2016)

Few issues are receiving a more insipid—and thus more harmful—treatment in our public discourse than world trade. Along with immigration, "free trade" is now the foremost symbol of a supposed either/or choice between globalism and nationalism.

"Globalists" generally hail the liberal marketplace as the engine of economic prosperity and assail its critics as uneducated and irrational isolationists, while "nationalists" instinctively identify trade with economic decline (or at least the loss of good working-class jobs), rising inequality and a general loss of control over the future. As CNN host Fareed Zakaria put it after Britain voted to leave the European Union, "the new politics of our age will not be Left versus Right, but open versus closed." This framework risks closing off our best possibilities for building a progressive economic future. We need a new paradigm.

Some historical perspective is first in order. That is the only way to account for the fact that those forces—call them white working class—today most deeply resentful of the open market were among its loudest champions during the first three decades after the Second World War.

In these early years of globalization, what we today call the Global South mattered mainly as sources of cheap raw materials or as markets for Western-produced goods. But in an age of transportation and communication revolutions, geography proved less and less a haven for higher-cost home producers against distant competitors—and, to be sure, not even that distant. By the North American Free Trade Agreement (NAFTA) era of the mid-1990s, U.S. workers were making ten times the average wage of their Mexican counterparts. If placed in direct competition, how could they possibly hold onto their jobs?

NEW WORLD ORDER

Oddly, most other problems of world economic integration have found solutions through compromise, whereas trade has remained the province of extreme either/or.

In finance and currency crises, for example, either the International Monetary Fund or World Bank (or both) regularly intervene to protect a national currency from abrupt free fall. In oceanic mining and fishing, worldwide agreements limit territorial overreach to prevent the exhaustion of vital resources or whole species. However inadequately, even on the climate crisis, world powers have accepted the principle of limits and the need to discipline fuel consumption and carbon output.

Yet, there is no such movement toward an adoption of mutually agreed international principles on matters of trade. In a politically suffocating manner, one is either pro–free trade (most big business and most Clinton-Bush-Obama policies), anti–free trade (Donald Trump with a proposed 45 percent tariff on China), or stumbling in the middle (Hillary Clinton, who at first supported and then opposed the Trans-Pacific Partnership). The TPP, in particular, attempts to overcome First World skepticism with side agreements on labor, affecting workers in Vietnam, Malaysia, and Brunei, but the record of enforcement for such guarantees is spotty at best

The options here present a silly, self-defeating set of choices and one that both workers and consumers in the United States and Europe need quickly to transcend.

Interestingly, as early as the time of the 1944 Bretton Woods Agreement, there were voices calling for a better international architecture when it came to world economic integration. The left-of-center Congress of Industrial Organizations (CIO) even got initial support from the administration of Harry Truman for the creation of an International Trade Organization (ITO) that would coordinate further bilateral or multilateral trade openings with tangible commitments regarding employment, development, and investment. Hopes for the ITO collapsed when conservative Republicans captured the Congress in 1950. No similar idea has been seriously considered since.

In the spirit of the ITO, we need a return to the quest for a new world order as undertaken at Bretton Woods, but this time with a more encompassing agenda. Not just financial stability, but the regulation of trade and debt must be on the agenda.

In the case of proposed NAFTA or TPP-type agreements, one could imagine an actualized ITO insisting on a step ladder of wage increases in the cheaper-labor countries as well as plans for displaced workers in the higher-wage countries before approving massive shake ups. In return, poor countries could count on significant debt relief.

Absent a move toward what we might call progressive internationalism, we are forced to choose between "globalists," heedless of the consequences of development for those outside the professional and financial classes, or "nationalists," suspicious of and hostile toward the world beyond our borders. Neither posture holds out much prospect for economic renewal, either at home or abroad.

CHAPTER TWO

The Rich Change the Rules

By Rick Perlstein

You know that one scene that shows up at the end of every heist movie, where the crooks recline on the beach with Mai Tais in hand, the ocean lapping peacefully in the background, both flashing that incredulous grin, astonished that they managed to pull off their audacious scheme? Those were our friends the capitalists, back in the summer of 1981, when the Republicans under President Ronald Reagan proposed massive cuts in the tax rates for unearned income, capital gains, and income tax rates even for the rich and the Democrats responded by pushing for even more massive cuts.

In his 1981 article "Whose Side Are Tax Cutters on?" John Judis reported to *In These Times* readers that Democratic Congressman Dan Rostenkowski put forward a tax package that "would virtually eliminate corporate taxes as a source of federal revenue." Or, as Rostenkowski put it, "Business is entitled to their decade, and I will try to help them get it." This chapter's first two pieces show such help from Democrats was well underway in the late 1970s—for, as Manning Marable put it in 1979, they were becoming the "governing wing of the GOP." Quite a contrast to the scene back in 1969, when Richard Nixon signed a tax package that increased capital gains taxes, slashed shelters, and skewed rates to put more money into the hands of the working class.

What happened? Inflation, for one thing, which shoved working families into tax brackets originally intended only for the affluent. And then there was an accident of history: in California, antitax zealots exploited an unfair property-tax assessment system to convince voters to pass the radical Proposition 13 referendum in 1978.

Finally, the most important factor: *propaganda,* in which hack economists who sketched fairy tales on cocktail napkins claimed that tax cuts would yield miracles greater than Jesus Christ's trick with the loaves and the fishes. And so, in 1981, Ronald Reagan was able to sign into law a tax cut so radical that, as David Moberg wrote in *In These Times*, "even Reagan's big business buddies are beginning to share some of George Bush's original assessment" that this was all "voodoo economics." And the tax cuts went hand-in-hand with big cuts to social welfare programs.

All the while, *In These Times* was there to record the madness and plot a path back to sanity. In 1982, economic historian Richard Du Boff pointed out, prophetically, that reversing the decline in both the quantity and quality of infrastructure—such as the water systems that poisoned residents of Flint, Michigan—could create genuinely equitable economic recoveries. Two years later, Frances Fox Piven made the case for the harmony of cross-class interest between warriors for economic justice and feminists and suggested that they "chain themselves again" to "statehouse columns" to protest Reagan's budget cuts just as they had years earlier for the Equal Rights Amendment (Bernie Bros and Hillarybots, unite!)

In the 1990s, *In These Times,* along with the broader Left, saw a cultural turn. Brash, broad confidence about the failure of capitalism and the possibility of radical economic transformation gave way to an emphasis on the power of language in *normalizing* inequality—for instance, in propagating the dangerous myth of the "classless" society even though, as David Futrelle noted in 1993, "more than half of all working Americans are unskilled or semi-skilled laborers." Or, in Thomas Geoghegan's poetic formulation, that "we are all waiters now."

In These Times shares a hometown with the dreaded University of Chicago economics department. One alumnus of the university wrote eloquently in 2009 about the self-evident intellectual failures, and simultaneous political success, of the "Chicago School's" greatest avatar, Milton Friedman.

The free market ideology is plain to see in David Sirota's invaluable documentation of how tax cuts in the 2000s eviscerated the budget surpluses of the 1990s—in lockstep with devastating cuts to infrastructure spending. "When the rainiest day of them all came"—Hurricane Katrina—"our country was left totally—and unnecessarily—vulnerable," he writes. Jeffrey Winters's absolutely brilliant "Oligarchy in the U.S.A." describes the depredations of America's "wealth defense industry," which includes a "mercenary army of professionals" who rape the tax code.

And that brings the reader roughly up to the present—another period in which we're suddenly brash again about transforming the economy. That University of Chicago alum who wrote about Milton Friedman in 2009? That would be U.S. Senator Bernie Sanders, an *In These Times* reader and contributor for decades, who last year became the most successful socialist presidential candidate in the history of the United States.

But not, alas, successful enough.

What kind of politics can get more Americans voting in their economic self-interest? One that trusts the people—and ignores the propagandists and the pundits. In 1980, the year Ronald Reagan was elected to his first term, the Republican pollsters at the Opinion Research Corporation asked voters whether "too much" was being spent on the environment, health, education, welfare, and urban aid programs. Only 21 percent thought so, the same percentage as in 1976. Even in 1984, when Ronald Reagan voodooed 59 percent of the population into re-electing him in a forty-nine-state landslide, polls showed that only 35 percent favored cuts in social programs to reduce the deficit. It's still pretty much the same: in an April 2016 Gallup poll, in contrast to Hillary Clinton's tax-hike timorousness, 61 percent of respondents thought that upper-income Americans were paying too little in taxes. The time of *In These Times*, which has been fighting the undemocratic redistribution of wealth up the economic food chain all these years, might be coming yet.

"THE BUSINESS OF THE U.S. IS..."

By John Judis (1978)

What has been surprising about the Carter administration is its reaction to business displeasure. No Democrat since Grover Cleveland has been so eager to please and so ready to serve. The climax came in January 1978 with Carter's budget message and economic program, which in the obeisance it paid to the private sector recalled the homilies of Calvin Coolidge.

To stimulate the economy, Carter chose the path of least business resistance—a tax cut. The job of stimulation is reserved for a reduction of the corporate profit tax from 48 to 44 percent and an increase in the investment tax credit. The effect of these proposals will be to redistribute national income to corporate profits and those whose income is most directly tied to them. They aim to stimulate "business confidence" by redistributing income away from workers to business.

AN ACCIDENTAL DEMOCRAT

Carter is now affirming the early perception of him as an economic conservative. In an interview with the *New York Times*'s Robert Shrum, one Carter aide described him as an "accidental Democrat. When he started out, you had to be a Democrat in Georgia. I think he could be a moderate Republican. He's convinced the key economic goal is reassuring business."

But more than a philosophical orientation led Carter to his subservience to business pressures. With business, Carter fears that the current recovery may be stunted and that a recession could occur in 1979. Besides creating immediate political problems, such a recession would probably preclude his re-election.

Carter evidently felt he had no choice but to opt for the traditional economic strategy of attempting to "win business confidence" through redistributing the nation's wealth in its favor.

But this strategy probably will not work for Carter. It is likely that our recession in the verbal clothing of recovery will drag on. And besides that, it is to be hoped that labor and minority organizations will not permit Carter's experiment in Democratic Republicanism to continue.

"DEMS ARE BECOMING GOVERNING WING OF THE GOP"

By Manning Marable (1979)

We are privileged to live in a time of unparalleled political crisis. Neither the traditional spokesmen of the Negro middle classes nor the dominant social forces that control the government and the economy are fully equipped to understand the nature of this crisis. Unlike Watergate, this is not a crisis of executive leadership or credibility. Unlike the Vietnam War, this is not an external crisis created by domestic political contradictions. The crisis involves the realignment of both major political parties toward the right, without a realistic electoral alternative for the majority of the American people. Since the McGovern debacle of 1972, the entire Democratic Party has shifted from its internal agendas toward the right.[1] Democratic candidates running for office last November began sounding like Republicans; Democratic office-holders running for re-election swore that they were "born again" tax cutters and anti-inflation fighters.

The move toward the right was caused by many factors, including the following:

1) the Nixon electoral triumph of 1972, which resulted in the purging of McGovern-Kennedy liberals from leadership positions within the Democratic Party hierarchy;

---

1   Democratic nominee George McGovern was beaten by Richard Nixon in foty-nine states in the 1972 presidential election *[Ed. note]*.

2) the Watergate scandal, which forced Nixon to resign in 1974 but (ironically) created the conditions for the election of independent and conservative Democrats from normally Republican districts—new politicians who weren't tied to the traditional leaders;

3) the nomination and election of President Jimmy Carter, the most conservative Democratic chief executive since Woodrow Wilson;

4) the real decline of popular cultural and political activism outside electoral politics since the late '60s;

5) the failure of organized labor, traditional middle-class black and Hispanic leaders, liberals, socialists, and intellectuals to promote a realistic alternative against the movement toward the right; and

6) the "tax revolt" of the white middle classes, culminating in [California's] Proposition 13 and similar legislation.

The further to the right the Democratic Party moves, the more "Republican-oriented" the Congress and executive branch of government become. Compounding the problem is that the Republicans are prisoners of their own extreme right wing, led by Ronald Reagan of California, Jack Kemp of New York, and many others.

The Democratic Party's leadership has charted a course reverting to the economics of Adam Smith, involving massive welfare cuts and inevitable recession. Unless organized labor, minorities, environmentalists, public service employees, feminists, and others build a united front, the rightward drift will accelerate in the '80s. It is no longer a question whether this should occur. It now has become only a question of when.

"Whose side are tax cutters on?"

By John Judis (1981)

Tax politics, like meetings of the Federal Reserve's Open Market Committee, have a certain soporific quality. But the results of the desultory debates in Congress affect the distribution and growth of wealth in the United States.

The two bills presently competing for Congress's favor—a Republican bill authored by the Senate Finance Committee and a Democratic bill drafted by the House Ways and Means Committee—would *both* precipitously widen the gap between rich and poor, encourage speculation, and make federal spending dependent upon a shrinking personal income tax base. These bills, says Robert McIntyre, the lobbyist for the Citizens for Tax Justice, "are the biggest catastrophes for tax finances in the history of the code."

Tax politics also can reveal the real inclinations of politicians who claim to be tribunes of the people. It has been a Democrat from a low-income Chicago district, Representative Dan Rostenkowski, the chair of Ways and Means, who has produced a comprehensive Democratic package that would virtually eliminate corporate taxes as a source of federal revenue.

Rostenskowski's bill only makes the Republican proposal *less* regressive. It will continue the shift of the tax burden from the wealthy to the less fortunate. "The Democrats apparently agree with the Republicans that only Democrats should pay taxes," one tax lobbyist quipped.

But the reduction in corporate taxes is even more important than the regressive reductions of the personal income tax. Contrary to current mythology, federal corporate taxes tend to come out of stockholders' dividends rather than consumers' pockets. Any shift from corporate to personal income tax tends to redistribute income upward.

When the various credits and deductions are figured in, the effective corporate income tax in the Democratic plan on most large corporations would be less than 10 percent.

Both the Democratic and Republican bills also include special plums for the wealthy. They raise the amount of inheritance exempt from estate taxes from $175,625 to $600,000.

Business United

In addition to the Reagan administration's expert salesmanship, several other factors contributed to the current tax debate. Previously, corporate lobbyists from the American Council for Capital Formation (ACCF), the Business Roundtable, the Chamber of Commerce, and the National Association of Manufacturers have quarreled over specific measures. This year the lobbyists, dubbed the "Carlton Group" for their breakfast meetings at Washington's Carlton Hotel, united.

On the other hand, labor has been singularly ineffective in its opposition to the Kemp-Roth Republican plan and the corporate tax reductions.[2] "Labor's position on the bill as a lobbying force is the lowest it has been in fifty years," one labor lobbyist admitted. "Nobody fears [AFL-CIO president Lane] Kirkland. He can't scare an eighty-year-old lady."

But perhaps most important, House Democrats, who as members of the

---

2   The Republican-sponsored Economic Recovery Tax Act, signed into law by President Reagan in August 1981, slashed income, estate, and corporate tax rates *[Ed. note]*.

majority party became used to corporate contributions, have continued to hew the business line on tax issues. "Business is entitled to its decade, and I will try to help them get it," Rostenkowski told a meeting of the ACCF.

"REAGANOMICS: ONE DOWN, THREE TO GO"

By Richard B. Du Boff (1982)

What lies in store for the U.S. economy in Year Two of Reaganomics? Reaganomics Year One—1981—hatched the second, and more serious, of back-to-back recessions that have brought us almost three years of uninterrupted economic stagnation. The trough of the first recession occurred in May 1980; the low point of the second seems to be approaching. This means that the expansion phase between these twin slumps lasted barely a year—easily the shortest recession-to-recession recovery span since the Second World War.

Two forces are at work in the present dismal economic picture: the chronic weakness of private-sector demand and the stifling effects of high interest rates. Both are being reinforced by Reaganomics. As an offset, the 1981 tax and regulatory giveaways to business will do little to spur capital spending. It is, in fact, unlikely that Reagan and company engaged in any serious study of the determinants of private investment before embarking on their "economic recovery" program. Their chief goals were not positive (even by capitalist standards) but negative—to get back at the poor and underprivileged, welfare mothers, university intellectuals, environmentalists and occupational safety advocates, social workers, and legal aid practitioners.

The real objective was to roll back the advances made between 1963 and 1972 by an array of reformist pressure groups that successfully used federal power to override the legendary reaction and corruption of state and local governments and vied with corporate economic power on its own terrain— the nationwide economy. In their zeal to restore to corporate America its rightful privileges, the Reaganomics hit squads may have convinced business that it had been "right" all along and that now, at last, the federal "bureaucracy" would be stopped from "interfering" with short-run profit maximizing, asset-enhancing merger activity, and overseas expansion.

Furthermore, the Reagan assault on the public sector will chip away— and perhaps periodically break down—the strongest single economic support for private-sector production and sales.

On the transfer payment side, the "war against the poor" threatens to soften economic activity even more and prolong the recession. Food stamps, aid for low-income families with dependent children, and Medicare are all being slashed. Unemployment insurance payments have also been decreased.

The contradictions of Reaganomics are plain for all to see. An administration promising "reindustrialization" is damaging our national productivity with actions that will accelerate the deterioration of our public capital—mass transit and railways, highways and port facilities, water, sewage, waste disposal, and postal systems. Even before Reagan, the United States probably had the most dilapidated and decaying public infrastructure of any industrial capitalist nation.

What never ceases to amaze in this grim scene is the enormous capacity for ideological self-delusion exhibited by the American business community at large. Their belief that Reagan is "good for business" reveals myopia of the highest order. It may be too much to expect a long-run view from the power centers of American capitalism: Can a leopard change his spots?

But for the American Left, large questions loom. As Reaganomics fouls up the economy badly enough to make Jimmy Carter and crew look competent by comparison, what alternatives are available for the bottom two-thirds of the income scale who will bear the costs of Reagan's vain effort to recreate the economy of the '20s? How can the Democratic Party be denied the rewards of the electoral victories that may flow its way for (at best) doing nothing at all? What visions of a more secure and less demeaning economic life can be proposed?

"THE POOR STILL GETTING POORER"

By David Moberg (1984)

The Declaration of Independence proclaims that all men—and, we would now emphasize, women—are created equal. If so, it's a fleeting experience. Even before Ronald Reagan came to the White House, the United States was the most unequal of major industrialized countries in the distribution of wealth and income. In the late '70s, the small steps toward greater equality taken during the War on Poverty already were being eroded, but in the Reagan years the polarization of American society has been intensified with a vengeance.

It has always been folk wisdom that the rich get richer and the poor get poorer. Folk wisdom now has ample statistical support. Not only have the numbers and proportion of the poor increased, thanks to deep budget cuts, regressive tax changes, and a prolonged recession, but also the ranks of the "middle class" worker are being threatened. Meanwhile, income and wealth for the professionals and managers as well as the tiny elite of the truly rich have surged upward, in many respects as an almost direct transfer from the pockets of the poor.

Much as Ronald Reagan deserves credit for this march toward greater inequality, it would be a mistake to see it as linked to Reagan alone. The tendencies were already present under Jimmy Carter. The challenges are not simply matters of fine-tuning government policy. More fundamentally, a changing economy will push toward greater inequality without dramatic intervention. Yet there has also been a political change.

As Thomas Byrne Edsall argues in an intriguing new book, *The New Politics of Inequality*, the major parties and the functioning of the political system have changed in ways that shift even more political power to the upper class and to a conservative, class-conscious Republican Party in confronting a divided, confused, and spineless Democratic Party. The rich are using that power to increase inequality even further. They have succeeded in part because their money buys power but also because they have been able to define the agenda of political debate and the prevailing political culture, taking away the initiative that the Left momentarily seized in the '60s.

Unabashed apologetics for inequality now are increasingly commonplace. It was Reaganite common sense that the poor could only be motivated by greater poverty and the rich motivated only by greater riches. It has now become widely accepted that workers are all paid too much and that the cure for economic ills is to tax capital (that is, wealth) much more lightly.

A simple inversion of this new common nonsense would not be a bad start.

"WOMEN'S COMMON GROUND"

By Frances Fox Piven (1984)

Imagine what might have happened. It is summer 1981. A new Republican administration, with the acquiescence or active support of most Democrats, enacts a program of massive cuts in social programs for the poor. Indignant feminist leaders, quickly realizing that women and their children will be the main victims, initiate protest marches in New York, Los Angeles, Chicago, Philadelphia, and Boston. The TV networks feature Gloria Steinem, Betty Friedan, and Bella Abzug holding aloft banners proclaiming the rights of mothers and children to food or health care or housing or heating fuel.

The ranks of the marchers are not numerous, but outrage spreads, demonstrations continue, the ranks swell, and the cameras turn to the increasing numbers of poor women and women of color hauling their infants and toddlers with them as they walk alongside the skirt-suited women from downtown offices.

Meanwhile here and there sit-down strikes break out among women staff members in health and welfare agencies who refuse to implement new restrictions in the Maternal and Child Health Program and the Women, Infants and Children Feeding Program.

This scenario is to me entirely credible. It could have happened. And it could still happen. The potential for political resistance among American women is enormous, as signaled more than anything else by the poll data on the "gender gap." But it hasn't occurred. True, women's organizations regularly issue statements denouncing current national policies, and they are often the only ones to do so. They lobby, too, and they work to promote women candidates for political office. These are welcome efforts in a gloomy political season, but they are puny beside the vast political potential suggested by the gender gap.

WHO LIKES WELFARE?

Why isn't much more happening? Why aren't more women human-services workers registering their clients or staging sit-ins to protest program cuts? I think the answer is that the institutional turf on which I am proposing to fight makes many of us who are the potential leaders very uncomfortable. We are not proud about the involvement of women with social welfare programs, and you cannot lock arms and stand firm if you are not proud.

Put bluntly, we don't like "welfare," and we don't like to contemplate organizing within the framework it creates. Many feminists share the prevalent American bias against the welfare state as such. They have come to associate emancipation with entry into the market and upward mobility within it. There is irony in these leadership attitudes (as there is in the similar attitudes expressed by some black leaders), given the increasingly impoverished circumstances of so many women and the unlikelihood of their escape from the low-wage service-sector jobs to which the market consigns them. The irony is compounded because more middle-class constituents of feminist organizations work for welfare state agencies than banks, or advertising companies, or Silicon Valley entrepreneurs.

This bias among feminist leaders is not unmotivated. A good many women leaders, like black leaders, are trying to build their organizations by operating in political and business spheres where a spirited defense of the welfare state would not open doors or win points. So we have conflicting ideas, and we are deeply ambivalent: women object that women are being made the victims of program cuts, but we are not quite willing to defend the programs that are being cut. Our denunciations are neither bold nor passionate, and that means we are failing to articulate and release the depths of moral indignation embedded in the gender gap. Our ambivalence is thus producing narrow and short-sighted calculations of organizational interest, for it rules out the possibility of creating a new political force capable of opening doors and winning points on its own terms. It rules out the possibility of activating and leading a movement that includes poor and working women.

"Stuck in the Middle with You"

By David Futrelle (1993)

It has been the peculiar genius of middle-class ideology to deny not only that it is an ideology, but that there are even such things as classes. America, we often hear, is a land of equality—or at least a land of opportunity. No one is trapped by his or her circumstances, and anyone can make it to the top. Americans, historian Louis Hartz once suggested, find it almost impossible to imagine the logic of class analysis. "[A] triumphant middle class," he noted, "can take itself for granted."

And, from the beginning, it has. "There is no permanent class of hired laborers among us," Abraham Lincoln once asserted. In Lincoln's view, "the prudent, penniless beginner in the world" might need to work for a time for wages, but only until he could set up shop as a businessman himself. "If any continue through life in the condition of the hired laborer," he proclaimed, "it is not the fault of the system, but because of either a dependent nature which prefers it, or improvidence, folly, or singular misfortune."

Today the argument is still propounded with vigor, often spiced with an unacknowledged and usually euphemistic racism: if you removed a few archaisms, added the word "empowerment" in a few spots, inserted a derogatory reference to the urban "underclass," and threw in a couple of well-cooked statistics, Lincoln's hoary platitudes would be indistinguishable from any number of recent pronouncements from the Washington think tanks.

If we set aside the ritualistic, largely meaningless denunciations of the rich that pop up during election season, there are only two classes that matter in American political discourse—the middle class and the "underclass." As in Lincoln's day, the middle class is seen, almost, as America itself, the repository of all that is good and true, the embodiment of our democratic promise. Politicians fight over this class like dogs for a bone.

As for the underclass, well, it's something else indeed. Wallowing in a "culture of poverty," trapped by their own dependency, the poor have only themselves to blame for their misery, and they hardly deserve the same rights as the rest of the polity.

But however neat this two-class division, it bears little resemblance to the facts of American life. According to sociologist Erik Olin Wright, more than half of all working Americans are unskilled or semi-skilled laborers, by all definitions working class. Far from being a land of equality, America has one of the most skewed class structures in the developed world. The top fifth of the population earns as much as all the rest put together. In the popular consciousness, families making $100,000 or more are still described as middle class—and heaven forbid if you suggest raising their taxes!—but in reality they're pretty close to the top of the heap.

But if American politicians have made too much of the idea of the middle class, those on the Left have made too little of it. If American mythology holds that the middle class is (or should be) all, Marxist mythology holds that there is no such thing. Marx saw the world as divided, quite starkly, into two classes, proletariat and bourgeoisie, defined simply by who owned capital and who did not. By these standards, nearly everyone counts as working class—from mechanics to office workers to burger-flippers at McDonald's.

Politically, alas, this kind of analysis is almost useless. It matters a great deal if autoworkers and office workers think of themselves as middle class— or, even if they don't, if they believe in the American mythology of success. Oppression may be conditioned largely by "objective" factors, but it is experienced subjectively—and if those who are oppressed blame themselves for their economic "failure" as wages drop and jobs disappear, they won't even recognize the injustices they face.

For American politicians, the ritual invocation of the middle class has been a proven winner. But for America itself, the mythology of the middle class has been a disaster, diverting attention from the real injustices of a system that is far from egalitarian, ensuring that government remains in the hands of one or the other of the two, increasingly indistinguishable, political branches of America's bipartisan elite. We can't get beyond this morass until we can start talking, clearly and forthrightly, about class—or, to put it more bluntly, about exactly who is screwing whom. We're not all in this together.

"WELCOME TO NEW ORLEANS"

By David Sirota (2005)

When President George W. Bush kicked off his bid for re-election in the spring of 2004, he proudly promoted the trillions in tax cuts he had passed as supposedly helping the economy. Then he went on the attack. "The tired, old policies of tax and spend," Bush said, referring to Democrats, "are a proven recipe for economic disaster."

The implication in Bush's statement is one America has been hearing for years from the Right: namely, that conservatives' agenda of tax and spending cuts is not tired, but rather somehow "new" and (most important) a path to success.

But with New Orleans residents still bailing water from their streets, that seemingly impenetrable axiom of American politics has crumbled almost as quickly as the infrastructure supposedly protecting our Gulf Coast during Hurricane Katrina. "Tax and spend" was not the recipe for economic disaster—tax and spending cuts were.

This is a reality visible in the numbers. Year after year, the Bush administration insisted on massive tax cuts for the wealthy. And year after year, the White House refused to provide the funding government experts said was needed to strengthen levees, beef up hurricane preparedness, and get federal emergency response ready for an onslaught from Mother Nature. America's budget surplus, built in the 1990s to serve as a rainy day fund, was robbed to provide more and more giveaways to the rich. When the rainiest day of them all came, our country was left totally—and unnecessarily—vulnerable.

2001 AND 2002: DENIAL

Casual observers wouldn't expect Mike Parker to serve as a de facto spokesman for how the Republicans' tax-cuts-at-all-cost agenda has weakened America. As a conservative GOP congressman from Mississippi in the 1990s, Parker was an outspoken advocate for giving tax breaks to the wealthy.

Parker was rewarded for his Republican service by President Bush, who appointed him to head the Army Corps of Engineers on June 7, 2001. That was the very same day Bush signed his massive $1.3 trillion income tax cut into law—a tax cut that severely depleted the government of revenues it needed to address critical priorities. As Parker soon learned, one of the priorities that would be sacrificed was flood and hurricane protection.

Overall, Bush's first budget introduced in February 2001 proposed more than half a billion dollars worth of cuts to the Army Corps of Engineers for the 2002 fiscal year. This 2001 budget proposal came in the same year that, according to the *Houston Chronicle*, federal officials publicly ranked the potential damage to New Orleans by a major hurricane "among the three likeliest, most catastrophic disasters facing this country."

By the beginning of the 2002 congressional session, Parker had enough of sitting in silence while these tax and budget decisions were being made. In a meeting with White House budget director Mitch Daniels, Parker demanded that the Bush administration restore the critical money for flood and hurricane protection.

But as Parker noted, "It made no impact on [the White House] whatsoever." In February 2002, the president unveiled his new budget, this one with a $390 million cut to the Army Corps. The cuts came during the same year the richest 5 percent (those who make an average of $300,000 or more) were slated to receive $24 billion in new tax cuts.

When Parker headed to Capitol Hill for annual budget hearings in February 2002, he couldn't hide the truth. Under questioning, he admitted that "there will be a negative impact" if the President's budget cuts were allowed to go forward. The White House fired Parker within a matter of days.

Some Republicans came to Parker's defense after he was removed. Rep. David Vitter (R-La.) said the administration was "in denial" about the cuts. "There's no two ways about it that [the corps] are very underfunded," he said, noting that "southeast Louisiana flood control [is] our most obvious example."

Vitter was right—but he was also "in denial" about his own culpability: just weeks before, he and his Republican colleagues voted for a brand new business tax cut package, costing the federal government $43 billion in revenues that could have gone to fill the budget gaps Parker identified.

Inadvertently foreshadowing just how closely tied the tax cuts and budget infrastructure negligence really would be, Bush signed this new tax cut two days after firing Parker.

2004: TEMPTING FATE

The *Washington Times* headline on January 20, 2004, told it all: "Bush Wants Tax Cuts to Stay." The article reported that even with a war, record budget deficits, and dangerously crumbling infrastructure, the president would make a new, $1 trillion tax cut plan the centerpiece of his State of the Union address.

And once again, just days after the speech, the White House on February

2 released a budget with another massive cut to infrastructure and public works projects—this time to the tune of $460 million. As the *Denver Post* later reported, "the Southeast Louisiana Flood Control project sought $100 million in U.S. aid to strengthen the levees holding back the Mississippi River and Lake Pontchartrain, but the Bush administration offered a paltry $16.5 million." Meanwhile, budget cuts forced the corps to delay seven projects that included enlarging critical levees.

These latest cuts came just as the previous ones were starting to wreak havoc. By June 2004, the *Times-Picayune* reported that "for the first time in thirty-seven years, federal budget cuts have all but stopped major work on the New Orleans area's east bank hurricane levees."

"We are doing everything we can to make the case that this is a security issue for us," Jefferson Parish emergency manager Walter Maestri said at the time, desperately begging the Bush administration to reevaluate its budget decisions.

2005: CATASTROPHE STRIKES

The weeks and months leading up to Hurricane Katrina were more of the same. The White House focused on a multi-trillion-dollar plan to privatize Social Security and a plan to repeal the federal estate tax.

Meanwhile, as the *Financial Times* reported, the president proposed a budget that "called for a $71.2 million reduction in federal funding for hurricane and flood prevention projects in the New Orleans district, the largest such cut ever proposed." In addition, "the administration wanted to shelve a study aimed at determining ways to protect New Orleans from a Category 5 hurricane."

By the time Katrina struck on August 29, the disaster was already a fait accompli. Though politicians feigned shock and outrage at the federal government's hurricane preparations, there was nothing to be surprised about. The disaster was the consequence of years of putting tax cuts above everything else—even above a catastrophe we knew was coming.

THE AFTERMATH

In the wake of Katrina, the D.C. political establishment has tried desperately to prevent any discussion of tax cuts and budget priorities as the culprits in the disaster.

At first, President Bush claimed, "I don't think anybody anticipated the breach of the levees"—an insult to the experts in his own administration and elsewhere who had been warning about exactly that for years. On Capitol Hill, Republicans simultaneously criticized those who were "playing politics" with the disaster, while pointing fingers at Democratic state and local officials.

Democrats—many of whom had voted for some of the Bush tax cuts—attacked the pathetic government response to the catastrophe but largely refused to hammer the underlying tax and budget decisions that created the conditions for disaster. And the media ate it up, without putting any of it into the context of tax and budget decisions.

It is downright criminal for Congress and the media to pretend that the Bush administration's tax cut binge and subsequent budget cuts had nothing to do with the catastrophe. Experts roundly agree that had the administration made different budget decisions, the impact of the hurricane could have been reduced.

Mike Parker told the *Washington Post*, "You have watched during a period of seventy-two hours a modern city of New Orleans [become] a Third World country, and it is all because of the disintegration of infrastructure."

Still, even after Hurricane Katrina, conservatives continue to push forward with tax cut zealotry, as if nothing happened. In his first interview just days after the disaster, President Bush made sure to tell ABC's Diane Sawyer that he will not consider rolling back his tax cuts to deal with the disaster or beef up infrastructure.

And that prompts a critical question: When will this madness end? If a city submerged under water can't shock the insulated political establishment into reevaluating its tax and budget priorities, what can? The answer is patently clear: The only thing that can prompt a serious debate about taxes is a political opposition that is willing to step forward and draw the tax cut contrast—an opposition that has not yet coalesced.

Politicians love to put signs up next to the projects they create saying "your tax dollars at work." The only way for the United States to have the desperately needed debate over budget priorities is if Democrats find the courage to plant a figurative sign in New Orleans's flood-drenched streets that says "your tax cuts at work." Then, and only then, will America's tax debate transform from a theoretical one that features terrific-sounding promises into a concrete one that highlights the very real consequences of a political system that seeks only to enrich the already rich, no matter what the cost to society.

"WE ARE ALL WAITERS NOW"

By Thomas Geoghegan (2006)

We are too scared to tax the rich. And the more money the rich take from us, the harder they are to tax.

It's not that they "buy off" the politicians: they don't completely. It's not, as sociologists believe, that people think, "Oh, in America, I could be rich, and I don't want to pay the tax." Sociologists claim someone making $50,000 a year, or $25,000 a year believes: I can be like Gates or Soros. Or my kids will be.

It's burned into our brains that Americans believe this.

I have a question: In your own life, do you know anyone out there in a suburb with a mortgage who believes this? I sometimes go out to barbecues and parties with clients, and I think of "businessmen" and guys in sales and ask myself, "Do they believe that?"

No, not for themselves. Or their kids. Usually they're disappointed in their kids. Over age forty, people know they aren't going anywhere. Under forty, from what I can tell, the young are even more bitter. Yet they're terrified to tax the rich, and far more terrified on the whole than their ancestors of the New Deal and post–New Deal used to be. So why, if they have everything to gain from taxing the rich, are they so terrified?

Because the more money the rich take from us, the more it changes our moral character—we lose the courage it takes to engage in self-government.

I borrow an old idea of the French writers like Rousseau, Voltaire, Tocqueville, Guizot, and many others. They believed that the particular "constitution" or form of government—monarchy, aristocracy, etc.—literally shapes our personality. We don't have monarchy, or aristocracy—but it's not a democracy. Most of the time, as in the latest election, most of us don't vote. Most of us don't know the names of our local candidates for Congress.

Even if you do know the names, don't think you're better than the rest. You are still living under a form of government where most people don't vote. Even if you're different, our collective disconnect with our own government has some bearing on your moral character as well.

Aristotle would not call us a democracy. Or a republic, really. I believe Aristotle and the Greeks would describe the America of this century as a plutocracy. The top 1 percent has nearly all the wealth. That's our form of government.

Classical plutocracy.

I take on the personality that lets me fit into a plutocracy. I'm not the owner of a business or a farm. I'm not a member of a labor union. I'm a servant, or a salesman. I sell myself to people in one way or another. In a plutocracy, everyone is a salesman. Everyone is a waiter. We live off not wages we negotiate but on commissions and tips. In this new economy, we don't even see how our character is changing, or how we are constantly selling ourselves for bigger tips: "I hope you like me." But it's turning us effectively into waiters in restaurants. There's a problem with waiters, which George Orwell notes: they identify with the diners, and they vote for the Right. Orwell hated waiters. He liked the back of the house. That's where the minorities and foreign workers are.

Unlike Orwell, I like waiters. It's partly because, in the America of 2006, I have had to adapt my own personality to the plutocracy we're in. But as much as I try to sell myself and please others, I wonder what it's doing to me and to so many others. If we're spending all our time trying to figure out how to please the rich, how to seduce them into giving us money, how to say, "I'm Bob, I'm your waiter for the evening," we aren't likely to be the people to confront them politically.

Many a sociologist has it wrong: It's not that I expect that I or my children will live like the Super Rich. It's rather that I have to like the Super Rich—I have no choice but to like them if I want a big tip.

It's a variation on a point that sociologist Richard Sennet makes. We bow, we scrape, but now we do it in the corporate world as a "team." People learn to be flexible, which means "likeable." As we get more income inequality and more "service" jobs, all our business majors really learn is how to be flexible and likeable—to sell ourselves, to seduce, so we can be Donald Trump's apprentice.

We need to put down the Toqueville. It's not like that any more. It's not the America of Jefferson: we aren't small farmers. Or the America of Lincoln: we aren't the free-labor, free-soil types. Or of FDR: we aren't the industrial workers organizing for higher wages. It's the America of the Bush family, of big country clubs and estates. It's the America where even the so-called "middle class" are more or less waiting tables.

So we adapt our personality. If we vote to soak the rich, they may cut back their tips! I lose out. It's because I don't believe in mobility (mine or yours) that I dare not soak the rich.

Besides, if I try to soak the rich, what good will it do me? Let's suppose I confront them. I put in a government that raises their taxes. There's no guarantee I'm doing any good for me. That is, there is so much inequality, the money may go to the poor. Or just as likely, it may go back to the rich. If the government raises my taxes, how do I know they will spend it on me, in the middle? That's why it is easier to raise taxes in Germany or Sweden, or even Canada. People know: if they spend it, they have to spend it, like it or not, on people like me.

So the more inequality, the more unnerving it is to raise taxes. It destroys the presumption that those in the middle will get it back. Whatever the motive, the result is the same. People are afraid in a plutocracy to raise taxes on the rich. The more money held by people in the top 1 percent, the more impregnable they are to progressive-type taxation.

"THE FAILED PROPHET"

By Bernie Sanders (2009)

The late Milton Friedman was a provocative teacher at my alma mater, the University of Chicago. He got his students involved with their studies. He was a gifted writer and communicator. And he received a Nobel Prize for his contributions to economics.

But Friedman was more than an academic. He was an advocate for, and popularizer of, a radical right wing economic ideology.

In today's political and social reality, the University of Chicago's establishment of a $200 million Milton Friedman Institute (in the building that until now has housed the renowned Chicago Theological Seminary) will not be perceived as simply a sign of appreciation for a prominent former faculty member. Instead, by founding such an institution, the university signals that it is aligning itself with a reactionary political program supported by the wealthiest, greediest, and most powerful people and institutions in this country. Friedman's ideology caused enormous damage to the American middle class and to working families here and around the world. It is not an ideology that a great institution like the University of Chicago should be seeking to advance.

Those who defend the Milton Friedman Institute will assure us that it will encourage a free and open exchange of ideas. That may very well be true. But if the goal of the institute is simply to do nonideological research, there are a lot of names that one could come up with other than that of the most polemical and ideological economist of his time.

My suspicions only deepen when I read on the University of Chicago website that donors who contribute more than $1 million to the project will have a special relationship with the institute as members of a Milton Friedman Society and will be expected to facilitate the institution's "connections to leaders in business and government."

I work in Washington, D.C., and I know about the power that big money has over process. When the insurance companies and the drug companies and the oil companies and the banks and the military-industrial complex make contributions to political campaigns, we usually know exactly what it is they want in return.

The timing of this project is a little ironic. Friedman earned his bread by denouncing government at virtually every turn. He, like his acolyte, former Federal Reserve Chair Alan Greenspan, believed that a largely unregulated free market constituted the most superior form of economic organization imaginable. Well, the tune of the right-wing free marketeers has changed a bit in the last few months.

My colleagues in the Senate and I are now picking up the pieces of a banking system brought to the edge of collapse by this theory of deregulation and by the insatiable greed of a small number of wealthy financiers playing in the market and engaging in incredibly risky—if not illegal—behavior.

In the rush to bail out Wall Street, we saw President Bush, Treasury Secretary Henry Paulson, the people in the U.S. Chamber of Commerce and the Business Roundtable—folks who loved Friedman's ideas and who, no doubt, would be prepared to financially support a Milton Friedman Institute—reverse their longstanding rhetorical opposition to government intervention.

Instead, they demanded that we come to the rescue of the financial firms that had lined up in front of Congress for their emergency welfare checks.

For years, all of these people, including the president of the United States, have been telling us that government should not be involved in ensuring health care for all Americans as a right of citizenship. ("What a terrible idea!") They have been telling us that the government should not be involved in making quality education affordable to all people; that the government should not be empowered to ensure that we reverse green-house gas emissions; that the government should not regulate pollution that contaminates our air and water and land; and that the government should not provide a strong safety net for our children, for our seniors, or for the disabled.

Well, it turns out that when the shoe is pinching their foot, they have become the strongest believers in government intervention—especially if working people and the middle class are bailing them out.

But the issue here is not just economic policy. It goes deeper than that. It touches on the core of who we are as a society and as a people. Are we as human beings supposed to turn around and not see the suffering that so many of our brothers and sisters are experiencing? Are we content to be living in a nation where, thanks in part to the Friedmanite ideology, the richest 1 percent owns more than the bottom 90 percent and the top one-tenth percent owns more than the bottom 50 percent?

With all due respect to the late Milton Friedman, his economic program is nothing more than a wish list for the greediest, the most monied interests in our society. At the same time that this ideology is supported by the rich and powerful—except when they're lining up in Washington for their welfare checks—this same ideology is almost unanimously opposed by working families and middle-class people across this country.

What would some of the items on Friedman's wish list be? First of all, the Friedmanites would be supportive of the concept of a culture of greed. They want people making billions of dollars on the covers of *Time* and *Newsweek* because these people are supposed to be our national heroes. We are not supposed to recognize a teacher who makes $40,000 a year opening up the minds of young people. We are not supposed to recognize a childcare worker who makes $18,000 a year giving poor children an opportunity to grow intellectually and emotionally. Those jobs are not considered important work.

But if you're a billionaire on Wall Street creating exotic financial instruments that end up being worth nothing, you are considered a hero. The fact that this culture of greed has permeated our political culture means that corporate CEOs can now earn more than 400 times what their workers earn without fearing a political backlash.

Now we have a case study for what happens when the ideology of Milton Friedman becomes the operating ideology of the government. Under Bush, the median family income has declined by thousands of dollars. Millions of Americans have entered the ranks of the poor. Some 7 million have lost their health insurance. Some 3 million have lost their pensions. And the gap between the very rich and everybody else has grown much wider.

Our country is due for a transformation. We have endured years of right-wing ideology, and we are eager to move in a different direction. I believe that we will see a major reordering of social and economic priorities and that this last general election represented a repudiation of right-wing economic arguments.

In the Bush era—a period in which some of Friedman's greatest admirers managed the U.S. economy—the top 400 families in this country saw their wealth increase by $670 billion.

Yet we have children in this country who have no health care, children who are undernourished, and children who sleep out on the streets. From an economic perspective, from a moral perspective, and from a philosophical perspective, the ideology of Milton Friedman is dead wrong.

"OLIGARCHY IN THE U.S.A."

By Jeffrey A. Winters (2012)

In 2005, Citigroup offered its high-net-worth clients in the United States a concise statement of the threats they and their money faced. The report told them they were the leaders of a "plutonomy," an economy driven by the spending of its ultra-rich citizens. "At the heart of plutonomy is income inequality," which is made possible by "capitalist-friendly governments and tax regimes."

The danger, according to Citigroup's analysts, is that "personal taxation rates could rise—dividends, capital gains, and inheritance taxes would hurt the plutonomy."

But the ultra-rich already knew that. In fact, even as America's income distribution has skewed to favor the upper classes, the very richest have successfully managed to *reduce* their overall tax burden. Look no further than Republican Mitt Romney, who in 2010 paid 13.9 percent of his $21.6 million income in taxes that year, the same tax rate as an individual who earned a mere $8,500 to $34,500.

How is that possible? How can a country make so much progress toward equality on other fronts—race, gender, sexual orientation, and disability—but run the opposite way in its policy on taxing the rich?

For an explanation, we need to look more closely at the relationship between wealth and political power. I propose an updated theory of "oligarchy," the same lens developed by Plato and Aristotle when they studied the same problem in their own times.

SO WHAT'S AN OLIGARCHY?

Across all political spectrums, oligarchs are people (never corporations or other organizations) who command massive concentrations of material resources (that is, wealth) that can be deployed to defend or enhance their own property and interests, even if they don't own those resources personally. Without this massive concentration of wealth, there are no oligarchs.

In any society, of course, an extremely unequal wealth distribution provokes conflict. Oligarchy is the politics of the defense of this wealth, propagated by the richest members of society.

Contemporary America (along with other capitalist states) houses a kind of "civil oligarchy." Even oligarchs, who can be disarmed for the first time in history and no longer need to rule directly, must submit to the rule of law for this modern "civil" arrangement to work. When oligarchs do enter government, it is more for vanity than to rule *as* or *for* oligarchs. Good examples are New York City Mayor Michael Bloomberg, former presidential candidate Ross Perot, and former Massachusetts Governor Mitt Romney.

Whatever views and interests may divide the very rich, they are united in being materially focused and materially empowered. The social and political tensions associated with extreme wealth bond oligarchs together even if they never meet, setting in motion the complex dynamics of wealth defense. Oligarchs do overlap with each other in certain social circles that theorists of the elite work hard to map. But such networks are not vital to their power and effectiveness. Oligarchic theory requires no conspiracies or backroom deals. It is the minions hired by the oligarchs who provide structure and continuity to America's civil oligarchy.

THE U.S. WEALTH DEFENSE INDUSTRY

The threats to wealth that oligarchs face, and want to overcome, create the enormous profit-making opportunities that motivate the wealth defense industry (WDI). In American oligarchy, it consists of two components.

The first is the mercenary army of professionals—lawyers, accountants, wealth management agencies—who use highly specialized knowledge to navigate 72,000 pages of tax code and generate a range of tax "products" and advice, enabling oligarchs to collectively save scores of billions of dollars, every year, that would otherwise have to be surrendered to the state.

The second component of the WDI is the nitty-gritty legwork that keeps the tax system sufficiently porous, complex, and uncertain enough to be manipulated. Some oligarchs do this work themselves, speed dialing public officials to directly complain about laws and regulations, but most do not. Instead, WDI professionals, motivated to earn a share of annual oligarchic gains, constitute a highly coherent and aggressive network for political pressure. These lobbyists fight to insert favorable material into the tax code, cut sections that cause problems, and block threats on the horizon.

The WDI, arising naturally from the opportunities and risks created by enormous wealth, has spawned its own pile of these opinion-makers, free to spread their ideas through a compliant corporate media while oligarchs themselves are free to look on.

OLIGARCHY, OR DEMOCRACY?

To argue that the United States is a thriving oligarchy does not imply that our democracy is a sham. There are many policies about which oligarchs have no shared interests, and their influence in these areas is either small or mutually canceling.

Though it may strike at the heart of elitism, greater democratic participation is not an antidote to oligarchic power. It is merely a *potential* threat. Only when participation challenges material inequality—when extreme wealth is redistributed—do oligarchy and democracy finally clash.

The answer to the question of inequality, then, is troubling. Wars and revolutions have destroyed oligarchies by forcibly dispersing their wealth, but a democracy never has.

Democracy and the rule of law can, however, tame oligarchs. Of course, this hasn't happened in the United States.

But it is endlessly fascinating that we're now in a moment when Americans are once again asking fundamental questions about how the oligarchic power of wealth distorts and outflanks the democratic power of participation.

"WHO IS JOHN GALT? NOW WE KNOW!"

By Slavoj Žižek (2013)

What is the ongoing U.S. government shutdown really about? In the middle of April 2009, I was taking a rest in a hotel room in Syracuse, New York, and jumping between two channels: a PBS documentary on Pete Seeger, the great American country singer of the Left, and a Fox News report on a country singer of the antitax "Tea Party," who was performing a populist, anti-Obama song full of complaints about how Washington is taxing the hard-working ordinary people to finance the rich Wall Street financiers.

There was the weird similarity between the two singers. Formulating an anti-establishment populist complaint against both the exploitative rich and the government, they called for radical measures, including civil disobedience. It was another painful reminder that today's radical-populist Right strangely reminds us of the old radical-populist Left.

The difference is the fundamental irrationality of the Tea Party agenda: to protect the interest of the hard-working ordinary people by way of privileging the "exploitative rich" and thus literally countering their own interests. One of the weird consequences of the 2008 financial meltdown and the measures taken to counteract it (enormous sums of money to help banks) was the revival of interest in the work of Ayn Rand, the closest one can come to the ideologist of the "greed is good" radical capitalism. The sales of her magnum opus *Atlas Shrugged* exploded again. According to some reports, there are already signs that the scenario described in *Atlas Shrugged*—the creative capitalists themselves going on strike—is being enacted.

The ridicule of this reaction is that it totally misreads the situation: Most of the gigantic sums of bailout money went precisely to the Randian deregulated "titans" who failed in their "creative" schemes and thereby brought about the meltdown. It is not the great creative geniuses who are now helping lazy ordinary people, but the ordinary taxpayers who are helping the failed "creative geniuses." One should simply recall that the ideologico-political father of the long economic process that ended up in the 2008 meltdown was Alan Greenspan, a card-carrying Randian "objectivist." Now we finally know who John Galt is—the idiot responsible for the 2008 financial meltdown and, consequentially, for the ongoing shutdown.

How long will this masterful ideological manipulation continue to work?

CHAPTER THREE

Busted: The Decline of Unions

INTRODUCTION

By Nelson Lichtenstein

The world was a very different place when *In These Times* began covering the labor movement forty years ago. Twice as many Americans worked in the manufacturing and mining industries, and the impact of global trade was just beginning to be felt. You could still buy an inexpensive TV or pair of blue jeans from a unionized American company. The U.S. automobile industry still built the great majority of cars purchased in the country and was a bulwark of union power. With almost 1.5 million members, the United Automobile Workers (UAW) still played a potent role in American electoral politics and trade policy.

But no more. The top line statistic that most observers use when charting labor's fate is "union density"—the proportion of all nonfarm U.S. workers enrolled in a union. This has fallen from about 24 percent when *In These Times* began publishing to just over 11 percent in 2015. These dismal statistics actually understate the precipitous decline in labor's power within corporations, because public-sector unions now enroll more workers than their private-sector counterparts. Huge nonunion firms like Walmart, McDonald's, FedEx, and Microsoft employ far more workers than did the unionized giants of the mid-twentieth century, like Ford and RCA. In 2015, private-sector unions covered a minuscule 6 percent of all workers. And they have little clout: when a trade union represents but a small minority of workers in a competitive industry, those workers no longer have the leverage to raise their own wages and benefits or to set a pattern for their employer's nonunion rivals. Although foreign competition and the economy's weak performance have dampened wages and working conditions, the demise of industry-wide unionism has contributed even more to the wage stagnation that, in the second decade of the twenty-first century, has finally gotten due notice.

Why have unions suffered such dramatic losses? In the 1970s and 1980s, most observers blamed a newly globalized capitalism. But there are other culprits: fierce corporate union-busting, backstopped by an increasingly anti-labor Republican Party, has thwarted all but the most heroic organizing drives. This chapter's second piece, "Equal Time for Union-Busting Firms," illuminates the tough odds facing organizers. And for too long, too many unions were too complacent, failing to focus on organizing in fast-growing service sectors like retail, healthcare, finance, and fast food.

In These Times was well ahead of the curve reporting on these developments.

Indeed, the labor reportage of longtime senior editor David Moberg and other *In These Times* journalists offered readers not merely an account of the travails faced by the labor movement, but an analysis of how to overcome them. In the 1970s and 1980s, labor partisans thought the key to a more powerful labor movement lay primarily in a democratization of a set of large unions whose potential militancy was subverted by their stolid leadership, Cold War outlook, and bureaucratic structure. (In a 1976 article, "Labor Movement: Stuck but Stirring," Moberg reported on those old radicals in the labor movement who now looked to the Sixties generation to revive a set of institutions now seen by many as stolid and complacent, and racist and sexist.) American Federation of Labor and Congress of Industrial Organizations (AFL-CIO) support for the Vietnam War had enraged many on the labor Left, along with the failure of many unions to champion African American civil rights demands or defend shop-floor militancy. In this era, *In These Times* writers reported frequently on opposition movements within key industrial unions like the UAW, the Steelworkers, and the Teamsters.

In These Times writers' commitment to union democracy never wavered, but the crisis set off by President Ronald Reagan's destruction of the Professional Air Traffic Controllers' Union (PATCO) in 1981 made clear that militant and democratic unionism by itself could not provide a bulwark against the growing onslaught from the Right. As Moberg reported in "As PATCO Goes, So Go the Unions," a portrait of the striking air traffic controllers, the union was composed largely of former military men. It was hyperdemocratic and increasingly prone to strike action, not unlike other rank-and-file insurgents of the 1960s and 1970s. Indeed, such heroic militancy remained commonplace in the post-PATCO era at many companies where union-busting managers and investors confronted trade unions head on. Moberg's "Striking People in a Sticky Situation" in this chapter reports on a heartbreaking strike by Hormel meatpacking workers in Austin, Minnesota, who fought both a company determined to slash wages and their own union's top leadership.

But in these well-chronicled fights, even the most creative forms of rank-and-file militancy could but rarely triumph against a free market–oriented neoliberal legal and financial regime linked to an increasingly globalized capitalism. "Concession bargaining," as it was called, eroded the wages, pensions, health benefits, and vacations of the working class, whether organized or not. Another Moberg article here, "To Concede or Not to Concede," explores this dynamic in the auto and trucking industries.

The unions had to begin organizing again and firmly ally themselves with people of color and women, whom in a service-oriented economy increasingly constitute the heart of the twenty-first-century working class. The AFL-CIO labor federation began moving decisively in this direction in the mid-1990s, but renewed efforts to organize workers did not halt the decline in union density. They also didn't prevent a schism over the labor movement's structure and organizing strategy. In 2005, a handful of major unions left AFL-CIO to form the rival federation Change to Win, a gambit analyzed by Moberg in "All Apart Now." But in the retail, health care, and other service sectors where unions hoped to make a breakthrough, many major organizing campaigns still foundered against managerial intransigence. Christopher Hayes's "Symbol of the System" looks at Walmart's particularly virulent brand of anti-unionism.

But this did not mean that changes in the labor movement have had no meaning. By the start of the new century, most of the big American trade unions stood clearly on the left side of American politics. They opposed the war in Iraq in 2003, welcomed Barack Obama to the presidency, and have supported the Occupy, Dreamer, and Black Lives Matter movements.

With new organizing difficult and collective bargaining increasingly marginal to labor's fate, the unions turned to a political strategy to boost the "social wage." The union-backed Fight for $15 campaign (detailed in Chapter 9), along with successful state and local initiatives to guarantee sick leave and provide paid time off after childbirth, all demonstrated how organized labor could once again provide the backbone of a genuinely social democratic policy regime and political movement.

None of this has staunched the institutional decline of the unions, which were under assault in the public sector as well as the private after the Great Recession. Wisconsin Governor Scott Walker's successful move in 2011 to strip public-sector workers of most collective bargaining rights is described in this chapter's final piece, "Capitol Offensive." Walker emboldened conservative Republicans to triumphantly pass a wave of anti-union right-to-work laws in labor's historic heartland: Michigan, Indiana, Wisconsin, and West Virginia. Meanwhile, federal labor-law reforms designed to protect unionism and make organizing possible have failed to become law.

And for more than three decades, the courts have marched steadily to the right on key labor issues.

So are we entering an era when American liberalism revives itself, when Democrats and those to their left finally tackle issues of wealth inequality and stagnant wages, but the trade unions continue their steady march toward marginality? Although little is happening now to contradict such a prospect, two centuries of industrial history argue to the contrary. Since America's Gilded Age, the union cause has been integral to a radical democracy struggling to be born. Trade unions are the one institution that firmly links together the worlds of work, politics, and multicultural social integration. Without them, liberalism too easily transforms into a species of neoliberalism. A revival of the unions therefore remains essential to the revival of progressivism. The sooner American liberals recognize this strategic imperative, the better.

"LABOR MOVEMENT: STUCK BUT STIRRING"

By David Moberg (1976)

"A lot of young people ridicule the labor movement," Mary Beth Guinen complained. "They see it as old guard, racist and fusty."

Before joining the staff of the Service Employees International Union (SEIU) a few years ago, she felt that way too. Now the faults look less glaring. "At first when I came in," she said, "it seemed like there was a locker room atmosphere. Here were all these crewcut guys out of the '50s telling 'funny' sexist jokes. Hadn't they heard of the cultural revolution?

"But they'd change—and deep. On Monday they'd be macho, but later in the week they'd hold a picket sign for the Equal Rights Amendment. These guys really can change. I've never seen any deep racism or sexism. They're really tuned in to human rights."

Conflicting images cloud the picture of trade unions in this country. Most people have contradictory impressions of unions, and the labor movement itself is a most peculiar animal of many inharmonious parts.

If the labor movement drift since the postwar purges has been toward caution, collaboration, conservatism, and occasional outright corruption, it is impossible to write off the entire movement in those terms.

Union bureaucracies certainly have become entrenched at the expense of members, minorities, women, and the unorganized. Even when active they usually have at heart the interests of members only and not other workers. Frequently they devote organizing time and money to raiding other unions.

Yet they are also changing, either under pressure from their ranks or in response to economic vicissitudes. Even though they lack a sense of mission, they still represent by far the strongest voice speaking on behalf of American workers. Even though they have consistently acted as brakes on more radical social change, and as buttresses of capitalism, they have been instruments of beneficial reforms. Their members often bitterly hate their union, but their members will also vigorously fight anyone who would destroy it.

A BAD PUBLIC IMAGE

As saintly and sinful, unions have had a complex but generally unfavorable public image. Nearly all surveys of public confidence in leaders and institutions rank unions and their leaders near the bottom.

That does not mean that most people are against unions. Roughly two-thirds of the public supports workers' right to strike or identifies themselves as being "in favor of" labor.

The gangster image of labor leaders produces much of the negative reaction. But there is also a schizophrenic feeling among many workers who identify with labor at times but also see themselves as antagonistic members of the "public."

Alternatively "the union" may mean, even for a member, either the bureaucracy or the rank and file. Unions (or, more accurately, unionism) does give workers a sense of "we" that is one of the main balances to the American cultural emphasis on "me." Despite union bureaucracies that are unresponsive and despite contractual provisions that cater to individualism, workers still draw the lesson of strength through solidarity from the labor movement, its history, and its ideology.

A union steward training session at a SEIU local recently demonstrated how elementary unionism conflicts with the individualism and distrust prevalent in American culture. Responding to a sample question about how a steward should handle his or her own grievance, a black woman said, "As a union steward, we'd have to say all grievances are equal. As a human being, we might push our own grievance a little harder. But as a union steward, we shouldn't. Persons are elected to steward to represent others. You're chosen to act for them, not to feather your own nest."

Ultimately, the impact of unions in America today is not only to win wages and benefits but, perhaps even more important, to give workers a small measure of security, a feeling of power, a sense of self-worth, defense against arbitrary management authority, and a belief in solidarity with other workers.

"EQUAL TIME FOR UNION-BUSTING FIRMS"

By Richard Kazis (1980)

"We make a serious effort to be like a marriage counselor between employees and employers." That is how Herbert Melnick, chairman of Modern Management, Inc., described his firm's activities during a House Subcommittee on Labor-Management Relations oversight hearing on "Pressures in Today's Workplace," held in Washington in February 1980.

Fred Long, chairman of West Coast Industrial Relations, Inc., put it slightly differently. "I'd rather use the analogy of doctors. We find out what ails the company and then cure it. After that, we suggest preventive medicine to keep the company healthy."

But people who have been on the receiving end of these firms' efforts to help management implement (as Melnick puts it) "effective and meaningful programs for communications with employees" are neither so metaphorical nor so sanguine. Robert Muehlenkamp, Director of Organization for District 1199 of the National Union of Hospital and Health Care Employees, followed Melnick's testimony. "What you heard today is a lie," he began. He went on in his statement to say, "Mr. Melnick's business is to lie and to coerce."

The business that Melnick, Long, and others like them are involved in is union-busting—and business is booming. The American Federation of Labor and Congress of Industrial Organizations (AFL-CIO) estimates that $100 million will be spent this year for the services of firms that, as Representative Dale Kildee (D-Mich.) noted, "have replaced the blackjack and the lead pipe with the briefcase and the ballpoint pen."

Two days of hearings were intended to give several of the most well-known and often-attacked management consultants a chance to defend and explain their activities. A full panel of Modern Management top brass and Fred Long not only defended their activities but mounted a smooth counterattack.

Melnick and Long gave similar testimonies. Each claimed to have engaged in no illegal activities. Each stressed that his firm was neither anti-union nor against collective bargaining. Both emphasized the importance of fostering cooperation between workers and management. Long claimed that when his firm's work is completed, there is a "happier and more motivated workforce."

Several witnesses and members of Congress challenged the consultants' testimony. William Lively, who was personnel director at California's Woodview Hospital during an anti-union campaign run by West Coast Industrial Relations (WCIR) in 1977, testified that WCIR put pressure on him to falsify records so that anti-union supervisory personnel would be allowed to vote in the election. He also explained how WCIR consultants had illegally initiated a campaign to decertify Local 399 of Service Employees International Union (SEIU), and how they had boasted that they could keep any election decision in the courts for years before it would be enforced.

The reaction of the members of the subcommittee was disturbing. Most of the more liberal Democrats were not in attendance. Except for Ted Weiss of New York, Democrats on the committee seemed either unprepared for battle or convinced by the consultants' seamless testimonies. Only Robert Muehlenkamp addressed the heart of the matter.

There were few challenges to the basic assumptions of Herbert Melnick, Fred Long, and others like them. These men in fact are anti-union and anti-labor. They see unions as obstacles to productivity and profit and, perhaps more important, as threats to the employer's total control over his workforce. Their model is not democracy in the workplace, but enlightened despotism, with their firms serving as well-rewarded advisers to the kings.

It is unsettling that the basic right of workers to organize and to act in their own self-interest received so little defense during these two days of hearings and that the proponents of unrestricted prerogative for employers were given such a polite and sympathetic reception. The boldness of Melnick and Long as they sat before the subcommittee is a clear indication that the attack on labor's right to organize is no longer confined to specific workplace campaigns. It has become a broad ideological offensive.

"As PATCO goes, so go the unions"

By David Moberg (1981)

Ask the average American why the air traffic controllers went out on strike and the odds are that he or she would say, with little sympathy, that those characters making $30,000 to $40,000 a year were greedily after even more money—a $10,000 a year increase, for starters.

But ask the average air traffic controller this question and the answer is quite different. I asked Carl Conant, the thirty-three-year-old vice president of the Professional Air Traffic Controllers Organization (PATCO) local at Stapleton airport in Denver, why he decided to make the leap: "I'm frustrated by not having the best health plan, and I even have to fund 40 percent of it myself, and besides, I don't have a dental or eye plan. I have a 90 percent chance of not making it to retirement. I have no voice in the policies I am subjected to. Every week there are new regulations, and I don't have a voice in the things I do.

"Money is definitely not the issue. If I could have a retirement plan, a shorter work week, good health benefits, good equipment, and a voice in job procedures, I wouldn't want that $10,000."

But eventually the talk always comes back to the unique characteristics of the job that attract, and exhaust, the intense band of people who guide the nation's commercial and private planes through the skies.

"When the traffic builds, your adrenalin heightens," said Mike Fahey, thirty-three. "Then the mental stress comes into play because of the adrenalin flow and the fatigue." Stories abound—of ulcers, nervous breakdowns, jitters carried home, and coworkers who simply could no longer take the job.

Controllers tend to be young men who thrive on challenge. The daily camaraderie, often involving instantaneous coordination and trust of one's colleagues, reinforces their sense of being a "special breed of people." Since four-fifths of them came into their jobs through the military, and many of those now on the job served in Vietnam, they have an additional sense of commonality. All that contributes to a natural solidarity that was nurtured in recent years by their growing sense of frustration over abuse by their supervisors, increasing workloads with insufficient staffing, faulty equipment that would go on the blink—suddenly leaving them with a darkened radar screen with a couple dozen planes floating in a narrow air space—and continual repudiation of their demands by the Federal Aviation Administration and Congress, leaving them far behind counterparts in other countries.

Eventually they felt they had no choice. "It was either go on an illegal strike and get fired," Dave Rambeau, thirty-five, said, "or stay there under the harassment of the Federal Aviation Administration and get fired for union activity or else never make it to retirement." Like many other controllers, he considers even the firings and threats he now suffers to be not much worse than staying on the job under previous conditions.

THE NO-STRIKE CLAUSE

But what about the controllers' pledge not to strike? What about the government's broken promises and contracts? Conant replied, ticking off a few earlier defaults by the Federal Aviation Administration and Congress: no adequate retirement plan, no funding for the promised training for a second career, no up-to-date equipment.

Most of the controllers at the Denver airport voted for Ronald Reagan, on the basis of a pledge the union received from his top campaign staff to treat controllers fairly; only a few would have supported him otherwise, they said. Most seemed not to be political, but there are scattered sympathies for conservative positions. The strike has changed their view not only of Reagan but also of the United States.

"There's something wrong with America when a man on strike is taken to prison in shackles," Conant said. "There's something wrong when people with $30,000-a-year jobs risk those jobs to go on strike. I love America, but if they tear down the unions, you might as well move to Russia. Here's the same man who wants to get government out of our personal business destroying our union. It seems like a contradiction."

Editor's note: Two days after PATCO's strike began, President Regan fired nearly all of the union's members for refusing to return to work. The unprecedented executive action broke the union and set the tone for labor relations throughout the 1980s and beyond.

"LABOR'S PROBLEMS ARE THE NATION'S PROBLEMS"

By Nicholas von Hoffman (1981)

The decimation of the air controllers strike can be written off as the ineluctable reaction of Reaganism to uppityness by public employees. Call it Republicans being Republicans, but when Democrats are being Democrats, it can be as devastating. It was the Democrat Jimmy Carter who smashed the coal strike by declaring a serious national emergency and did damage to the union from which it has yet to recover. It was the pro-labor president who advertised himself as a tender-hearted, empathetic wimp who sent the federal marshalls up into the hollers of West Virginia to serve papers on men who spit to see if the first symptoms of black lung will fly out of their mouths.

Since unionism isn't built into the party, Democrat attitudes toward labor organizations wax and wane with the prevailing public moods. Often there is no fixed, overall policy; rather each union must deal for itself so that as Carter was doing his best to destroy the coal miners he was creating a new, special, cabinet-level department for the National Education Association, the dominant teachers' union.

For the unskilled and the replaceable, successful union organization only began when government power was shifted over to the workers' side with the enactment of the Wagner Labor Relations Act. Without it, organizing a company, much less winning a strike, was occasional and heroic. But changing conditions and the whittling away of the act's protections has, over the course of many years, come close to nullifying it.

Reversing community hostility to unions and reinvigorating the Wagner Act cannot turn the trick by itself. Chrysler limps along to remind us that a completely organized work force in a company spurting red ink can't, no matter how strong and intelligent its union leadership, separate itself from the dying company.

The dislocations and changes in every aspect of employment are far beyond the power of even the strongest union to handle. Most employers are as helpless as unions in that they don't create their competitive situations—they react to them. Even industrywide bargaining is of little help in a low-tariff, free trade nation like ours. The disasters that have overtaken the American rubber and tire industry would not have been avoided by a different bargaining setup or different bargaining demands.

The crux of these matters are society-wide, not industry-wide. They must be handled through national policy and national planning, not by our friendly business agent with four unsmoked stogies tucked in his vest pocket, pleading with a senator to "give us the secondary boycott back and you'll never see us again."

"To concede or not to concede"

By David Moberg (1982)

Should workers make concessions to save troubled companies or industries? Tough-minded trade unionists, accustomed to scrapping with their employers for every tiny step forward, understandably flinch at the prospect. "You don't go down the ladder, because it will take you forever to climb back up," argues Don Douglas, president of the 9,000-member United Automobile Workers (UAW) Local 594 in Pontiac, Michigan, and a leader in the newly formed Locals Opposed to Concessions.

Among workers at General Motors (GM), which is expected to be profitable this year, the sentiment appears to run deep: despite urgings by UAW leadership, 43 percent of the union's GM council voted against resuming the talks with GM that had broken off two days earlier.

For many, the contract and those battles enshrined in it are sacred. But there is also the strategic bet that nothing can be gained, especially in bad times, that is worth the concession price. (The UAW bargainers, on the contrary, argue that when the companies are desperate, the union may be able to extract their own quid pro quo concessions.) But if the trade-offs were good enough—say, lifetime jobs in exchange for a few pennies less an hour—principle would take the hindmost.

The new Teamster contract, however, appears to fulfill the worst fears about what the concession game produces. The Teamsters agreed to freeze wages (but theoretically can reopen that portion of the contract), reduce the number of cost-of-living payments and divert part of that money to pensions, reduce pay for new workers, cut back some pension payments for part-timers and guaranteed pay for other workers, and change work rules to allow some direct delivery of freight in cities by over-the-road truckers.

Teamster leaders claim the contract will save jobs. But some of the work rule changes will probably reduce jobs.

Although the Teamsters have lost work to nonunion drivers in truckload freight hauling, where it is easy for an owner-operator to enter, they still have the vast majority of truckers working for the big national companies that emphasize less-than-truckload shipments (LTL). With regard to these companies, a Standard and Poor's industry survey concluded, "Any union concessions would serve primarily to bolster long-term profitability, rather than preserve Teamster jobs. In the short-run, a uniform reduction in costs for all LTL carriers would not ensure a more vibrant industry. Only higher tonnage levels and a shakeout of excess capacity can accomplish that."

Trucking is not a dying industry, Teamsters for a Democratic Union (TDU) organizer Ken Paff emphasizes, even if it is in a recession slump and a phase of competitive restructuring; there is no question from other transportation modes. "The big thing is: Can the union organize the unorganized?" Paff says. Many observers wonder how the Teamsters—or the UAW or any other union—can appeal to unorganized workers if it is giving up its past gains.

The autoworkers face a more difficult and complex situation. If the industry is to be competitive, it will have to automate much more, and the wave of robots could easily displace a quarter million jobs by 1985. Without some form of local content requirements for cars sold in the United States, job loss as a result of imports and a declining percentage of U.S. parts in cars assembled by domestic producers could reduce employment by as much as an additional 200,000 jobs.

"STRIKING PEOPLE IN A STICKY SITUATION"

By David Moberg (1986)

Austin, Minnesota—It was late at night in the basement of the union hall. There a mural sketched the history of American workers from slavery through Congress of Industrial Organizations (CIO) organizing to present-day depictions of air controllers on strike and farm auctions, culminating in a triumphal portrait of United Food and Commercial Workers Local P-9 and its leaders. Tom (not his real name) was making popcorn, which has always been available along with coffee, soup, and other staples for the meat-packers at Geo. A. Hormel & Co. during their six-month strike. He was in his usual good spirits, maintained by retreating to his home woodshop as well as by keeping in touch with fellow strikers at the hall. Under great pressure some of them had abandoned the strike; next to their names on the work schedule people had scrawled the epithet "scab."

Now fifty-four, Tom had worked eighteen years at Hormel after abandoning farming. "I won't cross that picket line no matter what," he insisted. "Life is too short to be a scab all your life. I don't want my boy to go to school and have somebody say his dad's a scab." But his convictions have had their price. He'd been reluctant to get food from the union's food shelf or to ask for money raised through its "adopt-a-family" support appeal. He always figured someone else needed it more. Then one day he was hit with two notices that shocked his hardworking self-image. "I almost lost my car and had my utilities cut off," he said, his voice suddenly breaking, his face reddening as he fought back the tears. He turned away for a moment to regain his composure.

With the company now hiring replacement workers and several hundred of the 1,420 P-9 members crossing the picket lines, tension has grown throughout this small community. It is not uncommon for people suddenly to break into tears or to speak out in angry frustration. "These are ties that bring out the best and the worst in us," said community-college teacher George Hillberg—one of the few community people who is publicly sympathetic to the strikers.

STICKING WITH IT

On a Thursday morning late in January 1986, a group of workers who were wavering in their loyalties had gathered in the union hall to voice their fears. And during their meeting with local officials and stalwart strikers, it appeared that most were—for the moment—ready to stick with the union.

"I've been a union member of thirty-five years," Billy said afterward. "It's hard to cross a picket line of people you know. But why should I roll over and play dead for a cause I don't believe in?" He wouldn't have what he had now without unions, but they weren't needed as much now, he argued. Besides, he wanted freedom to do as he wanted. As a "good worker" he didn't really need the union or could always find another job, he believed. He'd give the strike another two weeks.

The battle fought between the company and the local union and within the community and the international union is fought out in each worker's mind as well. For example, Jerry Simes had thought of crossing the picket line that day. "But I didn't cross," he told friends at the hall, "because I'm a goddam union man. That's the secret line I will not cross. My kids want me to cross. My wife wants me to cross. I don't agree with everything in my union, but I'm a goddam union man. When the union goes down, we'll have a dictatorship." But the decision has taken its toll. "Goddam," he mutters, "I didn't want it to come to this."

Roger (he asked that his real name not be used) finally reached his decision to cross. "I knew it was over," he said of the strike. "It's awfully tough. I've been friends with most of them all my life. I played sports here. Some people look up to me. To see me crossing disappointed a lot of people. I've been in sports and the army, but going down that ramp, it's the worst thing that's ever happened to me, going across that picket line. But number one is your family."

Three things convinced him the union was losing: the company hiring permanent replacements, "the international [selling] us down the river," and the arrival of the national guard. With a partial disability, he feared he couldn't get another job. And the union didn't seem to have the power it needed. "If the international had more power and Jim Guyette [president of Local P-9] was the leader instead of [international President William] Wynn, he might do well. He's intelligent. What he's saying is right. But he doesn't have the clout here."

Back on the job, Roger refuses to associate with the new hires, whom he blames for undermining the strike. With a rationale that remaining strikers reject, he does not consider himself a "scab," since he feels he's not taking someone else's job, simply trying to save his own.

Other crossovers said that many of the new hires—reportedly mostly young and not from Austin—were very happy with jobs that paid as much as twice what they had been making, even with the company-imposed pay cuts. Some are farmers who have been hit hard by low prices, drought, and debt pressures. Gary Harrison told of a farmer friend who had taken a job at Hormel. "It's killing him," he said. "He was in tears. He's got a wife and four kids. He's losing his farm. He's a proud man, and he feels he has to take care of his family. I can't condemn him for that, but I want him on our side. But with Reaganomics and the economy the way it is, Hormel is in the driver's seat. But I think America is getting damn tired of it."

"Working it out"

By David Moberg (1993)

Bill Clinton wants to help American workers be successful high-skill, high-wage competitors in the global economy. To pursue that goal, Secretary of Labor Robert Reich commissioned a panel of labor experts to suggest changes in labor laws and institutions by next year that would "enhance workplace productivity through labor-management cooperation and employee participation."

This mission statement enshrines improved economic performance of individual businesses as the overriding goal of labor law. The ten commission members are all sympathetic to unions. But Reich's directive not only risks giving short shrift to many of the historic goals of the labor movement but also may, surprisingly, not even be the best way of strengthening the overall economy and reaching Clinton's goal.

In the Depression, union organizers gave workers leaflets saying that President Roosevelt wanted them to join a union. Asked on the *MacNeil-Lehrer Newshour* whether he would recommend that workers with problems organize a union, Reich said he would first suggest that management and workers "come up with ways of working together constructively." The administration does not favor increased unionization, he said. "We don't want to load the deck in either direction."

Reich argues that workers must have a "voice" for businesses to maximize their productivity. At their best, unions have been a voice for justice on the job, higher wages, and solidarity—goals not necessarily related to international competitiveness. But many labor strategists think their best bet for labor-law reform is to argue that unions are good for the economy.

It is silly to argue whether labor–management cooperation in itself is good or bad. Workers inevitably cooperate with their employers simply by going to work, and some problems can be solved through rational dialogue. The real question is: To what ends and on whose terms should workers and employers cooperate?

Yet there are real differences of interest and power between workers and employers. Unions attempt not simply to provide workers a means of expressing their views but also to give them some power. Any approach to labor-law reform that glosses over the grossly disproportionate power of bosses and workers is a fraud. Cooperation is meaningful only when each party has a meaningful right to say either yes or no to proposals—in other words, only when there is the possibility for conflict.

Research over the past decade has shown that unions tend to increase productivity in firms. Indeed, economists Maryellen R. Kelley and Bennett Harrison found that unionized metalworking firms were more efficient and provided more job security for workers than nonunion firms with employee involvement. So it might seem that the work of Reich's commission is straightforward: it should figure out what will promote unionism.

"LEXUS AND THE RIGHT TO PEE"

By Barbara Ehrenreich (1999)

The right to organize is a little like the right to buy a Lexus. It exists—theoretically and on paper, thanks to the National Labor Relations Act of 1935—but is of almost no practical value to the average working person. A few years ago, for example, an organizer I know almost had convinced the employees of a confectionery warehouse in Queens to exercise this right—when management got wind of their intentions. The boss marched in, plucked out the two most vociferously pro-union workers, and pistol-whipped them in front of the terrified work force. End of organizing drive.

More commonly, in your larger and better-funded workplaces, management brings in a union-busting firm—sometimes at a price greater than several years of wage increases—and institutes a campaign of brainwashing. Employees are forced to attend "meetings" where they listen for hours as skilled union-busters explain why organizing would, in effect, ruin their lives: because unions are huge, corrupt, mob-like structures bent on extorting dues from gullible workers; because their pro-union coworkers are twisted, power-hungry wretches; because unionization will force management to relocate to Guatemala; etc. In a tragically high proportion of cases, these Orwellian tactics work.

John Sweeney's rejuvenated American Federation of Labor and Congress of Industrial Organizations (AFL-CIO) is launching a broad campaign for labor-law reform that would make the right to organize a little less theoretical. This is exciting and long overdue. It just doesn't go far enough.

What the AFL-CIO campaign leaves out is that the right to organize isn't the only human right missing in the American workplace. Take freedom of speech: a couple of years ago, I read about a Dallas grocery store worker being fired for tactlessly wearing a Green Bay Packers T-shirt to work. Ho ho, I thought, they won't get away with this. I was wrong. You can be fired for anything, so long as it does not constitute discrimination on the basis of race, sex, disability, or religion. (And Packer fandom is not yet recognized as a legitimate religion.) Yet antifeminists still like to argue that sexual harassment laws limit male workers' "freedom of speech." In the American workplace, there is no such freedom.

Ditto freedom of assembly: management is free to assemble the work force as a captive audience for anti-union harangues, but the work force is not free to assemble for its own deliberations. And you can't ever count on having a break, even to pee. There is no federal guarantee of the right to take a break on a shift of any length—an omission, as explained in Marc Linder and Ingrid Nygaard's extremely useful book *Void Where Prohibited*, that has an ugly effect on bladder and kidney health.

The most egregiously missing right is the right to any kind of privacy. American workers, supposedly proud heirs of the Revolution of 1776, can expect to have their phone conversations and e-mail monitored, their purses searched for contraband or stolen goods, and their private lives surveyed for unhealthy practices—such as smoking or motorcycling—that could be costly to the company health insurance plan, if there is one. Even more degrading, 70 percent of major companies now require employees to undergo urine tests for drugs.

It would help, in the coming struggle for the right to organize, if the unions were a little more militant about all the other missing workplace rights—if they had, for example, firmly resisted the encroachment of chemical fascism in the form of drug-testing. Maybe to hard-pressed union staff these seem like peripheral issues. But if you can't speak freely at work, assemble, or even safely carry union literature in your handbag, you're not in any position to organize.

More insidiously, the dictatorship of the bosses breeds submission in its victims. Why don't more self-respecting workers disrupt those union-bashing, captive-audience meetings? Because, after years of surveillance and monitoring and urine testing, they may not feel so self-respecting any more.

What we need is much more than a campaign for the right to organize. We need a new civil rights movement—this time for workers of all colors and genders—upholding the idea that the rights of free citizens are far too precious to check at the workplace door. If it wants to squash the management image of unions as dues-eating parasites, the AFL-CIO should lead the way.

"SOUTHERN BELLWETHER"

By Ian Urbina (2002)

"Organize or die" is the labor movement's mantra. Yet there still seems to be little strategy for one of labor's biggest and most enduring obstacles— organizing in the South. "Most unions are simply not yet willing to commit to campaigns in these states," says Nelson Lichtenstein, a labor historian at the University of California, Santa Barbara. "But they can't afford to wait."

Aside from being the main source of the hemorrhaging of factory jobs overseas, the South drags down national standards in working conditions and wages. Northern victories in organizing, job security, livable wages, or improved labor laws can only be temporary with the entrance to a Third World free trade zone at the Mason-Dixon line.

The obstacles to organizing in the South are huge. Since the North American Free Trade Agreement (NAFTA), southern employers have gone unmatched in using the illegal but highly effective threat of plant closure to discourage workers from organizing.

Southern managers are also far more apt to use race to divide union support. "When unions arrive, the very first thing many Southern bosses do is tell white workers to get ready for all black managers," says Stewart Acuff, a deputy regional director of the American Federation of Labor and Congress of Industrial Organizations (AFL-CIO). Right-to-work laws—which exist in twenty-two states, allowing workers in a union shop to opt out of paying dues—act as further disincentive for unions to head south.

Anti-labor sentiment tends to be much more overt than in the North. "Organizers down there are often completely on their own," Acuff says. "Mention the word union, and southern politicians of all shades disappear into thin air."

An added barrier to southern organizing is the lack of collective bargaining rights for government workers. In the North, labor laws provide at least marginal protection for the right of both public and private sector employees to organize. Since the government is less apt than private employers to get into dirty anti-union fights, public workers have joined unions in high numbers. As a result, the northern public sector offers a strong base of support as unions initiate campaigns in difficult industries.

But in much of the South it is illegal for public sector workers to bargain collectively, and thus there are no safe zones for union organizing. "The right wing in the southern states remains on high-alert regarding unions," says Paul Booth of American Federation of State, County and Municipal Employees (AFSCME), which represents public employees. "They believe that if they can cut organizing off at the public sector, it will never have a chance to spread to the private sector."

"ALL APART NOW"

By David Moberg (2005)

The old hymn of organized labor—"Solidarity Forever"—has rarely seemed less appropriate. Three big unions recently left the American Federation of Labor and Congress of Industrial Organizations (AFL-CIO) to forge a coalition with four other unions under the banner of Change to Win (CTW), which is launching an alternative federation in late September 2005. It makes the lyrics about labor unity ring a bit hollow.

But old as it is, the idea that strength for workers comes through collective empathy and action is still the strategic heart of the labor movement. And despite hard feelings on both sides, the split itself reflects an ongoing search for the most effective forms of solidarity in a world where global corporations and global labor markets rule, employment is becoming less secure, and the sentiments of mutual support among American workers have been diminished by market-driven culture and politics.

The challenge for unions is not simply to organize more workers, although that is crucial if labor is to regain power. It is to create relationships of understanding, support, and action among workers at various levels—in their workplaces, industries, and occupations; with fellow employees of far-flung corporations; in the community; at different levels of government and politics; and internationally.

Much of the fight leading up to the July 2005 AFL-CIO convention was ostensibly about the structure of the labor movement—mergers, jurisdictions, and dues rebates. In the end, the CTW unions said that the changes AFL-CIO President John Sweeney and his supporters were willing to make weren't big enough. The Sweeney camp retorted that the remaining differences were minimal, but the CTW unions left because other unions would not guarantee that Sweeney would step down early and let them pick his successor.

Now the question is not just how much the split will hurt the labor movement but whether either side can find a way to make the movement a bigger and more effective political force for working people.

The split may disrupt political mobilization of union members, but it is not a big ideological rupture. Unions on both sides of the divide, for example, pointedly attacked the fifteen Democrats who voted for the Central

American Free Trade Agreement. And both also insist they want to be more bipartisan—as if there are many pro-labor Republicans to support.

But the threat remains that the split could lead to organizational raiding. For example, Service Employees International Union (SEIU), the lead union in CTW, is recruiting domestic childcare workers away from a California branch of American Federation of State, County and Municipal Employees (AFSCME), the largest union remaining in the AFL-CIO. Meanwhile, AFSCME could launch retaliatory raids elsewhere against SEIU.

No EASY ANSWERS

Solidarity at the state and local level also remains a problem. In response to worries about federation rules that locals of disaffiliated unions could not belong to central labor councils or state federations, Sweeney offered a way for them to continue their membership. But the conditions—including a special assessment and rules for locals and their officers—were unacceptable to the CTW unions. To a degree, each side of the split is trying to shift the responsibility for breaking up the solidarity at the state and local level to the other side. But destroying the effective state and local labor groups established with great effort during the past decade over the national strategic battle serves no worker's interest.

"Hopefully, one of us is right," UNITE HERE President John Wilhelm says of the split. "If the AFL-CIO is wrong, and we're wrong, then workers' lives in this country are ruined." But it may be that each side has some of the truth. What is needed is openness to every way of strengthening solidarity. Without that, workers—and the labor movement—could indeed be ruined.

"SYMBOL OF THE SYSTEM"

By Christopher Hayes (2005)

There's a moment in the documentary *Walmart: The High Cost of Low Price* that serves as a perfect metaphor for the entire battle between organized labor and the country's largest private employer.

Josh Noble, an employee of the Tire and Lube Express division of a Walmart in Loveland, Colorado, is attempting to organize seventeen of his fellow workers into a union. As the National Labor Relations Board (NLRB) election approaches, we see Noble with a United Food and Commercial Workers (UFCW) advisor going through the list of employees, discussing who's with them and who's not. Noble says it looks about 50/50. Later, the organizer cautions Noble that he may have lost the vote of his friend Alicia. "No," Noble says. "I've talked with her quite a bit. She's just kind of hard to read … I hang out with her on the weekends. But she's definitely into it. She's real strong." Cut to: Alicia Sylvia in her car. Management's putting the squeeze on and she's now equivocating. We know what will happen. It's like watching David sent out to battle Goliath, blindfolded. Without a sling.

When election day finally rolls around, Noble loses the election—17 to 1.

It's not just that Walmart has been winning the ongoing fight with the UFCW, which has been trying to organize the bulk of the company's 1.2 million employees for the last six years. It's that its dominance has been so absolute that even the small victories the union has scored have proved to be Pyrrhic. In 2000, when seven of ten butchers in a store in Jacksonville, Texas, voted to join the UFCW, Walmart responded by announcing that henceforth it would sell only precut meat in all of its supercenters, fired four of the union supporters, and transferred the rest into other divisions. (Three years later, the NLRB ruled the decision illegal.) And in May 2005, when workers at a store in Jonquière, Québec, voted to unionize, Walmart simply shut the place down. "They wanted to send a message to every other store," says UFCW spokesperson Chris Kofinis: "'Don't you dare unionize.'"

BY ANY MEANS NECESSARY

There's little secret to Walmart's success. The company will simply do whatever it takes to keep workers from organizing. "Staying union-free is a full-time commitment," reads one of the company's training manuals. "[F]rom the Chairperson of the 'Board' down to the front-line manager … [t]he entire management staff should fully comprehend and appreciate exactly what is expected of their individual efforts to meet the union-free objective."

Managers are trained to call a special hotline at the first sign of suspicious behavior, including "employees talking in hushed tones to each other." After the call, the company's notorious labor relations division headquartered in Bentonville, Arkansas, will swing into gear, often dispatching a company jet to the afflicted store, bearing members of its crack team of union busters. Management will convene mandatory meetings with each associate and screen anti-union videos.

Former managers, like Stan Fortune, who worked for Walmart for seventeen years and then went to work for UFCW, say the store also illegally follows union sympathizers and spies on its employees with cameras in break rooms. "One of their favorite tactics is to say, 'We need to freeze all raises in the store because it can't appear that we're bribing anybody,'" Fortune says in the film.

And then Walmart will find a way to get rid of troublemakers. That's what spelled the end of Fortune's career as a manager at the company. In 2001 Fortune was managing a Walmart in Weatherford, Texas, when his boss instructed him to fire an employee suspected of talking to the union. "I told him 'I'm not firing him,' " Fortune says. "'That's illegal' ... He got in my face and said, 'You fire him or I'm going to fire you.'" A week later, Fortune was gone. "I filed for unemployment and the state found I was fired without cause. That's when I found out that means nothing in the real world."

Since 1999 the UFCW and others have filed more than 300 charges against Walmart with the NLRB, accusing the company of, among other transgressions, firing employees for suspected union activity in violation of the Wagner Act. In a third of these cases, the local NLRB office has issued a formal complaint and attempted to prosecute the company, but it hardly matters to the behemoth because even if the full NLRB rules against Walmart, the resulting penalties are a pittance. Walmart didn't return calls for comment, but generally they deny ever breaking the law.

In April 2005, the UFCW threw in the towel and decided to start from scratch. Instead of seeking to organize workers store by store, it launched WakeUpWalMart.com, a public awareness campaign designed to educate the public about Walmart's business impact and negative community effects. A coalition led by Service Employees International Union (SEIU), Democracy for America, and the Sierra Club has launched a similar project called WalMartWatch.com.

Walmart deserves just about all the bad press it gets, and its recent commercials stressing what a gosh-darn great place it is to work would suggest that these efforts are having some effect. But because there's been so much focus on Walmart's misdeeds, it's easy to surmise that the company is a kind of outlier and that the rest of corporate America would never stoop to such techniques. This is simply not the case.

"The right to organize in the United States is on the verge of extinction," says Andy Levin, director of the American Federation of Labor and Congress of Industrial Organizations (AFL-CIO) Voices@Work campaign. "Walmart's not a bad apple—it's the very symbol of a rotten system."

"Not your parents' labor movement"

By David Moberg (2009)

Workers of Chicago-based Republic Windows and Doors captured the nation's attention when they occupied their workplace in December 2008. Their employer gave only three days notice of the plant's closing and showed no intention of paying their accrued vacation pay or two months of back wages, as is legally required after a notice of closing.

Republic's bank, the publicly salvaged Bank of America, refused to extend credit to the company. In response, the 250 workers, mainly Latino and African American, occupied the plant, preventing the company from moving the machinery out until they received what they were owed.

Support poured in—from other unions, community groups, religious leaders and even president-elect Obama. Images of sit-down strikes from the Great Depression came to mind as the Great Recession deepened. Many observers thought Republic might be a harbinger of a new wave of labor militancy.

"These workers are to this struggle perhaps what Rosa Parks was to social justice fifty years ago," Reverend Jesse Jackson told a rally at the plant. "This, in many ways, is the beginning of a larger movement for mass action to resist economic violence."

A lackluster response

More than half a year later, that larger movement hasn't materialized. Why not? It's not for lack of reasons. Employers continue to shut down workplaces, cut wages, and fight pro-union legislation. Workers in other countries frequently take direct action to fight job losses. French factory workers hold managers hostage. Brazilian and Argentine workers seize and operate businesses and, in June 2009, British energy workers went on an unauthorized national strike.

The Republic sit-in has reverberated elsewhere, but only faintly. For example, workers at two Hartmarx men's clothing factories in Illinois and New York voted in May to stage a sit-in if the bankrupt company and its uncooperative bank, Wells Fargo, failed to sell to a buyer who would continue production in its domestic factories. (In June, the company announced it would sell to such a buyer.) In April, Southern Californian warehouse workers at a distribution center for mega-retailers staged sit-ins at a temporary staffing agency and blocked a prominent intersection.

Apart from these examples, few protests—let alone sit-ins—have occurred in response to widespread lay-offs and factory closings. "I think Chicago was the aberration," says Cornell University labor relations professor Richard Hurd. "We have very little tradition of labor militancy."

Since 1980, unions have rarely struck or taken other direct action in either good or bad times. Their current passivity reflects the evolution of American political culture, which has been shaped by corporate and right-wing hostility to workers' rights and unions. Elaine Bernard, the director of the Harvard Trade Union Program, says that the rarity of Republic-style sit-down strikes can be explained by the "tremendous repression" in the United States as compared to other countries. "I'm surprised in this country, with the high level of repression, how much is happening."

The political culture of American workers has also become even more individualistic. When unions were able to win strong contracts after the Second World War, many workers became comfortable with the gains from conservative business unionism. When the political Right gained hegemony after 1980, neither unions nor the Democratic Party effectively mobilized workers as a class.

According to University of Massachusetts sociology professor Eve Weinbaum, when workplaces close, workers tend to blame themselves. And workers today are often cynical about what unions or politicians can do for them. Most have little experience taking action themselves, as strikes and new organizing have declined. "The hurt and pain are still there, and you can see anger at executive pay," sociologist Dan Clawson says. "But people don't see how something might work and seize the opportunity."

LABOR UNION SHRINKAGE

As a result of employer hostility, globalization, weak legal protection, and the failure of unions to organize new workers, unions' share of the workforce and strength has declined. This has led many unions to retrench or find nonconfrontational ways to grow.

In many cases, unions have become closer partners with management than with the general public. Such development of a joint labor–management strategy made the autoworkers, for example, more isolated and vulnerable to attack and less likely to win better terms in the bailout—even if they had wanted to follow Republic workers' lead. "Autoworkers were not thinking of taking over plants and producing cars for fear the public would say, 'We tried to help. To hell with you,'" says Bernard.

Unions do turn out members to vote disproportionately for Democrats, but labor suffers from a general political demobilization. During the '60s, the Left pressured Democratic presidents to change course on foreign and domestic policy. Since then, political scientist Sheldon Wolin argues in *Democracy Incorporated*, the United States has evolved toward what he calls "inverted totalitarianism." In other words, America imposes a constricted free market model on policy while creating a controlled illusion of democracy.

Despite the current crisis of capitalism, the leadership of a new Democratic administration, and right-wing claims that Obama is a socialist, this free market economic model still dominates policy. This model denies the legitimacy of unruly democratic demands, such as a movement inspired by the Republic sit-in. A popular movement for economic democracy may develop, but it will need more than the militant disruption of business-as-usual in the workplace. It will require dismantling the debilitating, individualized free market mindsets of workers, unions, politicians, and the American public.

"CAPITOL OFFENSIVE"

by David Moberg (2011)

Madison, Wisconsin—The sheer number of people who marched around the Wisconsin state capitol building to protest Republican Governor Scott Walker's plan to cripple and kill public workers' unions was dramatic— around 100,000 on a cold, snowy Saturday in late February 2011.

They included members of nearly every union, farmers, small business people, and nonunion workers. A thousand unionized teaching assistants from the University of Wisconsin had come out early, jumpstarting the mass demonstrations within days of Walker's February 11 announcement of legislation that would end collective bargaining rights for the majority of the state's public-sector workers. Then they peaceably occupied the capitol, keeping it open for everybody. Police refused to evict them and then slept overnight with them in the hallways. Firefighters showed up wearing their helmets, accompanied by a drum and bagpipe corps.

Since Governor Walker announced his "budget repair" bill, there have been demonstrations by hundreds, even thousands, of workers and ordinary citizens in hundreds of small towns throughout Wisconsin.

Inside the capitol, the rotunda was a perpetual free speech zone, with protesters leaning over balconies to listen. A giant banner—"Tax the Rich"— hung above them.

Paul Woods, fifty-six, a nonunion carpenter and cabinet-maker, understood the issues of democracy and class conflict at the heart of this confrontation. "I'm definitely supporting the people," Woods says. "I feel like the middle class is being scapegoated and the corporations are having their way with us. If they want to fix things, they should grow the economy, not crush middle-class values."

THE BATTLE HAS BEEN JOINED

Walker and other Republican governors in at least a dozen states, including Ohio, Indiana, and Missouri, are engaged in a battle to destroy both public and private unions as a voice of workers on the job. Corporations and conservatives have crushed private-sector unions to less than 7 percent of the workforce with anti-union tactics, deregulation, globalization or outsourcing, and weakened labor laws. Today, public unions represent half the labor movement, most of its growth, and a disproportionate share of its political spending, making them a prime target for the resurgent Right.

Indeed, many on the Right want to eradicate or eviscerate unions to destroy the single most important source of financial and organizational support for the Democrats and what remains of liberalism—the weak American version of European social democracy.

The protesters were clearly motivated to defend the right of all workers to bargain collectively. Many people who were not in a union saw the labor movement as a defender of their interests. As the protests went on, polling consistently showed large majorities nationally and in Wisconsin supporting collective bargaining rights by nearly two to one.

"This is not a budget crisis," says Randi Weingarten, president of the American Federation of Teachers. "This is a power grab," as well as an effort "to foreclose public service workers out of a middle-class lifestyle by first taking away their voice and then doing as much as they can to minimize their political activity."

Because union leaders agreed to Walker's demand that state workers pay more for pensions and health insurance, much of the public appears to agree with Weingarten. Public workers often do have better insurance plans than many in the private sector. But research from the Economic Policy Institute and other investigators shows that public workers earn less in both wages and total compensation than private-sector workers with the same education, job tenure, and experience. That's true nationally and in Wisconsin and Ohio, where Republican Governor John Kasich pushed through legislation stripping public workers of collective bargaining rights.

Getting more workers to join a union would be the most appropriate rejoinder to the Right. The labor movement will need to implement organizing campaigns that are systematic and targeted, like those of the most successful unions. But the movement should also encourage and accommodate the more spontaneous self-organization that was common in the 1930s.

Despite the protests, Republicans are quite likely to pass anti-labor legislation in at least a few states beyond Ohio. Weingarten and United Steelworkers President Leo Gerard insist that they envision a long-term escalation of activity, even if there are interim defeats.

"The labor movement can't be wiped out of existence," Gerard says. "When there were no rules about creating unions, we still created unions. If you look at countries where workers have been isolated, whether it's Egypt, or whether it was Brazil during the military dictatorship—they form unions. So they may be trying to wipe us out, but it has brought us closer together."

In Wisconsin, unions will find it harder to operate if Walker's legislation passes. But they aren't going away, not in the state that was the first to authorize state employee unions. "Our view is we still have to have some form, some structure," says Rick Badger, executive director of American Federation of State, County and Municipal Employees (AFSCME) Council 40, which represents mainly local government workers in Wisconsin. "We have to plan for a world where unions are decimated. But either way, we'll still be standing."

Editor's note: Governor Scott Walker signed the Wisconsin Act 10 into law in March 2011. The number of union members has since declined precipitously in the state.

CHAPTER FOUR

Blowing Bubbles: The Rise of Finance

INTRODUCTION

By Dean Baker

The financial sector has developed a glamorous reputation. This is where ambitious Ivy League graduates rush to make their fortunes—a tragedy from the standpoint of the economy and society at large.

We should be clear about the role of the financial sector. It plays a tremendously important role in moving money around—from those who want to save to companies that want to invest or families that want to buy a home. But finance does not offer value in itself, the way housing, education, or healthcare do.

We should think of the financial industry the way we think of trucking. The trucking industry is absolutely essential for transporting the goods that allow our economy to function, but we want to accomplish this using as few trucks as possible—the most efficient trucking industry is a small one. The same goes for the financial sector.

Unfortunately, the policies of the last four decades have contributed to explosive growth in the financial sector. Depression-era regulations limiting banks' size and scope of activity were tossed out at the same time that computer technology allowed for an enormous acceleration of trading and a vast array of new financial instruments. The first five pieces in this chapter collectively tell that story, from deregulation on Capitol Hill (which led to the Savings & Loans crisis of the 1980 and 1990s) to the rise of hedge funds and companies like Enron. In the late 1990s, the financial sector profited enormously from the stock market bubble, followed later by the housing bubble. I described the growing menace of the latter in "Bursting Bubbles," which *In These Times* published in 2003.

The end result of all this was that by 2014, the narrow securities, commodities, and investment-banking sector constituted 2.4 percent of the economy, a nearly five-fold increase since 1970.

This growth was not associated with any obvious improvement in the financial sector's service to the productive economy. Developing an algorithm that allows someone to beat out other traders does not contribute much to society—but it's a good way to get very rich. A 2012 analysis of U.S. tax return data found that 18.4 percent of those in the top 0.1 percent were employed in finance.

In These Times writers warned repeatedly of the damage that could result from a financial sector run amok. But the industry was sufficiently powerful that the Federal Reserve Board and other regulators opted to look the other way. Even when the stock bubble burst in 2000–2002, the fallout was just laughed off, in spite of the fact that the recession led to what was then the longest period without job growth since the Great Depression.

Until 2008. The human toll of the housing crash is hard to quantify, but during the first two years of the Great Recession alone, about 8 million jobs were eliminated and more than 2 million homes lost to foreclosure. Both trends disproportionately impacted people of color, reversing decades of modest gains in closing the racial wealth gap. Two articles in this chapter, "The Subprime Bait and Switch" and "Killer Credit," show why.

Perhaps worst of all, the lesson remains largely unlearned.

The financial panic led to the 2010 passage of the Dodd-Frank Wall Street Reform and Consumer Protection Act, a somewhat serious effort at reform. The law has some positive features, such as making it more difficult for banks to speculate, but the industry was powerful enough to block any fundamental changes to the way it does business. For example, an amendment that would have broken up the big banks lost in the Senate by a vote of almost 2 to 1. Thus, the financial sector continues to dominate Washington, obstructing serious debate with mysticism about finance. Most people in Washington policy circles still believe, for example, that if we had not bailed out Wall Street in 2008, the gods of finance would have condemned the country to a second Great Depression in the form of a decade of double-digit unemployment.

The financial sector thrives on an aura of mystery—on the ability to hoodwink us into thinking that Wall Street knows best. Again and again, *In These Times* writers have attended to the task of declaring that the emperor has no clothes. The basic solution is straightforward: we need a small financial sector that serves the needs of the productive economy. We will know financial reform has succeeded when an ambitious graduate of Harvard is as likely to go into the trucking industry as to go to Wall Street.

"Bank Deregulation Threatens Stability"

By David M. Kotz (1986)

Until recently, bank failures were something you saw only in old newsreels. Now you see them on the evening news. Continental Illinois, once the eighth-largest American bank, collapsed and was effectively nationalized two years ago.

Several conditions of the '80s have contributed to the reappearance of bank failures. The generally dismal growth performance of the economy is one. Another is high and rapidly fluctuating interest rates. But a reversal in government policy toward banking—known as financial deregulation—has also been a key factor.

The passage of the Depository Institutions Deregulation and Monetary Control Act in 1980 firmly established deregulation as government policy, although some moves in that direction date back to the '70s. Interest rate controls have been eliminated. Restrictions on geographic area and services offered by banks have been loosened but not abolished. Government supervision of banks and Federal Deposit Insurance Corporation (FDIC) deposit insurance remain in force.

The regulatory system, inspired by the banking collapse in the Great Depression, had sought to assure a stable and relatively unconcentrated banking system. Despite problems, those aims were in large part achieved in the postwar period. Bank failures became a rarity, and the banking system, while moderately concentrated, was far less so than in other capitalist nations.

But over time the largest banks began to feel hemmed in by the regulations. They ran into growing competition from foreign banks and from less-regulated nonbank financial institutions, such as stock brokerage firms and mutual funds. In response, the big banks began to lobby for deregulation.

Soon large bank spokespeople were proclaiming deregulation was needed, not to benefit themselves, but to enable banking better to serve the public interest. A. W. Clausen, head of the Bank of America, invoked the 1789 French Revolution, predicting in 1979 that "Bastille Day is near" for the nation's "archaic laws and regulations" on banking. Less self-interested observers wondered whether a better historical analogy might be 1933.

To those wary of bank deregulation, proponents frequently proclaim that the process—whether good or bad—is inevitable. Chase Manhattan Chairman Willard C. Butcher insisted that, "Like it or not, the financial services industry is being transformed, almost daily, by market forces." No one can stop "the inevitable dismantling of the remaining artificial statutory and regulatory restraints," he argued. The corrosive impact of inflation, high interest rates, and financial innovation on the old regulatory system gave added weight to the deregulators' case.

Smaller banks and some other segments of the financial sector opposed deregulation, but the big banks had a key ally in the increasingly influential "free market" theorists. These economists argued that public regulation of banking was unnecessary and harmful. The unregulated free market, with the incentive of profit and discipline of competition, would produce an ideal banking system, they said. Donning a populist mantle, they even suggested that bank regulation was really a means to inflate bank profits at the expense of small savers.

GROWING INSTABILITY AND CONCENTRATION

The experiment in bank deregulation has served to remind us why regulation was originally imposed. Henry Kaufman, the executive director of Salomon Brothers and an astute observer of the financial scene, remarked that "there cannot be a true 'level playing field' among financial institutions," adding that a completely unregulated financial sector would "look more like a zoo with the bars let down."

The image of bulls, bears, sharks, and wolves running wild may be apt here. For while deregulation has been only partially carried out so far, harmful effects have already emerged. Perhaps most serious is renewed instability. Banks are not like other business firms: they are the guardians of people's savings and a major source of credit for businesses and households. Bank safety and stability are essential for social stability and the public welfare. Yet since 1980 the banking system has grown increasingly unstable.

One effect of the winner-take-all competition fostered by deregulation is a tendency for bank concentration to increase. The giant money center banks are now poised, ready to jump into new banking markets across the country when the gate is fully lifted. Some experts predict that one or two dozen giant financial conglomerates will then emerge in a dominant position in the entire financial sector, with perhaps a thousand small, locally oriented institutions playing a marginal role.

Editor's note: During the savings and loan crisis that began in the mid-1980s, more than 1,000 U.S. "thrift" banks failed, primarily because of risky mortgage lending. The federal government ultimately provided more than $100 billion in bailout funds.

"Bush's S&L plan would make us pay twice"

By James Weinstein (1989)

Like the environmental crisis caused by the Exxon Valdez oil spill, the savings and loan (S&L) crisis is the result of government deregulation. The Reagan–Bush idea that business knows best, and that if corporations are left to their own devices the public will best be served, turns out to be simply a means for the wealthy to feather their nests and the public be damned.

The S&L industry's despoliation of the public threatens in the end to cost the public even more than the Exxon Valdez incident.

It was deregulation that created the worst of the current crisis. In addition, most S&L failures have involved misconduct on the part of officers and directors. The General Accounting Office, the investigative wing of Congress, last month went so far as to call white-collar crime the main cause of the crisis. Regulators have reported that crime was a factor in 70 percent of insolvent institutions. All of this has been made possible by lax regulation.

The cost of cleaning up this government-aided mess will be enormous, because the federal government has an obligation to protect insured deposits. The cleanup should be paid for, in the form of added income taxes, by those who benefited from deregulation—financial institutions and the wealthy, as well as corporations that continue to avoid paying their fair share of taxes.

In short, it's time for working people to stop paying twice for the socially irresponsible greed of our corporate rulers. The least we can do now is force those who made the mess to pay for it.

"Easy money"

By Ralph Nader (1996)

How do Washington's big-time lobbyists prepare for major legislative efforts in the 104th Congress?

Last May, the American Bankers Association (ABA) offered a textbook study in influence peddling, treating key staffers from the House and Senate Banking Committees to a weekend at Virginia's lavish Homestead Resort, a playground for the rich and powerful. The ABA apparently assumed that Homestead was a perfect setting to make their pitch for a rollback of bank regulations. But the participants had their fun spoiled by ABC's Prime Time Live, which filmed the get-together for its October 18 show.

ABA lobbyists rushed forward to explain that it was merely "coincidental" that the event had been scheduled just days before the House Banking Committee was set to consider key regulatory "reforms." Not impressed, Prime Time Live called the Homestead frolic a "classic example of business as usual" in a Republican Congress that had promised change. Indeed, when the new Congress convened a year ago, lobbyists from both the banking and securities industries—the two giants of the financial community—arrived on Capitol Hill with briefcases full of pre-packaged deregulatory legislation.

Both industries realize that the 104th Congress represents their best opportunity in sixty years to roll back New Deal–era banking reforms and to slash the regulations and consumer protections enacted since then. So far, the nation's overeager bankers have been stymied in their efforts to undermine the banking industry's regulatory framework. But in late December the securities industry racked up a remarkable victory; the industry's lobbyists engineered passage of a controversial bill that makes it much harder to sue companies that lure investors by issuing misleading claims about their future prospects. Congress passed the sweeping financial "reform" over President Clinton's veto.

Of course, further deregulation would only accelerate the growing wave of banking mergers. Already, Chemical and Chase Manhattan are combining into a $300 billion bank. And more lenient banking laws seem certain to concentrate the nation's financial resources in the hands of a few conglomerates stretching across the country.

For consumers, the rise of such a colossus will mean fewer choices in the marketplace—and this will translate into higher fees, higher interest rates on loans, and lower returns on savings. For low- and moderate-income communities as well as minority neighborhoods, already limited banking services will disappear as branches close and lending decisions are processed by absentee managers.

The failure of even one large bank could never be handled by the current level of insurance reserves. This means that the new generation of banks, with hundreds of billions of dollars of deposits, will simply be "too big to fail." This policy mandates that the taxpayers will pick up the tab to save such institutions or to pay off depositors if they fail—much as they did in the wake of the collapse of the S&L industry. But the efficacy and safety of the regulatory and insurance system are getting virtually no attention on Capitol Hill.

Why haven't the banks—not exactly weaklings at the influence game— chalked up a major victory in the current Congress? Probably because the banks reached for too much too soon. Many of the GOP's most egregious banking provisions—like the wipeout of community lending laws—may die a deserved and ignominious death in the 104th Congress. But the big banks' most fervent dream—the repeal of the 1934 Glass-Steagall Act—remains very much alive. That landmark New Deal reform, which clearly separated the nation's banking and securities industries, helped stabilize America's financial markets during the Depression.

Unfortunately, memory is short in Washington.

Editor's note: Congress repealed the Glass-Steagall Act in 1999.

"Easy money and the rest of us"

By Juan González (1998)

"That's easy money," Phil Anderson, thirty-one, said with a breezy, knowing smile as he stood next to his Bloomberg computer terminal in shorts, sneakers, and sport shirt, talking about the see-sawing financial market in Hong Kong.

It was early September, and Wall Street was reeling from yet another of its many recent dives. A few feet away from Anderson, in a tiny one-room office in midtown Manhattan, sat Leonard Panzer, thirty, and Matt Rich, twenty-nine. They were feverishly working the phones, trying to calm anxious clients of the investment firm they manage, Kauser Capital LLC.

The casually clad trio seemed more like frat brothers on a New York City vacation than would-be masters of the universe. Still, if you want to understand the frightening gyrations that have swept financial markets the past few months, a good place to start is the secret, rarely examined world these young men inhabit—the world of hedge funds.

The Manhattan office building where Kauser Capital is located, 237 Park Avenue, houses so many of these newfangled firms that it's come to be known as the Hedge Fund Hotel. For several years, these funds have been the private secret of this country's super rich, proliferating in absolute silence in the closets of international high finance. If you were a multimillionaire and managed to put your money into one of these exclusive funds—they never advertise and aren't regulated—you made scads of money as these funds speculated that particular currencies or markets would go up or down.

George Soros is the king of hedge funds, and his Quantum Fund is the one all others seek to emulate. In 1992, Soros bet the British would be forced to devalue the pound. He was right, and thus became the first person to make $1 billion in a single year.

Since then, every whiz kid on Wall Street has been panting to leave his firm and start his own hedge fund. Ninety-five percent of the hedge funds that exist today are less than ten years old. Many funds reach enormous size very quickly. Because hedge-fund managers charge a 1 percent fee to their clients and take a commission of 20 percent of all profits, they can become very rich very fast, but they have to deliver huge returns to justify such outrageous commissions. Thus, they gamble big, and sometimes they lose big. When they do, millions of people suffer.

In late August, for instance, Soros lost $2 billion betting the wrong way on Russian bonds. He blasted Boris Yeltsin in public and told him he better devalue. A few days later, Yeltsin did just that, driving the Russian people into a poverty that has reached catastrophic levels.

Speculators and hedge funds that launch repeated "currency assaults" on countries by moving mountains of money in and out of world markets with the blink of a cursor have left devastation everywhere. The Russian economy has disintegrated. Indonesia, the world's fourth largest country, has 20 percent unemployment. Korea, Thailand, Malaysia, and now Brazil are reeling from the sudden flight of foreign investment. "No one talks about the social costs of these violent swings," says Marc Chandler, vice president and senior currency strategist at Deutsche Banks Securities. "A generation of sacrifice has gone out the window in many of these countries."

"The hedge funds are the bloodhounds," radical financial analyst Doug Henwood says. "They're the most extreme, volatile, and predatory form of finance capital. The fate of entire countries and industries depends on these people, and for the most part they're arrogant kids who know nothing about the real world."

Back in early September, the three whiz kids at Kauser Capital were still brimming with confidence. Hong Kong's fight to stave off the hedge funds would fail, Anderson assured me. The speculators would win. "It's a lay-up [in Hong Kong]," he said. "Easy money."

Then came late September, and the sudden bailout of one of the biggest hedge funds in the world, Long-Term Capital Management. The Federal Reserve Bank hastily convened a meeting of top bankers and pressured them to come up with $3.65 billion to keep wunderkind John W. Meriwether's fund afloat.

Meriwether, like Soros, had lost a few billion in Russia. But unlike Soros, he had borrowed enormous sums from banks, and his firm stood to lose trillions it did not have if it defaulted. So the Fed decided in the dead of night that Long-Term Capital was too big to fail. The entire world financial system would be threatened by the bankruptcy of a hedge fund few Americans had ever heard of and no government had ever regulated.

Easy money isn't so easy after all.

"ENRONOMICS 101"

By David Moberg (2002)

Even more than the dot-coms, Enron—the aptly nicknamed "crooked E"—was the star of the new "information economy." Tapping into and deceptively feeding the decade's collective delusion of unlimited wealth through computerized financial wheeling and dealing, Enron soared in a few years from a sleepy utility to the seventh-largest company in the United States—and one of the most widely praised.

The sordid tale of Enron's crash is a story with several themes: common greed that soared to uncommon dimensions; the failure and foiling of government regulation; duplicitous accountants, lawyers, bankers, executives, and politicians on the corporate take. But it also makes a compelling argument that the new information economy should really be called the disinformation economy.

In the *disinformation* economy, there is a systematic effort to hide, distort, and lie as a way of gaining wealth and power. In itself, this is old stuff, but the techniques for such deception are more sophisticated and elaborate than ever. Even though insider dealing is a crucial part of the disinformation economy, on the surface the economy relies heavily on public information, certainly much more than in the era of handshake deals between private capitalist titans. In this time of deregulation and globalization, as markets grow more all-encompassing and less constrained, failures of information can have much more dire effects. Even on capitalist terms, markets require full, accurate, and universally available information to guide rational decisions by investors, consumers, and citizens. Disinformation raises the level and cost of irrationality even as it promises a free market Utopia.

Enron's stock market success was based on systematic exaggeration of its financial strength. Its explosive growth and sudden collapse both were linked to the creation of more than 3,500 subsidiaries that were often used to keep debt off Enron's balance sheets, which in turn helped prop up its credit rating and reduce the cost of borrowing for further expansion. Unlike Enron shareholders, insiders—the corporate executives and selected investors, including divisions of banks that were lending to Enron—knew these subsidiaries were dubiously structured. But they ignored the dangers because Enron held out hope for fantastic returns—doubling their money or better in some years. The auditors for Arthur Andersen did not just overlook this chicanery. Like the lawyers who said it was all legal, the accountants were apparently paid well to help set it up. Nearly 900 of these subsidiaries were established in offshore tax havens like the Cayman Islands, notorious centers for money laundering and financial concealment.

Fundamentally, Enron transformed itself from an energy supplier into an almost totally unregulated financial institution. The profits Enron generated came mainly from its online trading of electricity and natural gas. The bulk of this trading was in "derivatives," complex financial instruments used to hedge or speculate about future prices. The derivative contracts were often opaque and confusing, even to experts. So this market was especially murky and open to manipulation.

To succeed, Enron needed markets—starting with energy—that were deregulated, volatile, and actively traded. Deregulation provided the instability that created an incentive for hedging and speculation as well as opportunities for Enron to profit, often by taking advantage of minor discrepancies in prices within the marketplace. Clear, predictable information about energy prices typical of regulated utilities hurt Enron; chaos and confusion were its manna. Keynes described financial euphoria as bubbles forming on bubbles. Enron was blowing its own bubbles.

The tentative moves emerging in Washington toward regulation of accountants, pension plans, accounting rules, and other troubled aspects of the Enron debacle are small, if necessary, steps toward the broader task of unmaking the disinformation economy. But the entire political culture has been so contaminated with disinformation that now—even in the wake of this scandal—both Republicans and Democrats are promoting further energy deregulation. Greed undermined professions that once claimed the public trust—accountants, lawyers, bankers—demonstrating the need for tighter regulation. But who can do that if government itself is corrupted?

"Bursting Bubbles: Why the Economy Will Go From Bad to Worse"

By Dean Baker (2003)

In 2000, President Bill Clinton could legitimately boast of the "best economy in thirty years." Unemployment was low, wages were rising at all income levels, and the poverty rate was headed downward at a rapid pace. But after President George W. Bush took office in 2001, the economy fell into recession, shedding jobs and causing real wage growth to slow and eventually stop altogether.

A convenient story explains this sharp economic reversal. According to the script, Clinton eliminated the deficit through progressive tax increases and spending restraint. This deficit reduction lowered interest rates and spurred an investment boom, which was the basis for the extraordinary growth of the late '90s. Then Bush came into office and quickly squandered the surplus with his tax cuts to the rich and military build-up. As a result the deficit skyrocketed and the economy tanked.

It's a good story, but the reality is quite different. The Clinton boom was built on three unsustainable bubbles. One of them, the stock bubble, has already burst. The dollar bubble is starting to deflate, and the housing bubble is perhaps just now reaching its peak. These bubbles created the basis for the 2001 recession and the economy's continuing period of stagnation.

The basic facts of the economy's rapid deterioration over the last two years are widely known. After creating an average of more than 3 million jobs a year from 1996 to 2000, the economy has lost more than 2 million jobs since March 2001. The economy's reversal was associated with a plunge in the stock market.

Of course, the stock market downturn should not be included among the economic failings of the last two and a half years. That downturn really was just a healthy return to reality.

As was the case in Japan in the '80s, the stock market bubble of the late '90s was accompanied by a housing bubble. It began as a result of people using their newly created stock wealth to purchase better homes. The rise in home prices since 1995 has outpaced the overall rate of inflation by more than 30 percentage points. This sort of run-up in home prices has no precedent in the postwar era.

Like stock wealth, housing wealth also spurs consumption. Families see the rising value of their homes as a source of wealth. They have been drawing on this wealth with a vengeance in the past two years, as plunging interest rates have led to an unprecedented surge in mortgage borrowing. As a result, the ratio of mortgage debt to home equity is at near-record highs.

This situation is frightening for two reasons. First, as a short-run matter, if housing prices fall sharply in some of the areas where the effects of the bubble are largest, new home buyers (and those who recently refinanced their mortgages and took money out) could find they have negative equity in their homes. If someone borrows $270,000 to buy a $300,000 home, and the price falls by one-third, this leaves them owing $70,000 more than the home is worth. When this happens, there is a huge incentive to just let the mortgage holder foreclose. If this were to happen on a large scale, the survival of many banks and financial institutions would be at risk.

The current high levels of mortgage debt are a problem for another reason. The population is aging, and many families are getting near retirement. With the front end of the baby boomers approaching sixty, many homeowners should be near to paying off their mortgage. The demographics indicate that mortgage debt should be lower than it has been in prior decades. But on the contrary, many baby boomers are likely to hit retirement—after having

just lost much of the wealth in their 401(k)s due to the stock market crash—
and discover that their homes are worth much less than they had expected.
These older baby boomers really need to be saving to ensure themselves
a sufficient income in retirement, but the illusory wealth created by the
housing bubble is preventing them from recognizing this fact.

The bubble will persist as long as people expect home prices to rise.

"THE SUBPRIME BAIT AND SWITCH"

By Alexander Gourse (2007)

In 2005, Betty and Tyrone Walker, a couple living in the Park Manor neighborhood on the south side of Chicago, took out a refinance loan with
Ameriquest. "All we wanted to do was to make our house more livable,"
says Walker, who is legally disabled and is raising a twelve-year-old adopted
daughter on her husband's salary as a mail clerk at a local medical school.
After being solicited by Ameriquest through the mail, the Walkers decided
to use some of the equity in their home to refurnish their basement.

The Walkers requested information about the loan numerous times, and
were confident that they knew what the terms of the loan would be when
they went to sign the closing documents. "We just kept asking them whether
we were going to remain on a fixed rate, and they just kept lying to us, telling
us we'd get a fixed rate," Mrs. Walker alleges in a lawsuit against Ameriquest.

As they later discovered, however, the terms of the loan were not as they
expected. Not only did the loan have an adjustable rate that can go as high
as 13.4 percent, but the Walkers allege that Ameriquest falsely told them that
their home had doubled in value since they had bought it a few years earlier,
thus qualifying them for a larger loan amount. Ameriquest didn't give them
copies of their loan documents at closing, and as a result the Walkers did not
realize that the terms had been changed until well after the three-day period
during which they could legally cancel the loan. They have since tried to
refinance, but have been unable to find another lender willing to lend them
the amount currently owed to Ameriquest; the artificially inflated appraisal
value has in effect trapped them in a loan with a rising interest rate.

"I felt so stupid after I realized that I had been taken advantage of," says
Walker. "I made them a lunch! I'm always cooking, so I offered them food.
I thought they were doing such a swell job of helping us that I cooked for
these people, oh lord." ·

The Walkers' story is all too familiar. Predatory lending is a particularly
widespread problem in low-income and minority communities, where a

complex history of housing discrimination, racial segregation, and a lack of access to affordable credit have left borrowers with few options. Though redlining, blockbusting, and other discriminatory practices were banned in stages between 1968 and 1977, most banks are reluctant to open branches in black neighborhoods, a vacuum that is filled by currency exchanges, payday lenders, and now subprime mortgage companies.

"Subprime lenders," says Geoff Smith, research director at the Woodstock Institute, a Chicago-based nonprofit that specializes in issues of community economic development, "are taking advantage of the fact that they're the only game in town."

According to "Paying More for the American Dream," a joint report from six national housing policy organizations, in 2005, black borrowers were 3.8 times more likely than whites to be placed in a high-cost loan, while Hispanic borrowers were 3.6 times more likely than whites to receive such a loan. Income disparities between white and minority communities account for some of this difference, but Smith says the disparity is too large to be accounted for by income alone. Low-income black borrowers in the Chicago area were four times as likely to be put in high-cost loans than low-income white borrowers.

"Killer credit"

By Adam Doster (2008)

Candace Angus is not one to break the rules. When she served on the Chicago police force for twenty-five years, it was her duty to maintain order. And as a longtime credit card user, she was never late on a payment and never in debt. So when she found interest on her Capital One balance considerably higher than she anticipated, she was irked.

A customer service representative explained that the charge was "residual interest" from two months prior that had not yet been applied. Although she didn't grasp the concept fully, Angus swallowed the news and paid her next bill in full. Thirty days later, residual interest was still on the statement, and higher than the month before. "[Capital One] caught me entirely by surprise," she says. "I'd never heard of that practice before."

What was this mysterious charge? Essentially, the payoff balance was obsolete by the time it reached Angus's mailbox because interest continued to build as her bill slid its way through the mail system. If her check took a week to reach the processing center, seven days worth of interest was eventually tacked on. And this caveat was hidden in the contract's fine print.

"It should be clear to the consumer that interest is being held up for a few months," Angus fumes. "Is it to the benefit of the consumer or is it to the benefit of the credit card company?" While she acknowledges that others have it worse than her—because her problem didn't lead to default or loads of debt—Angus's experience typifies those of many. "All the cards don't use that practice," she says, "but they all catch you somehow."

In the last quarter century, an unstable financial relationship was forged between Americans—grasping for an increasingly elusive middle-class lifestyle—and credit card companies that offer strapped consumers a lifeboat. But without adequate regulation, the industry has used deceptive techniques to hoodwink consumers and accumulate more than $30 billion in profits per year. Now, if legislators at the national level don't step in, some analysts fear that Americans' affection for credit may widen the existing credit crisis.

BEARING THE DEBT BURDEN

First, the facts. In 1970, 49 percent of Americans didn't have a credit card. Today, only 7 percent don't.

Coinciding with this rapid growth, the Supreme Court ruled in 1978 that banks could charge the maximum interest rate determined by state legislatures in the banks' home states, not the interest rate of the states in which they do business. Unsurprisingly, credit card businesses moved to Delaware and South Dakota—two states with virtually no interest caps—thus rendering state usury laws worthless.

Twelve years ago, the court applied the same logic to the size of fees a bank can charge. Congress has refused to step in at the federal level, enabling the industry's thorough deregulation.

With the freedom to act on their own accord, banks have implemented an array of confusing and punitive measures that bilk cash from clients.

"It's pretty extraordinary to see how the industry has essentially created a diluted regulatory environment, where they can basically do what they want to consumers," says Robert Manning, author of *Credit Card Nation* and a professor of finance at the Rochester Institute of Technology.

Before the '90s, most credit cards had one annual fee and a fixed rate. Today, they carry an assortment of charges that oscillate with the market and the cardholder's credit risk. If a borrower overdraws, instead of just declining the transaction from the outset, companies tack on a fee of $30 or more. Late fees are endless, as well. Banks charge the borrower until he or she breaks, as opposed to canceling a delinquent card, which was once an established procedure. Vanity is the banks' justification, claiming the practice allows customers to evade the humiliation of rejection.

For people with substandard credit scores or limited credit histories, often low-income people of color, intensely marketed subprime or "fee harvester" cards present a huge danger. These carry substantially higher interest rates and lower credit limits than cards granted to prime borrowers and are laden with fees. In fact, it's possible for subprime fees to absorb a borrower's entire limit, leaving him or her with nothing to spend.

"The issue is how you make credit card loans to people with bad credit, and how you make money off of that," says Jim Campen, executive director of Americans for Fairness in Lending (AFFIL). "And the solution is, basically, give them a credit card but don't give them credit, and charge them a lot of fees for doing it."

Even highly responsible customers are at risk. In some circumstances, borrowers are subject to retroactive price hikes, meaning banks can enforce higher rates on old balances as well as new ones, even if none of the original payments were late.

While it's unlikely that sensible consumers would ever agree to these outrageous terms, many opt in unknowingly. In 2004, *The Wall Street Journal* found that a standard contract in the '80s was one-page long. But weak disclosure requirements now allow banks to dole out thirty-page contracts in six-point font, often burying important stipulations, such as nonbinding legal arbitration, or omitting basic terms of credit.

Consumer advocates like Campen argue that credit card companies are counting on people to misunderstand the total cost of swiping a card. Angus agrees. "Once you start getting a little risky, a little in debt … they treat you completely differently," she says. "It's like they want to push you into dangerous waters."

And it has worked. Exploiting this asymmetry of information, credit card companies have reaped enormous earnings. R. K. Hammer, a California firm that evaluates credit card portfolios, found that the industry raked in $36.8 billion in net pretax profits during 2006. Meanwhile, credit card debt has more than tripled since 1990.

Plastic safeguard

If credit cards are a trap, why don't people abandon them entirely? Because, experts say, people must have their basic needs met, which credit cards make possible.

"The perception … is that credit cards are used for frivolous spending, that it's just easy money for people to use to buy their nice sneakers," says José Garcia, a senior researcher at the think tank Demos and author of a new study called "Borrowing to Make Ends Meet." "But they're not seen as a way that people have been dealing with economic shock."

Despite strong growth in labor productivity, hourly wages for most workers are not keeping up with inflation. In the last twenty years, incomes for the bottom 60 percent of households rose only 5 percent to 15 percent, according to the Bureau of Labor Statistics. Meanwhile, the average cost of living shot up 88 percent in that time.

Health care costs are a major contributor to this trend. But the problem extends further. As legislators disinvest from education, the average cost of college increased 165 percent between 1970 and 2005. What's more, the housing bubble pushed prices through the roof, leading to the doubling of median mortgage debt from 1989 to 2004. Childcare, transportation, and food cause concerns, as well. And as personal savings are drained, folks must choose between their plastic safety nets or financial ruin.

Until adequate regulations are put in place to safeguard consumers from their cards, and the need for borrowing is minimized by boosting earnings for working people, Americans will keep answering those mail solicitations.

"Why should anybody be allowed to put out unfair products," asks AFFIL's Campen, "which are simply designed to trap the unaware. In theory, we regulate toys, water, food, and drugs, and we don't want to have toxic products in any of those areas. We shouldn't have toxic credit products either."

"THE ONLY ROAD OUT OF CRISIS"

By Joseph M. Schwartz (2009)

Since taking office, President Barack Obama and his economic team have confronted a daunting financial crisis with a string of solutions that have been hard to sell to a wary public.

It's one thing to fix the current crisis, but preventing a repeat will require reflection on how this happened in the first place. The disastrous experience of financial deregulation demonstrates that without public regulatory restraint, finance capital will engage in irresponsible acts of speculative swindling during financial booms and resort to excessively conservative lending during financial busts.

The deregulation of the financial industry has been a thirty-year joint project of Republican monetarists and Democratic neoliberals. This "free market" project began with the Carter administration's deregulation of the Savings and Loans. It accelerated under the Reagan administration's gutting of the entire government regulatory apparatus, and culminated with the Clinton administration's abolition of the Glass-Steagall Act, which had separated commercial banks from investment firms. Now, the very banks that create risky financial instruments also market these instruments to their own clients.

To restore a sane credit system, the federal government must first take the fiscally prudent step of nationalizing and restructuring insolvent financial institutions. Then the Obama administration must recreate an effective regulatory system for domestic financial institutions and cooperate with governments of other advanced and developing economies to build a global financial regulatory system that favors productive investment over speculation.

The other story behind our current economic crisis is global neo-liberal capitalism's race-to-the-bottom. Transnational corporations that scour the globe for the lowest labor costs fail to pay workers enough to purchase the goods and services they produce. Only if Chinese and Southeast Asian workers can form independent trade unions will they be able to force employers to pay them wages sufficient to consume the goods they produce.

In developed nations, with wages failing to keep up with productivity increases, workers went into debt to forestall declining living standards, which temporarily put off the impending global crisis of overproduction and underconsumption.

In the end, restoring a stable global economic system will require raising the floor under global living standards and working conditions and creating global regulatory institutions that insure that investment and trade benefit all working people.

The era of deregulatory free market mania is crashing down upon us. We must revive the capacity of democratic governments to regulate the economy to serve people's needs rather than the speculative desires of corporate elites to recover from the current global economic nightmare.

"A NEW STRATEGY TO MAKE THE BANKS PAY"

By Laura Gottesdiener (2014)

When Maureen O'Neil took the job of chief code official and neighborhood improvement coordinator for Youngstown, Ohio, she realized almost immediately she had a problem: the city was littered with blighted houses caught in a legal limbo known as "zombie foreclosure."

It was 2011, three years into the worst housing crash since the Great Depression, and she and the rest of the code enforcement team were conducting hundreds of inspections a week of vacant homes across the city that had fallen into dangerous levels of disrepair. As the team started calling the homeowners into hearings, it quickly became clear that many had been pushed out by banks foreclosing on their homes and hadn't lived in the houses for years. They didn't realize that because the banks had never completed the foreclosure process, they were still responsible for the upkeep.

"It put us in a horrible position as human beings to say, 'Well, actually, the property is still in your name, and in all likelihood the bank just dumped it in the middle of the process,'" says O'Neil. "It's my belief that the bank would send a staff person or appraiser to drive by the property, and if that person saw that it was more of a liability and not something the bank was going to see much return on, rather than spend time and money on it, the bank wouldn't complete the foreclosure process."

Since 2008, foreclosures have caused a nationwide rash of blight, vacancies, and municipal shortfalls as city governments are forced to invest millions to maintain properties abandoned by banks, loan servicers, and lenders.

"Zombie properties" are especially costly for cities because they are almost always left unmaintained. According to a 2011 analysis by a coalition of community groups in California, from 2008 through 2012, each blighted foreclosed property cost the local government an estimated $19,229 in maintenance, inspections, evictions, and trash removal—which, in total, added up to tens of billions of dollars across the state.

The foreclosure crisis took an especially high toll on old manufacturing cities like Youngstown, which has already seen decades of depopulation since the steel mills were closed down. In 2010, the Mahoning Valley Organizing Collaborative, a nonprofit focused on housing and other economic justice issues, estimated that 40 percent of the city was vacant in some form. Faced with this staggering figure, O'Neil and a collection of grassroots organizers and city officials decided that it was time to take more serious action. They turned the problem into an opportunity to implement an innovative program to make the banks begin paying for their damage to the community.

In early 2013, the city passed legislation requiring any entity initiating a foreclosure process—be it a bank, mortgage servicer, lender, or individual—to post a $10,000 bond the moment the house becomes vacant (or immediately, if the house is already vacant). Unlike previous efforts by cities to impose fines on banks that weren't keeping their houses up to code, which forced cities to go chasing after big financial institutions with little interest in paying, this method makes the banks pay first—and then recoup their money later if they fulfill their responsibilities.

O'Neil says that when Youngstown first passed the bill, she and other city officials were convinced they'd be sued by alarmed banks.

"We thought, 'They're not going to let this go on, because it's going to sweep across the nation,'" she explains. "It was a real shock when they not only didn't take us to court, but actually did pay these bonds. I've talked to a number of municipalities that are looking to pass similar legislation, and they are basing much of it on what happened in Youngstown."

CHAPTER FIVE

Public Goods, Private Hands

INTRODUCTION

by Thomas Geoghegan

It is hard to know which is worse: the privatization of public services or the privatization of public property. The articles that follow track both dimensions of this trend in the United States, which began with the deregulation favored in the 1970s even among some liberals. Since then we've seen private companies cut wide swaths through what was once firmly held government territory. On the services side, this includes prisons, housing, schools, and defense. On the property side: highways, parking meters, and land.

Slowly but surely, we are liquidating the state. *In These Times* has been covering the auction since it began. This chapter's lead-off piece, "Central American Refugees for Profit," by Dennis Bernstein and Connie Blitt, shows us the Corrections Corporation of America near the dawn of the private prison era. (It's an era that may be cresting, at least at the federal level, given the U.S. Justice Department's intention to end the use of private prisons.) In "Corporate Caseworkers," Adam Fifield details an overlooked consequence of Bill Clinton's 1996 welfare reform law: Lockheed Martin and other companies scooped up contracts to "provide"—i.e., shrink—social services. In "War Profiteering and You," Christopher Hayes reveals the Bush administration's reconstruction contract bonanza after the invasion of Iraq. And Beau Hodai's "Publicopoly Exposed" shows how even the service provided by elected representatives—legislating—can be unofficially privatized. To a corporate-backed group intent on privatizing many government services, of course.

As a union-side labor lawyer, I sometimes see the sell-off of services, and its consequences, up close. "Increased efficiency" is often trumpeted to justify privatization, which can usually be translated as: pay workers less. I have a friend who used to do corporate consulting in Europe, which once had a wave of sell-offs of state enterprises. "Oh," he said, "I once thought these deals were about market efficiency and innovation. But one day I realized the only real purpose is union-busting." Otherwise no one would bother doing it.

That's what galls me about the way the Right rails at public unions. It's as if the solution to the decline of the middle class is to take what's left of it and drag it down as well. In recent years we've heard a lot about the charms of charter schools. If they really do much beyond paying teachers less, this has yet to be shown. But for the chance of union busting, it is an open question whether there would be charter schools at all. Yes, a few, I suppose—but those few mostly started by radicals on the Left, not billionaires on the Right.

Sure, there can be other government motives for privatization. In the case of private prisons, which now form a nearly $5 billion industry, at least one purpose is to escape the fetters of the Constitution and even the rule of law. While government-run prisons may degrade people enough, at least it is possible—sometimes—to drag the officials into court. Any kind of privatization makes it much harder to sue.

But what bothers me more of late is the sell-off of public property. In Chicago, where I live—and as Rick Perlstein describes in this chapter's final article, "How to Sell Off a City"—we've sold off public streets, or at least the parking meters, to the sovereign wealth fund of Abu Dhabi. Shouldn't we be going the other way, if only to save the planet? No one has said it better than Pope Francis: private ownership rights have caused our current environmental plight. To keep the air and water clean and temperatures stable, we need less private sprawl. Rather than shrink the commons, we need to develop a new sense that all owners of private property exercise a public trust. In this sense, the most dangerous privatization of all is to continue with a system of private property ownership that is warming up the planet.

While some on the Left deplore a strong national government and prefer not just local but even neighborhood control, it is the weakness of government at every level from which we have more to fear. Privatization of government—not just to big business, but to little not-for-profits that now deliver so many government-type social services—is just what we should expect in a country that has lost the nerve to tax. It's not enough to soak the rich: all of us should be paying more. Yes, it's a sign of trouble when even Bernie Sanders is paying an income tax rate of just 13.5 percent. We'll never get to Denmark until we pony up and pay real Danish-level taxes. And we'll just go on selling off the commons until we do.

"CENTRAL AMERICAN REFUGEES FOR PROFIT"

By Dennis Bernstein and Connie Blitt (1986)

Laredo, Texas—The Corrections Corporation of America (CCA) is Uncle Sam's right-hand man in Laredo. Private sector ingenuity coupled with governmental support has created a unique welcome for Central Americans arrested by the Border Patrol and taken to the Immigration and Naturalization Service (INS)/CCA Laredo Service Processing Center just outside this bustling border city west of the Rio Grande Valley.

Facility Administrator Tim McGuigan, a career expert in "correctional systems," has great confidence in this new union between the INS and the CCA. "We can marry the principals of good correctional practice with good business practices to make it a more efficient operation," says McGuigan.

The result is a sparkling new, state-of-the-art prison for profit. McGuigan says he feels "like a kid in a candy shop" every time he enters the glittering control "bubble" of CCA's fully automated facility that can detect on-site audio and visual motion as subtle as the flicker of a bird. And the other CCA officials are equally impressed. "A place like this is a correction man's dream," says the facility's security chief John Gonzales, a former Marine Corps stockade officer.

Others are less sanguine. According to Laredo attorney and refugee advocate Patrick Hughes, the facility threatens to end childhood for many refugee youth, and it introduces hundreds of adults to a futuristic technological world that creates for them a frightening, cultural non sequitur. "It's a cold and dehumanizing horror," says Hughes, founder of Refugee Legal Services, a not-for-profit organization that represents refugees detained in the facility. "It's an Orwellian nightmare with behavior modification honed to a science. There are microphones right in the ceiling that pick up everything that's happening."

According to McGuigan, it takes only four people to operate securely the 208-bed Laredo facility, although more are on duty during the daytime hours. Doors are opened electronically from central control—no one carries keys—and meals are served in the dorms, eliminating the need for a dining room and related staff. McGuigan says that this circumvents "problems inherent in moving large groups of detained people from one part of a building to another." He asserts that everybody benefits from a CCA prison in the neighborhood. The taxpayers save cash through the cost-effective nature of a privately built and run institution and even the detainees are better off.

Not everyone agrees that private prisons are a good idea. "They're in it for the money," says Hedy Weinberg, a staff attorney with the American

Civil Liberties Union (ACLU) in Tennessee, where CCA's home offices are located. "They're more concerned about incarceration than alternatives to incarceration," says Weinberg, "and they're going to be keeping people in so they can make a profit."

It's not surprising that some detainees become unruly with little to contemplate besides their often-traumatic pasts and highly uncertain futures. In its glossy brochure CCA claims to have a fully equipped recreation area. Yet a "real lack of recreation" was noted by Fernando Tafoya of the National Moratorium on Prison Construction (NMPC), who recently toured the facility on a fact-finding visit.

"What was considered recreation facilities was basically a slab of cement with some shade," Tafoya says. The small outdoor exercise pen is surrounded by a 14-foot cyclone fence topped with rolled barbed wire, which serves as the only clue to the traffic driving by that this pristine corporate-type building is actually a prison.

When he asked to see the gymnasium, Tafoya was shown a locker room "about the size of a one-person office, which had one exercise machine and a bench."

And the boredom created by limited recreational or educational programs at the institution plays right into the hands of another profit-stretching device employed by CCA, the use of "volunteer" labor.

SLAVING IS SAVING

Unlike other public prisons and INS-run facilities—where inmates are paid, if meagerly, for their work—it has been conveniently written into the INS/CCA contract that the company is forbidden to pay the detainees for their labor. Says INS Assistant District Director John A. Abriel, "Just by common sense, it would be a conflict of interest, in that the government is paying a contractor to provide a service to the taxpayer." He opposes paying the detainees, because the contractor would then be taking unfair advantage of the available labor pool to do jobs it contracted to do.

CCA administrator McGuigan has little trouble enlisting volunteers to work around the facility. "They want to do it," he says. "It's a way to spend their time, and obviously we let them do it." This "concept" of free labor works out smashingly well for everybody concerned except the detainees. Many refugee minors work long hours for nothing more than the privilege of, as Abriel puts it, "doing something for the general benefit of the people housed there."

Although McGuigan says the financial benefits of having refugees do laundry, prepare food, and clean does not figure in the company's balance sheet, the use of detainees to complete such tasks is clearly a substantial asset and a fundamental cost saver.

LOCKING UP PROBLEMS

The bond between the INS and private prisons is growing stronger, and immigration officials as well as CCA executives are pleased with the evolving relationship. The INS, through the use of such private concerns, can concentrate its efforts on routing out Central Americans and quickly deporting them before their growing presence casts doubt upon Reagan administration policy in Central America. "Our foreign policy is not working, so we're going to build more prisons and we're going to imprison the population that flees because of our [military] activity," says Tafoya. "We're a society more and more committed to locking up its problems."

"We're going to get tied into a system in which once we've turned our facilities over [to private entrepreneurs] the transition back is going to be nearly impossible," says Weinberg of the ACLU. The private corporations will then be in a position to charge whatever they want, she says, and even more seriously, be able to determine public policy as to who goes to jail and how long they stay.

"CORPORATE CASEWORKERS"

By Adam Fifield (1997)

In Los Angeles, deadbeat dads no longer answer to the government. Instead, they find themselves monitored by the Lockheed Martin Corp., the nation's largest defense contractor. Under a four-year, $50 million contract, the giant multinational corporation tracks them, summons them for informal hearings, and even draws their blood for tests.

Lockheed Martin is not the only big corporation that sees an opportunity to make a tidy profit delivering social services that once were the responsibility of public-sector employees. As the federal government abandons the welfare business, private companies like Lockheed are landing government contracts throughout the country to provide services ranging from child support collection to the administration of Medicaid.

"We're at a time when programs that provide subsistence benefits to the poorest people are being cut back, and at the same time, we're talking about spending some of those precious dollars to generate profits for shareholders of large corporations," says Henry Freedman, executive director of the Manhattan-based Welfare Law Center.

No state has welcomed private companies into the welfare arena as enthusiastically as Texas. Several for-profit companies, including Lockheed, Electronic Data Systems, and Andersen Consulting, have submitted bids on a $2 billion multiyear contract to administer the state's screening process for recipients of Medicaid, food stamps, and welfare; to computerize its welfare system; and to integrate the delivery of various benefits into "one-stop shopping" centers throughout the state.

The plan, dubbed the Texas Integrated Enrollment Service, was passed into law in 1995 with bipartisan support. As many as 5,000 state public sector workers may lose their jobs, while public control over vital, dwindling services to the poor has been put in jeopardy.

Texas is the latest and perhaps boldest example of corporate America's attempts to cash in on welfare reform. "The country is looking at Texas. What we get away with, they're gonna do," says Gene Freeland, a labor representative at the Texas Workforce Commission, a state job-training agency created in 1995 by consolidating the state's twenty-eight different job training programs, now called "local workforce districts."

The 1996 federal welfare law, which replaces much of the current welfare system with block grants to the states, has created a raft of new business opportunities for private companies that are vying for these funds by promising to reduce welfare rolls, place welfare recipients in jobs, streamline services, and eliminate public-sector jobs. Under the new law, states are allowed to keep federal welfare dollars they don't spend. The fewer people served, the larger the savings. In essence, the state is hiring private companies to pull the switch and purge the rolls.

"The private companies want to get all the funding streams for moving people off welfare and into jobs," says Debbie Goldman, a research economist at the Communication Workers of America. "They want to be the labor department and the welfare department."

Many states have already privatized certain welfare services. According to a recent industry survey by Andersen Consulting, private companies have contracts to perform welfare functions in forty-nine states. Contracts currently held or up for bid cover a range of services, including the screening of welfare applicants, administration of benefits, welfare-fraud investigations, automation of information systems, and job training and placement.

The largest player in welfare privatization is Lockheed Martin, a $30 billion corporate giant. Lockheed Martin Information Management Systems

Corp., the company's branch specializing in social services, parking, and transportation, has contracts in forty-five states.

Unions, nonprofits, and advocates for the poor argue that welfare privatization is really a fig leaf for further cutbacks. "A lot of the privatization is sold on the grounds of efficiency," says Freedman from the Welfare Law Center. "But a lot of the savings come on the grounds of a reduction of services."

"War profiteering and you"

By Christopher Hayes (2004)

So Vice President Dick Cheney's former employer Halliburton has been in the news a lot lately—bilking the U.S. government for millions in Kuwaiti oil imports to Iraq, turning the other way as employees take bribes, and overcharging the Army for food served in mess halls. It gets to feeling like the whole "reconstruction effort" is just some bloated, corrupt muddle of patronage and war profiteering.

But then comes "Rebuilding Iraq: Small Business Subcontracting Opportunities," convened in February 2004 near O'Hare Airport outside Chicago. Sponsored by the Small Business Administration (SBA) and featuring speakers from—you guessed it—Halliburton, among others, the daylong seminar was intended to show that profiting from the Bush administration's foreign policy is anyone's game.

"We are literally here at the direction of the president of the United States to make sure that each and every one of you has the opportunity to be involved in one of the truly major business undertakings of this century," said General Patrick Rea, regional administrator of the SBA. And it's some undertaking. The total value of contracts, Rea assured, "could move to the figure of a half a trillion dollars."

Reducing the Iraq war and subsequent occupation to a business opportunity is disconcerting enough, but far more bizarre was the subtle yet consistent message that Iraqi reconstruction constitutes a comprehensive domestic economic policy agenda. "We're all looking for what are those twenty-first century jobs," Rea told the crowd. "You're sitting in a room where they're going to unfold by the thousands."

Rea's right—there's an awfully large potential for profit. Both the conquest and occupation of Iraq have been the most heavily privatized military ventures in U.S. history. Thanks to an initiative implemented in the early '90s by then–Secretary of Defense Dick Cheney, the U.S. military now contracts out almost every possible aspect of its work, from food preparation to janitorial services to camp design and construction.

Now this very same approach is being applied to reconstruction, as the government bids out contracts on everything from school construction to power-plant design to water treatment.

In the last round of contracts alone, $8.6 billion was awarded to about two dozen companies, the majority of which are American mega-firms. (Only companies from "coalition member" nations are allowed to bid.)

But the Bush administration is committed to spreading around the wealth. It requires that all subcontractors partner with Iraqi firms for work on the ground. And the policy seems to be working. While big-time entities like Halliburton may get the massive original contracts, they don't do most or even much of the work. "We don't intend to swing the hammers ourselves," Halliburton KBR Small Business Liaison's Kimberla Fairley told the crowd. "We're going to subcontract out all the work."

This is where small businesses come in, at least in theory. Under the Coalition Provisional Authority's procurement guidelines, 10 percent of contract dollars must go to certified small business subcontractors. And as Jeannie Houston, program manager for Bechtel's Supplier Development and Diversity Program noted, competition is fierce.

The ostensible purpose of the conference, then, was to give attendees the inside scoop on beating out the competition. But representatives from Bechtel, Halliburton, Parsons, et al. had precious little in the way of advice to offer, outside of suggesting that firms register on a centralized database, encouraging owners to be persistent and instructing that they partner with Iraqi firms if they seek to complete work on the ground.

It was beginning to look like the Iraqi reconstruction contracts were structured exactly like the Bush tax cuts: while the wealth redounds overwhelmingly to the very richest recipients, the administration argues they're dealing everybody in. With Iraqi reconstruction representing one of the only signs of life in an otherwise dead economy, desperate small business owners, these walk-on players not already selected for Team Bush, were frantic to be drafted.

After Bechtel's presentation, Sal Hassanien, an Arab American small-business owner from Detroit, stormed to the mike as representative for a group of exile engineers who moved back to Baghdad to take part in reconstruction. "I've been trying to contact Bechtel. I've been trying to contact Parsons and it's impossible," he said. "[We] send e-mails, they never respond, call them by phone, they never respond."

Outside the conference hall, Hassanien voiced frustration with the trivial amount of money trickling down to small firms. "You get a contract that is worth, I don't know, let's say $100," he said. "You know by the time you give it to the Kuwaiti companies, it's $50. By the time you get to the real guys, the Iraqis who are actually doing the work, they get about $10 out of that. Everything else, $90, is going to administration, subcontracting, and subcontracting and so on. It's really screwed."

Referring to prime contractors like Halliburton that participated in the day, Hassanien laughed and continued, "The big boys, yes, have put up a dog and pony show."

"PUBLICOPOLY EXPOSED"

By Beau Hodai (2011)

On November 2, 2010, a radical cohort of Republicans swept into office in states across the country.

When the legislative sessions began in January 2011, this new breed of Grand Old Partier set to the task of breaking public employee unions, dismantling state government, and privatizing civic services.

While battles still rage in the nation's legislatures and statehouses, mainstream media attention peaked in February and March 2011 with the culmination of the fight over Governor Scott Walker's budget bill AB 11, which sought to curtail the collective bargaining rights of government employees and thus disempower Wisconsin's public sector unions. When on February 23 the *Buffalo Beast* published recordings and transcripts of a prank call to Walker from a Beast reporter posing as billionaire GOP donor David Koch, it became apparent how intimately involved brothers David and Charles Koch were in Walker's efforts to break public sector unions.

Subsequently, bloggers and editorialists began batting around possible scenarios involving myriad right-wing public policy foundations funded by the Koch brothers and proceeds of Wichita, Kansas-based Koch Industries (and other Koch-controlled corporations). During such speculation, one name arose as the favorite villain behind the multitude of bills aimed squarely at public employee unions. That name was ALEC: the American Legislative Exchange Council.

An exhaustive analysis of thousands of pages of documents obtained through public records requests from six states, as well as tax filings, lobby reports, legislative drafts, and court records, reveal that these suddenly popular anti-public employee bills were indeed disseminated as "model legislation" by ALEC.

The purported goal of this nationwide movement has been to reduce the budgetary burden posed by public employee salaries by limiting the right of public employees to collectively bargain for pay and other benefits. These restrictions, along with "paycheck protection" laws, curtail the political power of public employee unions by cutting off funds for political campaign and lobbying expenditures. These measures would effectively thwart attempts by public employee unions to resist privatization of government functions and to support candidates opposing elected officials who vote for corporate giveaways of public resources.

"PUBLICOPOLY" IN PLAY

ALEC contends that government agencies have an unfair monopoly on public goods and services. To change that situation, it has created a policy initiative to counter what it calls "Publicopoly." ALEC's stated aim is to provide "more effective, efficient government" through privatization—that is, the shifting of government functions to the private sector.

Though the specifics are secret and "restricted to members," ALEC openly advocates privatizing public education, transportation, and the regulation of public health, consumer safety, and environmental quality, including bringing in corporations to administer:

- foster care, adoption services, and child-support-payment processing;
- school support services such as cafeteria meals, custodial staff, and transportation;
- highway systems, with toll roads presented as a shining example;
- surveiling and detaining convicted criminals;
- ensuring the quality of wastewater treatment, drinking water, and solid-waste services and facilities.

To accomplish these initiatives, ALEC contends that "state governments can take an active role in determining which products and services should be privatized." ALEC advocates three reforms: creating a "Private Enterprise Advisory Committee" to review if government agencies unfairly compete with the private sector; creating a special council that would contract with private vendors if they can "reduce the cost of government"; and creating legislation that would require government agencies to demonstrate "compelling public interest" in order to continue as public agencies. (Who then oversees these committees to ensure that the private sector doesn't unfairly profit by monopolizing public goods and services? One can only assume it is the same "Private Enterprise Advisory Committee.")

ALEC NUTS AND BOLTS

ALEC is a 501(c)(3) not-for-profit organization that in recent years has reported about $6.5 million in annual revenue. ALEC's members include corporations, trade associations, think tanks, and nearly a third of the nation's state legislators (virtually all Republican). According to the group's promotional material, ALEC's mission is to "advance the Jeffersonian principles of free markets, limited government, federalism, and individual liberty, through a nonpartisan public-private partnership of America's state legislators, members of the private sector, the federal government, and general public."

ALEC currently claims more than 250 corporations and special interest groups as private sector members. While the organization refuses to make a complete list of these private members available to the public, some known members include Exxon Mobil, the Corrections Corporation of America, AT&T, Pfizer Pharmaceuticals, Time Warner Cable, Comcast, Verizon, Walmart, Phillip Morris International, and Koch Industries, along with a host of right-wing think tanks and foundations.

ALEC is composed of nine task forces. Each of these task forces, which serve as the core of ALEC's operations, generate model legislation that is then passed on to member lawmakers for introduction in their home assemblies. According to ALEC promotional material, each year member lawmakers introduce an average of 1,000 of these pieces of legislation nationwide, 17 percent of which are enacted. ALEC does not offer its model legislation for public inspection and refused to comment on any aspect of the material covered here.

Three of its model bills call for the creation of state "councils" or "committees" tasked with streamlining state agency performance and identifying services to be outsourced to the private sector. The Public-Private Fair Competition Act calls for the broadest scope of privatization. The act seeks to prohibit state governments from "engaging in any commercial activity of any goods or services to or for government agencies or for public use, which are also offered by private enterprise." It also calls for the creation of "Private Enterprise Advisory Committees." The committee members—the majority of whom are business owners or corporate officers—would review what services, if any, government should continue to provide citizens.

THE NONPROFIT ROACH MOTEL

Public records requests demonstrate a clear tradition of ALEC model legislation being passed from ALEC-member corporate lobbyists through the offices of ALEC's elected public-sector chairs to other lawmakers. In essence, ALEC has created a web of lawmakers and public employees who act as lobbyists/agents on their behalf and on behalf of their corporate and special interest members.

Yet ALEC, as a 501(c)(3) entity, is strictly prohibited by federal tax code from taking part in the formation of legislation. In the past year, ALEC has vociferously insisted that it simply passes model legislation along to lawmakers. As such, ALEC claims it is not engaged in the crafting of actual legislation, nor is it engaged in lobbying.

Despite such protestations, ALEC is a conduit, an intermediary between Corporate America and the Republican Party—a legislative roach motel controlled by corporations, special interest groups, and right-wing think tanks through which lawmakers (whose election campaigns are often funded by the same corporations and interest groups) gather model laws to take home and introduce in state legislatures.

Taken together, ALEC's efforts to shape legislation, beguile lawmakers, and privatize government services have one clear goal: to eliminate the public sector altogether.

"PRIVATIZING GOVERNMENT SERVICES DOESN'T ONLY HURT PUBLIC WORKERS"

By David Moberg (2014)

If you want to understand how privatization of public services typically works, Grand Rapids, Michigan, is as good a place as any to start.

The state operates a nursing home for veterans in the town. Until 2011, it directly employed 170 nursing assistants but also relied on 100 assistants in the same facility provided by a private contractor. The state paid its direct employees $15 to $20 an hour and provided them with health insurance and pensions. Meanwhile, the contractor started pay for its nursing assistants at $8.50 an hour—still billing the state $14.99—and provided no benefits for employees. This led to high worker turnover, reduced quality of care, and heavy employee reliance on food stamps and other public aid.

Yet despite the evidence from this useful—albeit unplanned—experiment, which showed that any savings the state made through privatization came at the expense of workers and their clients, the new conservative Republican state government decided in 2011 to complete the privatization of the provision of nursing aides to the home.

The experience with privatization at the Grand Rapids nursing home is in many ways typical among the rapidly growing ranks of public agencies in which the staff of private contractors replace government employees. And according to a new report, "Race to the Bottom: How Outsourcing Public Services Rewards Corporations and Punishes the Middle Class," privatization policies around the country have greatly contributed to the nation's growing economic inequality and to a decline in the quality of public services.

The report by In the Public Interest (ITPI), a resource center on privatization, concludes that in most cases, privatization policies lead directly to cutbacks in government investment in skill development and to reductions in workers' pay and benefits.

Regardless of level of government, the story of privatization remains much the same. Elected leaders, often under legislative or political pressure from voters, try to reduce spending or taxes by relying on contractors for services instead. This way, politicians can attempt to avoid responsibility for the pay cuts and worker eliminations that almost inevitably result from privatization.

Government privatizers turn over huge swaths of public service work to private contractors—jobs such as corrections officers, nursing aides, teachers, school support personnel, clerks, waste haulers, food service workers, and many others. Nobody knows precisely how much government work is now subcontracted, but New York University professor Paul Light estimates that there are about three times as many federal contract workers as civil service employees, with millions more at the state level.

Privatizers frequently claim that they charge governments low rates because they are especially efficient. In many cases, however, public employees are at least as efficient as private contract ones. Instead, if contractors' operational cost is lower, the savings stem from the comparatively low salary their employees receive.

Even if advocates of privatization admit that the savings through contracting result from lower pay, not greater efficiency, they typically argue that governments pay above-market wages. Contracting out saves money for taxpayers by eliminating that premium, they say.

But when governments properly account for all of their costs, subcontractors are often more expensive than public employees. Those costs stem from a variety of sources. Governments must frequently hire an additional layer of supervisors to make sure that contractors meet legal and other requirements. In addition, poorly paid contract employees often collect public assistance from supplemental nutrition programs, Medicaid, and other aid for the needy, whose costs should be attributed to the contract.

Contracting out public work also rolls back critical progress toward equality on the basis of gender, race, and income. Whatever their shortcomings, public employers in recent decades have opened up more opportunities and paid fairer wages to both African Americans and women than the private sector. Cutting public service pay, therefore, compounds the inequities of income in America, replacing the ladder of opportunity upward with a "downward spiral."

Economists argue over the degree to which broad forces such as technology development or globalization account for rising inequality in the United States, says Jared Bernstein, a senior fellow at the Center on Budget and Policy Priorities. But privatization, he says, is one major cause of increased inequality that "smart policy" could easily reverse.

As some first steps toward that smart policy, ITPI recommends that governments require contractors to show that their cost savings come from innovation and efficiency, not wage and benefit cuts. Contractors should be required to provide a living wage, health insurance, and other benefits, ITPI also suggests.

Mary Sparrow, a former custodian at the Milwaukee County Courthouse in Wisconsin, might have benefitted from such changes. She was laid off in 2009 in the depth of the Great Recession after a private contractor, MidAmerican Building Services, won a contract to clean the building. The company told her she could keep the job—but not the pay. They offered her $8 an hour, instead of the $14.29 she had been making, and none of her former benefits. She and her husband have scraped by since, she said at a press conference at the release of the ITPI report, her voice cracking with emotion—buying health insurance with unemployment insurance payments, exhausting life savings for their children's college to cover myriad expenses, contending with health worsened by stress, and watching former coworkers relying on food banks.

"Only the contractors come out ahead, not the middle class, the frontline workers," Sparrow told the assembled crowd. "Milwaukee County or any county that privatizes will not see the promised cost savings. Privatizing has a devastating effect on our communities, not only on what we earn but what we spend. This has been awful for us, and I hope any city, any state, will think twice before privatizing."

"How to sell off a city"

By Rick Perlstein (2015)

In June 2013, Chicago Mayor Rahm Emanuel made a new appointment to the city's seven-member school board to replace billionaire heiress Penny

Pritzker, who'd decamped to run President Barack Obama's Department of Commerce. The appointee, Deborah H. Quazzo, is a founder of an investment firm called GSV Advisors, a business whose goal—her cofounder has been paraphrased by *Reuters* as saying—is to drum up venture capital for "an education revolution in which public schools outsource to private vendors such critical tasks as teaching math, educating disabled students, even writing report cards."

GSV Advisors has a sister firm, GSV Capital, that holds ownership stakes in education technology companies like "Knewton," which sells software that replaces the functions of flesh-and-blood teachers. Since joining the school board, Quazzo has invested her own money in companies that sell curricular materials to public schools in eleven states on a subscription basis.

In other words, a key decision-maker for Chicago's public schools makes money when school boards decide to sell off the functions of public schools.

She's not alone. For over a decade now, Chicago has been the epicenter of the fashionable trend of "privatization"—the transfer of the ownership or operation of resources that belong to all of us, like schools, roads, and government services, to companies that use them to turn a profit. Chicago's privatization mania began during Mayor Richard M. Daley's administration, which ran from 1989 to 2011. Under his successor, Rahm Emanuel, the trend has continued apace. For Rahm's investment banker buddies, the trend has been a boon. For citizens? Not so much.

They say that the first person in any political argument who stoops to invoking Nazi Germany automatically loses. But you can look it up: according to a 2006 article in the *Journal of Economic Perspectives*, the English word "privatization" derives from a coinage, *Reprivatisierung*, formulated in the 1930s to describe the Third Reich's policy of winning businessmen's loyalty by handing over state property to them. In the American context, the idea also began on the Right (to be fair, entirely independent of the Nazis)—and promptly went nowhere for decades. In 1963, when Republican presidential candidate Barry Goldwater mused "I think we ought to sell the TVA"—referring to the Tennessee Valley Authority, the giant complex of New Deal dams that delivered electricity for the first time to vast swaths of the rural Southeast—it helped seal his campaign's doom. Things only really took off after Prime Minister Margaret Thatcher's sale of UK state assets like British Petroleum and Rolls Royce in the 1980s made the idea fashionable among elites—including a rightward-tending Democratic Party.

As president, Bill Clinton greatly expanded a privatization program begun under the first President Bush's Department of Housing and Urban Development. "Hope VI" aimed to replace public-housing high-rises with mixed-income houses, duplexes, and row houses built and managed by private firms.

Chicago led the way. In 1999, Mayor Richard M. Daley, a Democrat, announced his intention to tear down the public-housing high-rises his father, Mayor Richard J. Daley, had built in the 1950s and 1960s. For this "Plan for Transformation," Chicago received the largest Hope VI grant of any city in the nation. There was a ration of idealism and intellectual energy behind it: blighted neighborhoods would be renewed and their "culture of poverty" would be broken, all vouchsafed by the honorable desire of public-spirited entrepreneurs to make a profit. That is the promise of privatization in a nutshell: that the profit motive can serve not just those making the profits, but society as a whole, by bypassing inefficient government bureaucracies.

As one of the movement's fans explained in 1997, his experience with nascent attempts to pay private real estate developers to replace public housing was an "example of smart policy."

"The developers were thinking in market terms and operating under the rules of the marketplace," he said. "But at the same time, we had government supporting and subsidizing those efforts."

The fan was Barack Obama, then a young state senator. Four years later, he cosponsored a bipartisan bill to increase subsidies for private developers and financiers to build or revamp low-income housing.

Meanwhile, the $1.6 billion Plan for Transformation drags on, six years past deadline and still 2,500 units from completion, while thousands of families languish on the Chicago Housing Authority's waitlist. Be that as it may, the Chicago experience looks like a laboratory for a new White House pilot initiative, the Rental Assistance Demonstration Program, which is set to turn over some 60,000 units to private management in 2016. Lack of success never seems to be an impediment where privatization is concerned.

CHAPTER SIX

Welcome to the Precariat

By Rebecca Burns

In the gospel according to Silicon Valley, the day is nigh when we'll all be freed from the shackles of our nine-to-five jobs. Rather than dragging ourselves into the office each morning, we'll spend our days at the beck and call of smartphone apps, blithely shuffling from gig to gig. Whether we find that prospect exhilarating or terrifying is irrelevant: on-demand platforms like Uber, PostMates, and Airbnb are "the future of work," according to their proponents.

This makes it sound as though our lives will soon be the stuff of science fiction—either a Jetsons esque utopia or an Apple-manufactured version of the Matrix, depending on how sanguine you are about joining the digital warren of TaskRabbits.

The reality is closer to something that sci-fi writer William Gibson once said: "The future is already here, it's just unevenly distributed." In other words, the key features of the "gig economy"—unpredictable, often low-paid work with no access to benefits—have long been a reality for certain workers.

Agricultural and domestic laborers, for example, have always been gig workers considered undeserving of basic labor protections. Where hard-won minimum wage and overtime laws established a modicum of security in many industries, these two sectors, then predominantly black, were explicitly written out of New Deal–era legislation in order to appease Southern legislators. This ensured that a large swath of workers would remain precarious and isolated from organized labor. ("An Udderly Bad Job" and "Domestic Workers Emerging From the Shadows" in this chapter show how this marginal status creates a sense of worthlessness.) Right-wing assaults on labor law since then have successfully chipped away at protections for a number of other groups. For example, the Taft-Hartley Act of 1947 excluded so-called independent contractors and low-level supervisors from recently minted labor laws.

The growth of precarious work accelerated from the 1980s onward thanks to the decline of manufacturing (see Chapter 1) and the concurrent rise of lower-wage, often part-time service-sector jobs. Meanwhile, corporations devised a host of employer-friendly work arrangements. The temporary help industry sits at the intersection of these developments: since the late 1970s, temp agencies have become a fixture of the new economy as employers have aggressively promoted labor "flexibility" as a cost-saving strategy. While staffing agencies often portray temp hiring as a necessary short-term survival strategy in the wake of recessions, during the most recent recovery many companies saw no reason to reinstate permanent positions when they could continue using cheaper, more disposable temps. The number of temporary workers hit an all-time high of 2.9 million in 2015, according to the Bureau of Labor Statistics. The emerging new class of "permatemps" is dominated by the most vulnerable workers: African Americans, Latinos, and women are all overrepresented.

While temps are concentrated primarily in the service and manufacturing sectors, the model has also made its way into professionalized industries—IT, academia, and law, for example—disrupting some of the last bastions of stable employment. (Three stories in this chapter, "Temp Slave Revolt" and "Forever Temp?" and "The Adjunct's Lament," show temp workers in IT, manufacturing, and academia, respectively.) Labor activists debate whether we are witnessing the rise of a "precariat," a new, distinct class of workers characterized by insecurity and atomization and impervious to traditional organizing methods. They argue that as white-collar jobs undergo the same casualization long underway in blue-collar industries, adjunct professors in elite universities and temp workers in Walmart warehouses find themselves with common interests.

Is precarity the new normal? Because of varying definitions and a lack of available data, it's difficult to quantify exactly how widespread precarious employment has become. But a 2015 study by the U.S. Government Accountability Office (GAO) noted that "contingent" workers—when defined most broadly as all part-time, temp, and on-call workers, as well as the self-employed—may constitute more than a third of the total U.S. labor force. Contingent workers contend with greater job instability, less access to health insurance, and lower pay. The GAO estimated their median annual earnings were $14,963, compared to $35,000 for full-time workers. In short, it's clear that the bottom is falling out for a growing number of workers.

While deepening precarity has become the subject of growing notice and concern in the age of Uber, it's important to remember that its roots lie in the exclusion and isolation of vulnerable groups of workers—not in new technologies that have suddenly arrived on the scene. Nevertheless, the architects of the sharing economy are going to great lengths to convince us that thanks to technological changes, a fundamental shift in the way we work is underway, and the old rules no longer apply. A host of sharing-economy advocates are in the midst of a push to "modernize" (read: gut) labor law by carving out broad exemptions to existing safeguards for workers on Internet-based platforms—a solution that recalls past efforts to exclude farm and domestic workers. (Uber's fight to classify its drivers as contractors is also reminiscent of cab companies' push toward leasing in the 1970s, which we see in this chapter's opening piece.)

This isn't actually a vision of the future of work—it's one of the past, before the labor movement won key victories that created the protections in force today.

Conservatives, unsurprisingly, drool at the prospect of an unfettered free market future. During his run in the 2015 Republican primaries, Ohio Governor John Kasich repeatedly suggested that we "Uberize the government." But it has also won buy-in from some surprising quarters, including certain sectors of the labor movement. While there have been a few efforts to organize gig-economy workers into traditional unions, the more common approach is to embrace freelancing as an attractive alternative lifestyle, pending a few tweaks. Most notably, the 300,000-member Freelancers Union has pioneered what founder Sara Horowitz calls "a new form of unionism," focused on plugging holes in the safety net rather than traditional collective bargaining.

Widespread worker precarity presents daunting challenges for unions (see Chapter 9), but organizers must be wary of cures that are worse than the disease. In a world with few employees but a surplus of on-demand "independent" contractors and temp workers, collective action is hard to imagine—which is exactly what employers want.

"CAB COMPANIES USE LEASING TO BOOST PROFITS"

By David Moberg (1976)

Dangling an attractive offer to "be your own boss" and make big money before a job-hungry labor market, cab companies in Chicago and other cities are threatening to undermine drivers' unions, make the work more demanding and dangerous, and shift financial risk to the drivers.

The new gambit is leasing. Leasing was once common and never disappeared. But most cabbies work on a commission, earning between 40 and 50 percent of the fare, plus tips. Drivers and companies share the ups and downs of the market.

In response to a National Labor Relations Board complaint charging cab companies with unfair labor practices, an administrative law judge this year ruled that lease drivers were not employees and thus not covered by the union. The companies responded with a new drive to attract lease drivers, offering a variety of special deals.

Cabs lease for $18 to $23 for a twelve-hour shift or $32 for a full day. Once drivers "make their nut," or pay the leasing fee, they keep the rest of their fares. Leasing appeals mainly to young, inexperienced drivers who think they can make a lot of cash quickly. The feeling of greater freedom and access to a car for personal use also make leasing attractive to young drivers, mainly inner-city blacks. "You're really your own boss," said twenty-six-year-old Wade, who has driven cabs less than a year. "You do what you want to do. It's your car. If you don't make a quota, it's your business. I'm not the kind of guy who likes to sit in a cab line. I like to roll."

Although most drivers brag about how much more money they make, other drivers doubt that they can regularly do much better unless they work exhausting hours, hustle hard, and violate cabdriver etiquette and customs—cutting into cab lines, darting across busy streets for fares and bribing hotel doormen.

Very few longtime cabbies have switched to leasing. Leroy, a thirty-eight-year veteran cab driver who came to Yellow Cab Co. Twenty years ago when it first hired blacks, got his night-shift spotlight ready while we talked. "I got too much time in to switch. I would be crazy to lease and give up my benefits—pension, month vacation, health insurance. These young guys ain't got nothing going for them anyway. They may see the money there, but I don't. This way (on commission) if I don't get out this evening and make but $5 or $10 in fares, I got some of that."

Lease drivers have to pay for their own gasoline and the first $250 on accidents that are their fault. They have no union benefits and since they are not officially employees, the company does not have to pay for workmen's compensation. And with leasing, cab companies can protect their profits by passing on gas price increases to drivers and raising leasing rates.

Drivers have already felt the pinch of hard times—fewer riders and lower tips. In exchange for a fling with a loosely reined independence and a chance of more money, they are now also expected to put up with harder work, fewer benefits, greater insecurity, no union protection, and more mental pressure.

"MARGINAL WORK IS ON THE RISE AS TRADITIONAL JOBS EVAPORATE"

By Robert B. Carson (1977)

The pundit who observed that the next worse thing to being out of work in the United States was to have a job was right. Bad as unemployment is, the day-to-day problem of most American workers is work itself. The trouble is not just that labor is increasingly tedious and dull or "not fulfilling." Despite the hold of the work ethic in American life, work for the vast majority has rarely been "fulfilling." For most, it has always been brute and tiresome. In the past, though, there was often a sense of security and the hope of monetary or status advancement to blunt the day-to-day drudgery. In recent years, these aspects of work in the United States have been receding.

The workforce has almost doubled since the Second World War and real GNP has grown by about 120 percent. But this expansion has been accompanied by the shift of a growing percentage of workers into marginal industries and marginal occupations that provide little sense of economic security and practically no hope of upward movement. Understanding this change in the structure of labor puts the magnitude of America's unemployment problem in clearer perspective.

What specifically are the employment trends?

First, during the past twenty years there has been very little job growth in the old industrial occupations. Second, most recent job growth has been in the largely unskilled and lower skilled, labor-intensive service sectors. Third, these new jobs have been relatively poorer paid and, whether with or without the benefits of unions, are the least secure.

Thus, we can conclude that while more and more Americans are working, more workers are being pressed toward the margins of employment. For many, the transition from employment to unemployment, whatever the personal psychological jolt, is scarcely noticeable from the perspective of the economy as a whole. The "new jobs" then, contrary to conventional economists' claims, were never a sign of a vital economy but merely another measure (along with chronic unemployment) of the growing labor surplus problem of American corporate capitalism.

It is evident in looking at the performance of the American economy in the past quarter century that corporate capitalism is able to produce greater and greater levels of output with decreasing need for human labor. The actual labor of more and more people becomes irrelevant. Among the employed—especially those in labor-intensive jobs—the vulnerability to periodic unemployment, job insecurity, relatively lower wages, and degrading work can only be expected to heighten in a production-for-profit society. Within the limits of the system of corporate capitalism, there are no "economic" answers to the problem. Growing unemployment and the increased marginalization of the labor force can only be approached as political problems.

"IMMIGRANTS SWEAT IT OUT IN ILLEGAL GARMENT FACTORIES"

By Doug Turetsky (1990)

At 207 West 38th Street, a cold metal door opens into a narrow workspace. Long tables dominate the small, cramped room. Frayed electric wires dangle from the ceiling, and the floor is littered with scraps of fabric. The rapid-fire chatter of sewing machines fills the room as eight sewers stitch belts.

There is no desk, no filing cabinets—no place payroll records are likely to be kept. Wilfredo Zapata, the owner of the factory, says he's been in business just three weeks and pays his workforce—all Hispanic—in cash. The shop is not registered with the New York State Department of Labor. If a spark were to ignite the fabric strewn on the floor and tables, it would be nearly impossible for several of the workers to escape from the cramped room.

Nearly eighty years after the Triangle Shirtwaist Company fire took the lives of 146 immigrant garment workers, prodding government officials to crack down on factory conditions, sweatshops continue to plague the garment industry. In fact, according to investigators and labor unionists, the number of sweatshops may be on the rise in New York—the hub of the nation's garment industry—as well as in Chicago, El Paso, Los Angeles, and other cities.

A primary reason sweatshops continue to exist is the structure of the apparel industry itself. The manufacturer's label rarely belongs to the company that actually produces the garments. In the "rag trade," the manufacturer is really the outfit that owns and designs the material and markets the goods. Production is left to independent contractors who compete for the sewing jobs. It is these contractors who must bear most of the production overhead and must increasingly compete with low-cost factories—often established by U.S. companies—in Latin America and the Far East. Today's intense competition for manufacturing contracts is ultimately shouldered by workers in the form of reduced wages and poor working conditions.

Cities like New York, with their burgeoning immigrant populations, are ripe for sweatshop operations. It doesn't take a lot of money to set up a small shop—some loft space, a few rented or secondhand machines, and a few laborers willing to work for low wages. Many of these shops are started by

Asian or Hispanic immigrants who arrive with some cash and find workers among the poorer members of their communities.

Immigrant-rights advocates and unionists believe the 1986 Immigration Reform and Control Act, under which employers are fined for hiring undocumented workers, exacerbates the situation by forcing some immigrants to accept even lower wages and worse conditions. "It obviously hurts all workers when one sector of the labor force is driven further underground," says Marla Kamiya, public-policy director at the Center for Immigrant Rights.

Even many longtime garment workers make little more than $5 an hour. When undocumented workers are forced to accept below-minimum wages, the hourly wage made in hundreds of the city's nonunion manufacturing shops is ultimately driven down. The downward pay spiral can be even worse for workers paid by the garment. It is not uncommon for pieceworkers to be paid less than the price initially offered by the shop operator.

Members of the Garment Industry Development Corporation, created by city officials and management and labor leaders in 1984, contend that the garment trade will not survive simply by cutting wages and allowing factory conditions to decline. But, says International Ladies Garment Workers Union spokesperson Susan Cowell, for thousands of the city's rag-trade workers, "the trend has been back toward 1910."

"LIFE OF LEISURE EVADING THE AMERICAN WORKER?"

By David Moberg (1992)

As you prepare for the Labor Day weekend, perhaps reflecting on your summer vacation trip, here's a grim statistic that's hardly worth celebrating. While the average American enjoyed about two weeks vacation in 1992, most western European workers were guaranteed four to five weeks paid vacation by law—and often got several weeks more. The disparity in vacations is one big reason why Europeans work significantly less than Americans, whose work hours have actually been increasing since the late '60s. This is part of an overall trend that goes against the predictions of growing leisure time by both critics and apologists for advanced capitalism.

Even as most full-time employees have been working harder and longer, there's been a great increase in involuntary time off—people either unemployed or working less than they want. Much of the increase in average work time reflects women's entry into the work force and an expansion of the number of weeks they work each year. But time pressures have grown across the board—with workers experiencing more overtime, more moonlighting, and a bit less paid time off.

By calculating these figures on work time, Harvard economist Juliet Schor has helped bring the old issue of work time back into public debate with her book, *The Overworked American*. Schor's estimates of work time reveal that American living standards over the past two decades have slumped far more than is indicated by falling family income levels. Even this stagnation in U.S. living standards has been achieved only by more people working longer hours.

The increase in work hours in the United States over the past two decades has been especially hard on parents aged eighteen to thirty-nine with young kids. Although talk of family values in the presidential race is already thick enough to gag on, often there's a detachment from the realities of time, work, and money. Democrats at least support unpaid family leave, but that's hardly a sufficient answer to family needs. European workers— often both men and women—typically are guaranteed many months of paid leave to take care of new children.

A Leisurely Decline

Longer hours of work have been a consequence of the persistent, under-lying crisis of the American political economy over the past two decades. Corporations and the government failed to respond to new global challenges —such as the rise of strong, aggressive competitors and energy price shocks—with a coherent public–private strategy to improve the efficiency, technical sophistication, and social organization of American business. Instead, U.S. corporations attacked unions, fled to low-wage locales, and increased pressures on workers. That included squeezing more hours of work out of employees rather than "working smarter."

The collapse of the labor movement in the face of the employer onslaught—and its abandonment of its historic campaign for shorter hours of work—has undoubtedly been central in encouraging the employer strategy. If there were a national health insurance plan like Canada's, there would be less financial incentive for employers who provide health-care benefits to demand overtime rather than hire new employees, thereby taking on additional health-care costs. If there were a public consensus that people should have more freedom to choose leisure, the government could mandate minimum vacation, set an overtime rate of double normal pay, or require overtime payment in "comp" time off rather than money. Lawmakers could also mandate payment of proportional benefits for part-time workers and raise the minimum wage.

To reverse the trend to overwork, we need both to increase the nation's wealth through public policies that boost productivity and to guarantee a greater, more equitably distributed share of total wealth for workers. But equally important, Schor insists, people should be "free to choose," as Milton Friedman loves to say, whether to take their share of that growing wealth in money or time.

By voluntarily opting for a more frugal lifestyle, people can choose time over money. Or with the privilege of wealth, others can opt for leisure. But for the vast majority, the promise of freedom to choose work or leisure requires both strategies to increase national wealth and place new constraints on employers through public policy and union pressure.

In medieval Europe, as in most peasant and primitive societies, people worked far less than they did in nineteenth-century capitalist Europe, in many cases far less than we do today. The calendar was full of festivals, rituals, fairs, and other ceremonial and collective gatherings that held societies together and gave meaning to people's lives. Now the shrinking time people have away from work is channeled into the rites of consumption, from shopping to tending to one's past purchase. If it is possible for people to win more time, there will be yet other battles over the creation of a democratic and noncommercial culture that might give new meaning and coherence to people's lives and a new and desperately needed civility to American society.

"TEMP SLAVE REVOLT"

By David Moberg (2000)

Seattle, Washington—After a few weeks as a product designer at Microsoft, twenty-six-year-old Ed Campodonico wondered out loud to his office mate why there wasn't a union for temporary employees like them. "Dude," his partner replied edgily, "you can't talk about that."

But Campodonico, who grew up in a union family, did talk about it. So have a small but growing number of other skilled computer workers who hold temporary jobs in this global software center and do not have the rights and benefits of regular employees, even after years of working virtually full-time for the same company. Their innovative union, the Washington Alliance of Technology Workers, or WashTech, is confronting two of the most important trends in the American workplace—the information technology boom and the rising importance of contingent workers, a catch-all phrase for part-time, temporary, contract, lease, or other nonstandard employees.

WashTech was born in 1997 after a few Microsoft "permatemps" were outraged that the Washington Software Alliance, an industry lobbying group, had persuaded the state labor department to deny overtime pay protection to a large swath of well-paid software engineers. Now affiliated with the Communications Workers of America, WashTech organizers are seeking new ways of giving a voice to workers who do not fit into existing labor laws and organizations.

"We're trying to create a new model of unionism," says Marcus Courtney, co-founder of WashTech. "In this industry, collective bargaining is not an attainable goal right now. That's not going to preclude us from organizing and building power for workers on the job, at the legislative level, and in the community. If we play by the rules, we'll never win. So we're going to build a new kind of worker organization that works for this industry and new-economy jobs."

In May, WashTech joined with about forty other worker advocacy organizations, ranging from the American Federation of Labor and Congress of Industrial Organizations (AFL-CIO) to the Chicago Coalition for the Homeless, to form the National Alliance For Fair Employment (NAFFE). Although the day laborers, software designers, and adjunct professors represented by groups in the NAFFE might seem to have little in common, all contingent workers—about 30 percent of the workforce—lack many of the rights or legal protections of standard employees.

Much of the recent growth of contingent work reflects an attempt by the most powerful corporations to shift as many risks as possible to their employees and dependent businesses and to avoid responsibilities for workers and the potential claims they might make by organizing or demanding their legal rights. Indeed, it is often unclear who (if anyone) is legally considered their employer—which is precisely what businesses want.

While WashTech is still small—it has 260 dues-paying members, working at more than seventy Seattle-area companies, and 1,700 subscribers to its electronic newsletter—it frequently exposes abusive practices of companies like Microsoft and Amazon.com as well as the temporary employment agencies. Its criticisms have already led to improved employment agency benefit packages for temps. It has also launched surprisingly effective, if not yet victorious, legislative battles for investigation and regulation of the temporary employment industry, such as a proposal that agencies must reveal the fee they collect from each temp worker's contract.

Uᴘʜɪʟʟ ʙᴀᴛᴛʟᴇ

Unlike many temp workers who are immersed in poverty, most software engineers and editors, even the temps, typically earn $60,000 a year or more—and they often love their work. "We had to overcome this idea that labor unions were only for people who hated their jobs," Courtney says.

But temps are often upset about being treated as second-class workers and the parasitic role of the employment agencies. Often workers find their own jobs, then are forced to work through a specific agency that provides them nothing. Besides seeking health insurance and training to stay on top of a fast-changing industry, many software workers want some control over the long hours of overtime that have become the industry standard.

Still, the idea of collective action is alien to most young high-tech workers, especially temps who are often quite isolated from each other and rapidly churn through jobs. "We start not even at square one, but at negative three," explains Mike Blain, co-founder and president of WashTech. "The negative baggage is especially heavy in information technology, with its maverick, libertarian culture, which believes you succeed by being smart, working hard, keeping trained, and moving around—and if you don't succeed, it's your fault."

"Hᴇʏ ᴍɪʟʟᴇɴɴɪᴀʟs, ᴅᴇʙᴛ ʙᴇᴄᴏᴍᴇs ʏᴏᴜ"

By Mischa Gaus (2006)

The children of baby boomers are the new debtor class. Buckling under a heavy weight of debt, new workers step into an economy of low-wage and contingent work, a combination that makes the basics of adulthood increasingly unattainable.

"We grew up in the Reagan era where everything was fake, voodoo economics, and we're not seeing the connections," says Anya Kamenetz, author of *Generation Debt: Why Now Is a Terrible Time to be Young.* "I don't think we can continue treating people as disposable, not providing them with health care or the means to save."

Educational debt is the most visible—but not the only—barrier to the well-being of the "millennial generation," roughly defined as Americans born after 1978. Every gate on the way to middle-class life is now tougher to unlock. Mortgages, health insurance expenses, car maintenance, child-care, and tax loads for two-income families have all ballooned. The familiar combination of summer work, a part-time job during the school year, and a little help from home doesn't begin to cover today's college costs.

"Students are in a pretty deep financial hole," says Luke Swarthout, higher education associate for the State Public Interest Research Groups, which advocate on a variety of consumer, environmental, and good-government issues.

Some never emerge from their chasm of liabilities. The Supreme Court recently decided that retirees' Social Security checks can be garnished for old student debts, and changes to bankruptcy law last year make it nearly impossible to discharge educational loans.

For students who approach their working lives seeking returns beyond pure remuneration, rising debt loads postpone basic decisions. Even with a scholarship to American University's law school, Julia Graff, twenty-eight, started her career as a staff attorney at the Delaware American Civil Liberties Union last year facing $80,000 in debt. She anticipates paying lenders until she retires. Graff knew her ambition to pursue a nonprofit career meant she would forgo luxuries. But her debt-to-income ratio means trips to university dental clinics and taking on odd jobs like tutoring and translating Spanish. "I live paycheck to paycheck," Graff says. "Eventually I'm not going to want to live like I did when I was eighteen."

And when lives don't match up with debt schedules, the strain can be severe. After finishing community college, Mandy Minor, thirty, bounced around the University of South Florida before settling on business admin-istration. She graduated five years ago, picking up $60,000 in consumer and student debt along with her diploma. Minor owns a small writing and design firm with her husband and had a daughter five months ago. She pays $400 a month just to maintain her debt load and has given up on buying a house. She worries how to provide health insurance once her daughter no longer qualifies for Florida's state-provided care.

Ensuring economic security is not solely an issue of self-interest for young people. Because higher education remains the most important factor for predicting economic success—and thus an opportunity to bridge inequality—it is a social justice concern as well.

Struggling for a Living Wage

Once they've graduated, however, what really staggers young people is a one-two punch: saddled with loans, students have a hard time finding a stable job that will actually support them. Steady productivity gains have been swallowed by capital, stagnating wages for young people.

"Management has pulled a fast one," says Kamenetz. "They've gotten people to accept intangible benefits instead of old, actual benefits. We've all sort of followed this idea that we're all free agents." Flexibility and contingent labor have replaced the certainty of bargaining agreements and pensions.

The emerging generation's beliefs could offer an opportunity for reshaping the political discourse. Recent studies by the liberal New Politics Institute and a University of Maryland public policy center suggest that millennials are more likely to identify as progressive than any other age group. But unless they find political avenues to channel their discontent, they may soon find themselves screaming in the streets.

"FOR DISGRUNTLED YOUNG WORKERS, LAWSUITS MAY SPARK INTERN INSURRECTION"

By Michelle Chen (2013)

You'd have to be pretty desperate to offer to work for free, right? Or you could be just an enthusiastic young student who believes that toiling for little more than free coffee and a line on your résumé may boost your future career.

But recent research shows that unpaid internships are not likely to lead to a coveted job offer. A National Association of Colleges and Employers survey found that paid internships did boost job prospects, unlike their unpaid counterparts. A majority of paid interns received a job offer afterward. But the unpaid intern experience seems more of a time suck than a springboard; unpaid interns received future paid-job offers at about the same rate, just over 35 percent, as those who had not interned.

Now, some interns are taking legal action against bosses whom they say offered nothing in return for their labor. And the courts are listening. In June 2013, a federal judge in Manhattan cast a legal shadow over unpaid internships by certifying a class-action lawsuit against Fox Searchlight and Fox Entertainment Group. Two unpaid interns filed suit accusing Fox of denying them proper wages for the weeks they spent performing essentially the same duties as regular employees.

The suit reveals how youthful aspirants can be seduced into a crap job gilded with glamorous IOUs. Eric Glatt and Alexander Footman allege that as Fox Searchlight interns, they "took lunch orders, answered phones, arranged other employees' travel plans, tracked purchase orders, took out the trash and assembled office furniture," according to the *New York Times*. Juno Turner, an attorney with Outten & Golden, representing the interns in both the Fox and Hearst cases, tells *In These Times* that while the firm's first priority is to resolve the wage dispute, the bigger hope is that the suits will prompt more paid internships. These, she notes, "can be taken advantage of by a broader spectrum of individuals, including those unable to work for free, and in turn will open doors for career paths that might have been foreclosed to those who couldn't previously take internships."

David Yamada, a labor-law specialist at Suffolk University Law School, comments via email, "We'll probably never know how many people from modest backgrounds don't even bother applying for unpaid internships because they know they can't afford it. But there surely is a strong element of economic class bias in this practice."

It is unsurprising that the first major intern lawsuits would emerge in sectors built on fame and reputation, where the biggest, brittlest dreams go to die as promises of glamor fail to match up with unglamorous drudge work that drives these industries. The controversy represents deeper disillusionment rippling through an overeducated, underpaid workforce that is anxious, financially insecure, and increasingly outraged.

Their plight echoes the labor conflicts of early-modern times that stirred disaffected young apprentices to rise up against their masters. When young people realize that an apparent stepping stone is really an indefinite dead end, they learn quickly that their labor rights are not worth trading away for empty promises. Once the mask slips on the illusion of "making it" after college, they might even find common cause with other workers who already know how hard it is to get a fair day's pay.

"THE WAGE-THEFT EPIDEMIC"

By Spencer Woodman (2013)

Last October, Anthony M. Van Buren drove 135 miles south from his home in Charlottesville, Virginia, to the small town of Moneta in search of his former boss, Robert Brown, the owner of Star Valley Painting Contractors Inc. The visit was neither invited nor welcome. According to Van Buren, Brown's site manager had fired him, along with several others, after they'd complained about not being paid for their work on a large painting project. The company, he says, owed him more than $1,000 for three weeks of work. Struggling financially, Van Buren, fifty-nine, had tried and failed to work out a deal with his landlord to forestall eviction. He needed his pay, and fast.

Driving to Moneta was a last resort. Days before, Van Buren had called Virginia's Department of Labor and Industry to report his employer's non-payment, a crime under Virginia state law. To his disbelief, the agency told him they were no longer taking wage-and-hour claims and that it was up to him to investigate and prosecute the alleged crime. They referred him to a private lawyer, but the attorney's fees alone would have amounted to more than the sum he sought.

Van Buren brought along two other men: his cousin and another fired worker also seeking back wages from Brown. Having grown up in Harlem in the 1960s, Van Buren was no stranger to confrontation. Yet he did worry that the unannounced visit would attract the attention of the Moneta sheriff, an unappealing prospect for an African American out-of-towner entering a tiny municipality at the foot of the Appalachians. He even considered, briefly, alerting the local authorities of his plan. "I wasn't going up there for no trouble or anything," Van Buren says. "All I wanted was my money."

As the three men sped through the southern Shenandoah Valley in a 1989 Honda Accord, Van Buren prayed for two things: that he'd get his money, and that, in doing so, he wouldn't be harmed.

No ENFORCERS OF THE LAW

Even as the ranks of low-wage workers have swelled since the recession, Democratic and Republican legislatures in more than a dozen states have quietly slashed funding for the agencies that enforce minimum-wage law. Budget cuts are no surprise in an era of austerity. Yet the effect of these cuts on wage-and-hour investigative units—charged with examining and settling wage disputes—has seriously compromised an essential line of defense for already vulnerable low-wage earners, according to experts. State labor officials and researchers around the country tell *In These Times* that low-wage workers facing abusive employers increasingly have nowhere to turn.

The victims of nonpayment of owed wages—referred to as "wage theft"— are most frequently workers at the bottom of the income scale. The U.S. Department of Labor, which significantly expanded its investigative force under former Labor Secretary Hilda Solis, can take wage-theft cases, but it is less familiar with local particulars and is prohibited from investigating many employers covered by state laws. Most private attorneys are unwilling to take wage-theft cases, since they involve comparatively small sums of money.

Former investigators interviewed for this article say that budget cuts over the past decade have impeded their ability to perform meaningful investigations. They paint a stark picture of weakened enforcement divisions, lacking both necessary staff and funding, that regularly close claims of wage theft that appear legitimate. Such closed cases represent de facto wins for employers.

"This sends a powerful message to employers that they're not likely to get caught and that following minimum-wage laws isn't a priority," says

Catherine Ruckelshaus, legal co-director at the National Employment Law Project. "It's to the point where, in some industries, there's no minimum-wage floor at all."

Cuts to state minimum-wage investigative units have happened with almost no fanfare. The change reflects budgetary realities and also a successful decades-long attempt by business groups to frame employee protections as a partisan issue, not suitable for public dollars. As union ranks shrink and average wages decline, weakened labor-law enforcement represents yet another locus of power shifting away from the interests of the labor movement.

Virginia offers an extreme case. Last July, the state eliminated its entire wage-and-hour enforcement unit. All six of the state's minimum-wage investigators retired or were reassigned, leaving many wage-theft victims either to give up or—like Anthony Van Buren—to resort to vigilantism to retrieve pay.

Until last July, Bobby Myers worked as a wage-and-hour investigator in Virginia. During his last two years on the job, his caseload resembled that of other hard-hit departments around the country. When he first arrived in 2009, the staff was large enough that an investigator was usually available to focus on hard cases—and could even drive hours to personally visit a noncompliant employer. But by 2011, each compliance officer was solely responsible for some 250 wage claims a year, a job Myers describes as a chaotic race against a swelling backlog that often left him "just filing 'no'" on tough cases.

"Our powers were just really weak. We were constantly bluffing," says Myers. "Some repeat offenders eventually learned to call our bluff, and then there was very little we could do. That was when the claimant would see just how powerless we were to enforce the wage law of the commonwealth of Virginia."

Often, an accused employer would simply refuse to hand over essential, potentially incriminating documents, and after several attempts to coax the employer by phone and mail, Myers would have to close a case without further investigation. Thus, for at least several savvy employers in Virginia, Myers says, there was effectively no minimum wage.

"When someone's been screwed out of money that they've worked for and that's going to make a difference in how they're going to live—and you, as the investigator on the case, cannot help—it makes you feel hollow, just impotent," says Myers.

"FOREVER TEMP?"

By Sarah Jaffe (2014)

Betty McCray, fifty-three, has moved around a bit in her lifetime. She's worked as a chef, a nursing home attendant, and a welder. Throughout, she says proudly, she has "worked union," even in states with anti-labor right-to-work laws, such as Tennessee, where she moved in 2010 to be closer to her son.

That changed in 2011, when she found work at a Nissan auto plant in Smyrna, Tennessee, preparing parts for the assembly line. Not only is this job nonunion, but McCray doesn't technically work for Nissan—she's employed through Yates Services, a temporary staffing agency. She's one of a growing number of people who do the physically demanding work of manufacturing, but who, as temps, have none of the job security and few of the benefits that many Americans still associate with the sector.

McCray found the job through the local unemployment office, which referred her to Yates. As an "associate" (the firm's preferred term for temp), she works alongside permanent Nissan employees, but she is treated differently. She says she is paid less, gets no personal days, and has to bring a doctor's note if she is sick. Her job feels precarious, like she could be let go at any time.

The path to becoming an "employee," that elusive goal, is far from clear. Tracy Logan, thirty-four, worked through Yates on Nissan's assembly line for a year before winning a promotion to a position as a robot tender, overseeing the robots that spray paint on the car parts. To his surprise, he remained a temp. "When I first arrived at Nissan, that position was considered Class A—only Nissan personnel can hold that position," he says. "I put in for it, thinking that would be a way of getting on with Nissan. Somewhere in there, they changed the classification of the job, but didn't let us know."

Such experiences are increasingly common, according to Leone José Bicchieri, executive director of the Chicago Workers Collaborative (CWC), a nonprofit worker center that organizes low-wage and temp workers. Not only has temporary employment expanded into sectors that used to be sources of stable full-time employment, he says, but it's often no longer really temporary. Some temps are brought on for only days or weeks, others work for years at the same plant through the same agency.

Organizers in the field, Bicchieri says, now talk about "staffing agencies" rather than "temp agencies," and "direct-hire" workers rather than "permanent" employees. "It's not a 'temp' job," Logan says, "but it's temp status."

So is permatemping the new model in manufacturing? Nissan spokesperson Justin Saia maintains that temporary jobs can provide a route to direct employment. "Having contract workers enables us to further develop the skill sets of these employees to position them for direct employment opportunities with Nissan through our Pathways program," he writes in an email. But on the other hand, he notes, "The contract jobs in our business model are designed to be long-term, stable jobs with competitive pay and benefits."

Or, as Logan puts it: "They want us to be permanent temps."

FROM "KELLY GIRLS" TO "STRAPPING" MEN

Kelly Girl Service, a staffing agency founded in 1946, pioneered the temp industry. Temping was originally framed as a way for white middle-class housewives to earn a bit of extra money, says Erin Hatton, a sociologist at the State University of New York at Buffalo and author of *The Temp Economy: From Kelly Girls to Permatemps in Postwar America*. Married women weren't perceived as breadwinners in need of full-time hours or family-sustaining wages.

"That's how [temp agencies] gained entry into the labor market," says Hatton, "but once they gained legitimacy, they were able to spread out." She says that from the beginning, temp agencies had a toehold in manual labor and manufacturing, but they deliberately played up the "girls," in part to avoid conflicts with then-powerful unions. By the 1970s, though, they began openly targeting men. One ad campaign from Kelly read, "Obviously, we can't call ourselves Kelly Girl Service any more," as it touted its stable of "big, strapping" male workers.

Kelly Girl Service became Kelly Services in 1966, and today its work placements range from offices to universities to banks to factories—including another Nissan plant, in Canton, Mississippi. The temp business has ballooned, comprising some 17,000 staffing firms in the United States with a combined 2012 revenue of $117 billion.

A 2010 report from the Bureau of Labor Statistics (BLS) found that "while manufacturing's share of total national employment fell from 16.2 percent in 1990 to 9.8 percent in 2008, manufacturing's use of temporary workers greatly intensified." Because the BLS categorizes temp workers as service employees regardless of the kind of work they do, the agency has no good data on how many of those "lost" manufacturing jobs simply migrated over to staffing agencies. But according to a 2004 report from the Council of Economic Advisers, a third of all temp service employees work in the manufacturing sector. "If the official manufacturing employment statistics are adjusted by this amount," the authors found, "the decline in the level of manufacturing employment in the 1990s is eliminated." In other words, a good number of jobs were simply outsourced right here at home, offloaded from company payrolls onto staffing agencies.

For manufacturers, says Hatton, the logic is simple: "They have none of the costs of outsourcing with all of the benefits of outsourcing and all of the benefits of a native, English-speaking local workforce."

In many cases, that workforce is highly skilled, comprising workers like McCray who have years of manufacturing experience under their belts. While temp agencies once emphasized unskilled labor, these days some openly recruit skilled labor on the cheap. A job application obtained this fall from the Smyrna, Georgia, facility of gun manufacturer Glock lists six separate staffing agencies through which one can apply for a manufacturing or warehouse job. One of the agencies, Automation, recently posted a skilled machinist position on its website for an (unnamed) gun manufacturing company in Smyrna. The listing called for an array of skills:

Applicants must have experience operating the robotic machine, must be mechanically inclined, must have metalworking experience. Applicants must also be able to read specs and be technically skilled.

Applicants would also have to be extremely flexible: "This position rotates weekly between 1st and 2nd shift (this is a requirement)," meaning day and evening shifts. And the wages on offer for all those skills and flexibility? "$10 hour to start, but depending on experience, may go up to $13." According to the BLS, the mean hourly wage for a machinist last year was $19.65.

So much for the value of skilled labor. (Automation did not respond to repeated requests for comment.)

This should remind us that manufacturing jobs weren't good jobs because of the inherent value of the job, says Amy Traub, a senior policy analyst at the nonpartisan think tank Demos. "They were terrible jobs until people organized."

Despite the many drawbacks of a temp job, anemic job growth during the economic recovery has meant that many blue-collar workers have few options beyond putting in their time as a temp in the hope that they'll get hired full-time one day.

The lure of that elusive job is used to keep permatemps around. One of Nissan's direct hires, Matthew Thornberry, fifty-one, describes morning meetings at the company's Canton plant, where "temporary workers keep getting told, 'Nissan's going to hire you, Nissan's going to hire you.'" The American Staffing Agency claims that 43 percent of temp workers get brought on as permanent hires, but the temp workers and advocates I spoke to, such as Betty McCray in Smyrna, doubt that's true.

"We were promised to be hired on," she says. Yet she and her fellow workers have remained temps for years. "Lots of temp workers have lost hope."

"An udderly bad job"

By Joseph Sorrentino (2014)

New Mexico's dairies, like almost all dairies in the United States, never stop running. Cows are milked two or three times a day, every day. "Cows don't know holidays," says Alfredo Gomez, a fifty-six-year-old dairy worker in southeastern New Mexico. "Here, there's no Christmas." For the vast majority of dairy workers in New Mexico, as in most states, there's also no holiday pay, no overtime, no sick pay, and no workers' compensation. They work in dirty, difficult, and sometimes dangerous conditions for an industry they're convinced values milk over milkers. (Gomez and nearly all the other workers interviewed for this piece requested a pseudonym for fear of retaliation from the dairies.)

Dairy is big in New Mexico. Big in number of cows, with approximately 320,000 statewide; big in average herd size, with about 2,200 cows per dairy (the largest in the nation); and big in economic impact. Dairy is the number one agricultural commodity in the state. The value of New Mexico's milk production topped $1.5 billion last year. When you factor in milk processing, goods, and services purchased by the industry, and the wages workers spend locally, dairy's total economic impact on the state is over $4 billion annually.

Big Dairy goes to great lengths to project a small image. It portrays itself as comprising family farms and as an industry deeply concerned about its cows and its workers. Photographs on dairy co-op and lobbying websites show clean black-and-white Holsteins sprawled in lush green fields, with calves being bottle-fed by smiling young Anglos.

At best, that's a gross misrepresentation. Three-quarters of workers are Mexican, and most of the milk produced in New Mexico (and nationwide) comes from concentrated animal feeding operations. Cows don't graze in green pastures. Instead, they are kept in corrals, standing on dirt or, more frequently, in the muck that is generated by their urine and feces. A dairy cow expels as much as 150 pounds of manure a day.

"It's nasty [work]," says Matías Soto, a short, strongly built fifty-nine-year-old originally from Durango, Mexico, who has worked in dairies in southeastern New Mexico for three years. "We have aprons, [but they get] completely covered in manure and urine." The smell in a milking barn can be noxious. Just a few minutes in one can leave a lasting foul taste in your mouth. But, workers say, you get used to it.

Most of the cows are docile, but not all. "The younger ones are dangerous," says Antonio Jiménez, who worked in a dairy outside of Roswell during high school. "They don't know how to be milked and [they] kick. Sometimes the ones that have just given birth [are dangerous], too." The New Mexico Center on Law & Poverty (NMCLP) survey found that 53 percent of the workers interviewed had been injured on the job, often more than once, and sometimes seriously.

In March, Matías Soto was working as a milker at a dairy in southeastern New Mexico. Somehow, a bull had gotten mixed in with the cows and stuck in one of the milking parlor gates. As Soto was trying to free the bull, he says, "It lowered its head and attacked me, lifting me six or seven feet in the air. I hit my head on the concrete floor." His skull fractured. But, he says, he wasn't taken to the emergency room in Artesia, about forty miles away, for three hours. He then had to be airlifted to a hospital capable of handling his injury. The cost of the helicopter alone was more than $60,000, and Soto's hospital bills were in "the tens of thousands of dollars," says María Martínez Sánchez, a former attorney at the NMCLP who worked with Soto. And the dairy had no workers' compensation insurance.

Its medical insurance covered Soto's medical bills, but not all of the helicopter costs. Instead, says Martínez Sánchez, Soto went into debt, borrowing from friends and relatives, although he eventually received a small amount of money in a settlement with the dairy.

INJURIES: PART OF THE JOB

Workers' compensation is designed to cover a portion of workers' medical expenses and lost wages if they're hurt on the job. Requirements vary from state to state, and New Mexico has long exempted dairies and farms from having to insure field workers and people working directly with animals.

Without workers' compensation, "either the worker doesn't get medical care, they go into great debt, or they are so injured they have to go to the emergency room, and the taxpayer pays," says Martínez Sánchez. "As taxpayers, we're subsidizing the agricultural industry."

Workers in New Mexico's dairy regions don't have many options for work. In the southeast, it's the dairies or the oil fields, which pay better but are more dangerous and farther from workers' homes. In the south central region, it's dairies or farm work, which pays even less. So workers stay quiet and trudge in day after day, knowing how little they're valued. Every worker interviewed for this article was asked if they believed dairy owners valued cows or workers more. Without hesitation, each answered, "Cows."

Dairy worker Angelica Rosario adds, "They treat the cows like a person and the workers like slaves."

"Domestic Workers Emerging from the Shadows"

By Stephen Franklin (2014)

Domestic workers' stories about how they are cheated out of their wages, overworked, or not treated with respect often move Ania Jakubek. But every so often she hears a truly troubling story, like one offered by a woman who told her how a middle-income family made her live in their garage, sleep on a flimsy cot, and use a bucket for her toilet because they would not let her into their house at night.

"People treat their pets much better," said Jakubek, an organizer for the Arise Chicago Worker Center, which has served several thousand workers since its founding a dozen years ago.

Jakubek works with Polish domestic workers, who make up a large number of Chicago's domestic worker ranks, and with whom she has a special bond. She came to the United States from Poland to work as an au pair and was plunged into subminimum wages and a heart-breaking job.

Her description of the indignities faced by domestic workers came at a recent forum in Chicago at the University of Illinois-Chicago, sponsored by the National Domestic Workers Alliance and *In These Times*. She and others spoke of continued abuses but also the progress spawned by efforts to help domestic workers.

San Francisco–based labor lawyer and author Sheila Bapat described domestic workers' march toward their rights in the United States as an upward effort, with laws guaranteeing them protections passed in California, New York, Massachusetts, and Hawaii since 2010. It is an effort, she explained, that links the 2 million domestic workers in the United States with the domestics around the world, whose ranks have been estimated at from 50 to 100 million.

She lamented the long-term setback that domestic workers suffered when they were excluded from the pioneering workplace protections laid down by the Fair Labor Standards Act in 1938. Besides the lack of workplace protections, one of the major challenges domestics face is that "they are socially and culturally invisible," Bapat said.

The impact of their invisibility, said Jakubek, leads to a sense among domestic workers that "they are not worth much." As a result, Jakubek said she works to bring domestics together regularly to share their experiences as well as to help them bond.

That kind of outreach mattered to Magdalena Zylinska.

"It gave me hope and reason to believe that we are not alone," said Zylinskia, who began working as a maid soon after arriving in the United States from Poland. She has thrived, she said, when work was plenty, and suffered when people cut back on hiring her, sometimes canceling jobs without any notice. "Sometimes people who hire us don't realize that we are also people with bills to pay."

THE ADJUNCT'S LAMENT

By Rebecca Burns (2014)

"She was a professor?" That's the question an incredulous caseworker asked when confronted with the predicament of Margaret Mary Vojtko, an eighty-three-year-old French teacher who spent the final months of her life destitute and nearly homeless before dying in September. The story of her death has become the symbol of a surprising economic reality: "Adjunct professors are the new working poor," as one CNN headline proclaimed.

Vojtko taught for twenty-five years at Duquesne University in Pittsburgh, but, as an adjunct faculty member employed on a contract basis, she never received health or retirement benefits. And when the university informed her last spring that it would not be renewing her contract, it was not obliged to provide her with severance pay. Fighting cancer and unable to afford both the out-of-pocket costs for her radiation treatment and the heating and upkeep bills on her house, Vojtko's case was finally referred to Adult Protective Services (APS). Vojtko reacted to the summons from APS with shame and dismay. But before she could appear, she collapsed from a massive heart attack and died two weeks later, according to an account published in the *Pittsburgh-Post Gazette* by United Steelworkers (USW) counsel Daniel Kovalik.

The caseworker assigned to Margaret Mary before her death wasn't the only one who reacted to her desperate circumstances with disbelief. "Most people are under the illusion that the academy still provides people a good life," says Kovalik, whose union is organizing adjunct faculty in Pittsburgh. "But professors have been proletarianized." The USW is seeking to represent adjuncts at Duquesne—who voted last year to unionize, though the university has refused to recognize the union—and attempted to intervene with both the university and APS on Vojtko's behalf.

Indeed, the injustices that Vojtko's tragedy laid bare—an employer that treated her as disposable, a tattered safety net that offered her little assistance at her most vulnerable—are all too familiar. What shocked the public consciousness, instead, is who is now suffering them: contrary to the economic axiom that higher education is the pathway to prosperity, the highly educated may now end their lives as destitute as anyone else.

THE PROFESSORIAT'S DECLINE

Five years into the recession, the continued downward mobility of professionals is often portrayed as a droll example of class pastiche. A February 2013 *New York Times* article, for example, playfully describes adjuncts who travel abroad to pick up extra teaching work in the summer as "seasonal workers with Ph.D.'s."

But, in fact, adjunct faculty may have more in common with low-wage seasonal workers than with the tenured faculty at their own institutions. A 2012 analysis by the Coalition on the Academic Workforce, a research group, found that while salaries for tenure-track positions average $66,000 a year, pay for adjunct faculty—who now constitute as much as three-fourths of the teaching force in higher education—averages just $21,600. And like seasonal farmworkers and others who eke out a living moving from job to job, most adjuncts lack access to health insurance and retirement benefits. Both groups, too, have served as canaries in the coal mine of an economy increasingly structured around precarious employment.

But the freefall of the professoriat, once archetypal members of what Barbara Ehrenreich and John Ehrenreich have termed the "professional-managerial class," suggests an even bigger shift underway: the erosion of the professional class itself. Will the academy's penurious part-timers awake to this new reality?

In many cases, adjuncts, by virtue of their status as "professionals," fall through the cracks of even the meager protections provided to other low-wage workers. Historically, professional work has been marked by a degree of autonomy from employers, and federal and state labor laws typically exempt professional workers from minimum wage and overtime protection under the assumption that they can set their own terms of employment. But adjunct advocates argue that this assumption is an anachronous one that, much like the growing incidence of employers misclassifying their employees as "independent contractors," shifts all of the responsibilities of "independence" onto workers without allowing them any of the benefits.

When a group of part-time community college instructors in Washington state sought access to overtime pay, for example, under the rationale that their contracts didn't pay enough to do the work required of their positions, the State Supreme Court ruled that they are not protected by the state's Minimum Wage Act because they have control over their hours and working conditions. Similarly, adjuncts often have difficulty qualifying for unemployment insurance when one semester's contract is up under the rationale that they have reasonable expectation of being hired for the next academic term, even though stories abound of contingent faculty who are told just days before classes begin that their services are no longer needed.

This combination of precarious working conditions and exclusion from legal protections has long been the experience of migrant workers and other marginalized groups, notes Saket Soni, director of the National Guestworker Alliance. Its growing prevalence among other groups of workers suggests an alarming trend. "On our current path, we'll all end up as guestworkers," says Soni, "trapped in an economy of temporary, intermittent work, struggling with debt rather than building wealth, sourced into labor supply chains rather than climbing career ladders.

"Employers have long treated immigrant workers as disposable. Now, more American workers than ever know how they feel."

"In Search of Solidarity"

BY CHRISTOPHER HAYES (2006)

Solidarity: now there's an anachronism. The U.S. news media doesn't talk about solidarity; it employs the assured and peppy tone that speaks to the individual consumer: *After the break, we'll tell you how the strike will affect your morning commute.* Solidarity is the opposite of news you can use.

Enter the word into Google news and you'll find that in English-language papers from Lahore to Leeds, the word pops up frequently. Not so here. In American publications it appears, if at all, only in neutered form—the simple presence of group cohesion. A company sponsoring a retreat for its employees does so to encourage "corporate solidarity."

Yet the word retains a specific moral force. I remember the thrill I felt when I received a correspondence from a union organizer who signed off, "In solidarity." It felt, at once, a generous invitation to fellowship and a moral call to arms.

THROUGH OUR BLOOD IT RUNS

The *Oxford English Dictionary* defines "solidarity" as "The fact or quality, on the part of communities … of being perfectly united or at one in some respect, esp. in interests, sympathies, or aspirations." It comes from the same Latin root as "solid" and is adapted from the French *solidarité*, which by the nineteenth century had supplanted the *"fraternité"* of the French Revolution as the social glue for the impending era of enlightened utopia.

In the mid-nineteenth century, *solidarité* crossed both the English Channel and the Atlantic. Sven-Eric Liedman, a professor of intellectual history at Sweden's Göteborg University, writes that Americans were skeptical of the French import: in 1844, one American complained of "the uncouth French word, *solidarité*, now coming in such use." While the word never quite gained the same cachet it had (and continues to have) in Europe, the American Left quickly adopted it. *Solidarity* was the name of an early anarchist journal. Eugene Debs said solidarity was "a fact, cold and impassive as the granite foundations of a skyscraper." And, in 1915, Ralph Chaplin of the Industrial Workers of the World wrote the labor anthem "Solidarity Forever" to the tune of "Battle Hymn of the Republic."

Solidarity in the political vocabulary of the American Left became class solidarity, workers' solidarity, the banding together of laborers against bosses. But it possessed more than rhetorical resonance; it was also the foundation of the labor movement's most potent tool: the strike.

While in the United States, the word has been ghettoized in the labor movement, solidarity in Europe remains part of mainstream political vocabulary. The labor rights guaranteed in the European Union charter are collectively referred to as "rights to solidarity."

THE MUNDANE AND THE SUBLIME

As elusive as its meaning may be, from the amorphous cloud of centuries' worth of usage and citations, two general categories of solidarity emerge: the mundane and the sublime.

In its mundane sense, solidarity means a robust feeling of together-ness, a "one-for-all, all-for-one-ness" that holds fast a group of people in a common activity. It is best summed up in Benjamin Franklin's exhortation to his co-conspirators that they must all hang together or surely they would hang separately. This kind of solidarity is morally neutral. Union members refusing to cross a picket line exemplify solidarity, but so do white home-owners in a Chicago neighborhood signing restrictive covenants to keep black families out.

Sublime solidarity, on the other hand, embodies a powerful moral aspi-ration to realize the fundamental fellowship of humankind. The human subject imbued with full solidarity would treat each person the same way she would treat the interests of her closest kin. It is this solidarity Jane Addams described as "not philanthropy nor benevolence, but a thing fuller and wider than either of these," and what Gandhi referred to when he spoke of the "essential unity of all people."

What the great social movements of our time have been able to accom-plish is to find the sweet spot between the mundane and often blinkered solidarity of specific communities of interest, and the grandiose but vague notion of the solidarity of all humanity. From the labor battles of the '30s, to the Gandhian independence struggle, to civil rights and anti-apartheid movements, the most uplifting and effective social movements have ori-ented themselves toward sublime solidarity while remaining grounded in the mundane but robust cohesion of a specific group with specific aims and specific demands. We may remember moments of moral progress for their dramatic or transcendent quality, but they were first and foremost political victories born of a refusal to pull apart. Such solidarity is the Left's proudest tradition, both here and abroad: the unity of purpose and determined fellowship among those battling an unjust order combined with a constant effort to stretch that fellowship to ever larger groups of citizens.

As the American Right offers that redundant canard "moral values" as its lodestar, the Left should offer solidarity. Not retrograde brotherhood, or faith-specific fellowship, but something more robust and difficult and rewarding. The uplift of collective enterprise.

PART TWO

PUSHBACK

CHAPTER SEVEN

Solidarity Without Borders

INTRODUCTION

By Michelle Chen

All around us, borders are crumbling and sharpening. The global neoliberal order allows capital, goods, and services to flow freely, but no parallel "free market" system allows people to move across borders. So the corporate arbitrage of trade treaties and tax dodges is rarely acknowledged as a critical factor driving mass migration. Rather, as states and corporations exploit communities, those seeking freedom and dignity across borders are vilified as criminal and invaders.

But over the past twenty years, two radical movements have breached those borders.

The global justice movement, which crested between 1999 and 2003, opposed the rise of multinational corporations through trade agreements, deregulated markets, and quasi-governmental institutions of the international financial system. It began as a battle to reclaim public resources from corporate talons and morphed into an insurgency against militarism and government impunity. As a predecessor of the Occupy movement, the "horizontalism" undergirding the spectacle of mass protest gatherings presented a counterpoint to corporate power, through a kind of globalization of mass politics.

Soon globalization was more than just a protest theme: it was a lived reality embodied by the migrant rights movement. This came to prominence in 2006 when an effort to overhaul the dysfunctional immigration system collapsed in Washington. Years later under Obama, frustrated by broken electoral promises, continued legislative stagnation and a massive surge of deportations, immigrant-rights activists grew more militant. Undocumented youth who had previously avoided public exposure became visible. Mobilizing against neocolonialism at home and abroad, migrant activism's more radical strands have articulated a demand for real freedom of movement, to match the unbridled transborder flow of capital.

Although distinct, the movements for global justice and migrant rights represent parallel approaches to transnational solidarity and grassroots struggles against inequality.

David Bacon's dispatch from the December 1999 anti–World Trade Organization protests in Seattle, Washington ("Making History") underscores the sheer novelty of that moment. He describes a motley coalition of environmentalists, trade unionists, and others brought together to issue "an indictment, not of a particular company, or even a single country, but of a whole economic order."

The movement flourished after Seattle, building a youthful insurgency against neoliberalism and pushing global solidarity. The annual World Social Forum, founded in 2001 as an alternative to the World Economic Forum, attracted anti-globalization activists from around the world. Naomi Klein documented ("Take It to the Streets") how activists forged a populist laboratory for envisioning the "world as it should be" through a common language of resistance. But just as the movement was becoming a force to be reckoned with, it was abruptly overshadowed by a new militant incarnation of neoliberalism after 9/11. Borders hardened, the United States invaded Afghanistan and Iraq, and Washington soon co-opted authoritarian regimes across the Global South as brutal "allies" in the "Global War on Terror."

As Ben Ehrenreich observed from the 2003 World Social Forum in this chapter: "Gone [were] the not-so-distant days when the diminishing importance of the nation-state was on most everyone's lips in the global justice movement, when something called 'corporate globalization' ... appeared to have displaced imperialism as the common enemy of the Left." Facing the monstrosities of mass imprisonment and torture, along with military drone attacks and other emerging technologized atrocities, many activists saw antiwar protests as part of the larger struggle against the neoliberal order. The urgency was clear enough: when your chief occupation is sheltering your children from the next air raid, you can ill afford to worry about Walmart's transnational tax-dodging. The most visceral effects of globalization demand an immediate response that grapples with the everyday violence of sheer survival.

In "People vs. Empire," Arundhati Roy notes the spread of resistance movements across borders—and then sounds a stark warning. "Resistance as spectacle has cut loose from its origins in genuine civil disobedience and is becoming more symbolic than real," she wrote in 2005. Global summits can inspire on a symbolic level, but the challenge is to channel lofty inspiration into the grassroots aspirations driving the struggles that such gatherings represent, but can ultimately never resolve. Indigenous communities struggling to protect their lands from mining interests may feel the same outrage as South African mine workers demanding decent housing. They may encapsulate the same radical impulse as Black Lives Matter protesters facing down riot police. And the refugees of the Arab Uprising brave parallel waves of state oppression as their struggle for dignity migrates to the Global North. None of these groups consider "anti-globalization" to be their main goal. But they are all on the frontlines of a global uprising.

Perhaps the issues have shifted, but the warnings of globalization's early skeptics ring truer than ever today. As the North American Free Trade Agreement (NAFTA)'s imposition began, in 1994, Noam Chomsky presciently anticipated "a low-wage, low-growth, high-profit future, with increasing polarization and social disintegration." In the years following, millions of impoverished Mexicans crossed into the United States. It was perhaps inevitable that a migrant rights movement would emerge. In the spring of 2006, the streets of the United States erupted as migrants and refugees amassed to demand equality before the law after Washington again blocked reform. Organized by loose coalitions of labor and community groups, the massive nationwide May Day protests proclaimed migrants' humanity, showed they formed a vital pillar of the economy, and affirmed their right to the dignity of citizenship.

Undocumented youth activists found their voice as transnational rebels in 2010, demanding passage of the DREAM Act, which would provide a path to citizenship for those who had grown up "illegal," but now saw themselves as citizens without papers. Tracking the so-called "DREAMers" while they marched under the banner "undocumented and unafraid," Micah Uetricht observes how they shaped their movement around the right to sustain their communities on their own terms, not only within the United States, but also across their diasporas created by economic globalization. As Bacon points out, the "right to stay home" is a concept that our current border regime fails to contemplate.

The narratives included here begin to answer the questions we should be asking whether we're in the streets, at work, or in school. What kind of freedom do we seek, whether in tandem with or in contravention to market freedom? We've learned the idioms of civil disobedience, but the problems that animate us, such as free trade agreements and bailout packages, are not sown in public.

That may be where this chapter leaves us: facing a new frontier in radicalism. David Graeber pointed out in 2001 ("Wall Done") that the transborder protest rallies in North America against free trade deals represented a call for autonomy through solidarity: not "anti-globalization" so much as "a movement for real globalization, for the genuine free movement of people, possessions, and ideas."

Today we hold out hope for a new kind of global justice movement. The radical answer to globalization isn't about creating one unitary movement, but about globalizing ourselves. Moving from anti-globalization protests to migrant activism is hopeful progress, bringing us from ideology to the raw reality of borders. By rejecting the idea of walls, both real and symbolic, we look past borders to all of humanity. And we see that another world really is possible—not because we hold a sign heralding its arrival, but because we're already living in it.

"TIME BOMBS"

By Noam Chomsky (1994)

Major changes in the global order over the past quarter-century have led to a huge increase in unregulated financial capital and a radical shift in its use, from long-term investment and trade to speculation.

The effect has been to undermine national economic planning as governments are compelled to preserve market "credibility," driving economies toward what Cambridge University economist John Eatwell calls "a low-growth, high-unemployment equilibrium," with declining real wages, increasing poverty and inequality for the many, and profits for the few.

The parallel process of internationalization of production provides multinational corporations with new weapons to undermine working people in the West. Workers must now accept an end to their "luxurious" lifestyles and agree to "flexibility of labor markets" (i.e., not knowing whether you have a job tomorrow).

The triumphalism among narrow elite sectors is quite understandable, as is the mounting despair and anger outside privileged circles.

The New Year's Day uprising of indigenous people in Chiapas can be seen in this general context. The uprising coincided with the enactment of the North American Free Trade Agreement (NAFTA). The Zapatista army called NAFTA a "death sentence" for indigenous people, a gift to the rich that will deepen the divide between narrowly concentrated wealth and mass misery, destroying what remains of their society.

The NAFTA connection is partly symbolic; the problems are far deeper. "We are the product of 500 years of struggle," the Zapatista "declaration of war" stated. The struggle today is "for work, land, housing, food, health care, education, independence, freedom, democracy, justice and peace."

The indigenous people are the most aggrieved victims of government policies. But their distress is widely shared. "Anyone who has the opportunity to be in contact with the millions of Mexicans who live in extreme poverty knows that we are living with a time bomb," Mexican columnist Pilar Valdes observes.

There are many factors driving global society toward a low-wage, low-growth, high-profit future, with increasing polarization and social disintegration. Another consequence is the fading of meaningful and democratic processes as decision-making is vested in private institutions and the quasi-governmental structures that are coalescing around them, what the *Financial Times* calls a "de facto world government" that operates in secret and without accountability.

The protest of indigenous people in Chiapas gives only a bare glimpse of time bombs waiting to explode, not only in Mexico.

"Making history"

By David Bacon (2000)

Those who marched or stood or sat in the streets of Seattle made history, and they knew it. And like the great marches against the Vietnam War, or the first sit-ins in the South in the late '50s, it wasn't always easy to see just what history was being made, especially for those closest to the events of the time. Tear gas, rubber bullets, and police sweeps, the objects of incessant media coverage, are the outward signs of impending change—that the guardians of the social order have grown afraid. And there's always a little history in that.

Poeina, a young woman sitting in the intersection at the corner of Seventh and Stewart, waiting nervously for the cops to cuff her and take her away in her first arrest, knew the basic achievement she and her friends had already won: "I know we got people to listen, and that we changed their minds." It was a statement of hope, like the chant that rose November 30 from streets filled with thousands of demonstrators as the police moved in: "The whole world is watching!"

The Seattle protests put trade on the public agenda, making the World Trade Organization (WTO) a universally recognized set of initials in a matter of hours. But the greatest impact of Seattle will be on the people who were there. A certain understanding of the world was forged in the streets here—a realization based, to begin with, on who was there. Environmentalists came protesting the impending destruction of laws protecting clean air and water.

Animal-rights activists came to protect sea turtles. Trade unionists came fighting for jobs and protesting child labor. Fair-trade campaigners arrived ready to debate corporate domination of the process by which trade rules are decided.

Environmental activists in their twenties came with the tactics from the battles in the forests of Northern California and the Pacific Northwest. They carried giant puppets, dressed themselves in costumes rather than carrying signs, and laid down in busy intersections at the height of morning rush hour. In groups of twenty and thirty, they chained their arms together, slipping metal sleeves over hands and chains to make it hard for the police to cut them apart. Two years ago, this tactic was answered by Humboldt County sheriffs, who swabbed pepper spray directly into the eyes of protesters at Pacific Lumber Company. Even for veterans of civil disobedience, the chains are a tactic that demands determination and commitment to face down the fear of violent response. Later the same day, tens of thousands of union members marched into downtown to join the protest. Having shut down all the ports along the Pacific Coast from Alaska to San Diego, union members chanted and waved picket signs as they filled the streets as far as the eye could see. Each union's members marched together, each with its own color jacket or T-shirt, each carrying banners and hundreds of signs printed for the occasion. Many of the morning's young protesters were visibly impressed by the strength of their numbers and organization.

In the midst of the tear gas, it was not hard to see that this culture of protest is starting to spread, whether through union jackets on protesters in the redwood forests or giant puppets on union picket lines in Oakland. But underneath is the germ of an idea, a linkage. For unionists, the depredations of a global trading system have pitted workers in many countries against each other in a race to the bottom in wages and worker rights. Environmental activists see a system that values profit-making over laws protecting health and the environment. Rather than creating an atomized assembly—each group pursing its own interests in isolation—protesters came ready to see what they had in common.

Annie Decker, an organizer and observer at an intersection filled with sitting bodies, called her own realization liberating. "We don't have to just express an opinion on one issue," she said. "Trade and the power of corporations are affecting us in so many areas that we can all make connections, and see the common element behind the problems we share."

"WALL DONE"

By David Graeber (2001)

Editor's note: In April 2001, tens of thousands of people protested in Québec City, Canada, at the 3rd Summit of the Americas, held to negotiate the proposed Free Trade Area of the Americas (FTAA).

The single most dramatic moment of the protests in Québec came on the first day of the summit, when thousands of protesters who had marched through the city finally reached "the wall." Until that point no one had seen a single cop. Now, a phalanx of riot police, armed to the teeth with tear gas, pepper bombs, and plastic bullets, waited silently behind the chain-link fence. There was a momentary pause, and then hundreds of masked activists—ranging from black-clad anarchists to Mohawk Warriors—descended on the wall itself, produced grappling hooks and wire cutters, and began to systematically tear it down.

This was not simply a fortuitous target of opportunity: a month before, a call had gone out over the Internet—put out by anarchists and members of the newly formed American branch of Ya Basta!, originally an Italian group, which has been calling for principles of free immigration and global citizenship—for "all people held back by walls to converge in Québec City to take direct action against the security perimeter."

Attacks on the wall were echoed by actions against border posts across North America. In Vermont, there were "people's assemblies" along the border at spots where the Canadian government was systematically denying entry to anyone who so much as looked like an activist. Several hundred activists occupied the Peace Bridge in Buffalo; thousands rallied on both sides of the crossing between San Diego and Tijuana; in Blaine, Washington, 4,000 activists and union members from the United States and Canada marched across a border bridge and seized customs posts before finally being dislodged by the Royal Canadian Mounted Police.

Walls and borders were the perfect symbols: treaties like the FTAA allegedly promote a process that is making nation-states and national borders increasingly irrelevant. The reality is that corporate globalization is premised on exactly the opposite of a free flow of people, products, and ideas. Rather, it is based on keeping the majority of the world's population trapped behind increasingly fortified borders, within which even existing social services can be withdrawn, and then removing all restrictions which might have kept Nike and The Gap from taking full advantage of their resultant desperation.

In fact, the size of the U.S. Border Patrol has almost tripled since the signing of North American Free Trade Agreement (NAFTA), and the Immigration and Naturalization Service (along with police forces and prisons) is about the only branch of government that is actually growing. By fortifying the border and placing dozens of activists in arbitrary detention to prevent them from being able to express their ideas in Québec, the Canadian government was merely subjecting mostly white activists to the sort of violence most of the world's population face every day.

More than anything, the attacks on walls and borders demonstrated that the rapidly growing movement of global resistance is not an anti-globalization movement at all. It is, or is rapidly becoming, a movement for real globalization, for the genuine free movement of people, possessions, and ideas.

"Take it to the streets"

By Naomi Klein (2001)

It looks a little like one of those press conferences announcing a merger between corporate giants: a couple of middle-aged guys shaking hands and smiling into a bank of cameras. Just like on CNN, they assure the world their new affiliation will make them stronger, better equipped to meet the challenges of the global economy.

Only something is askew. More facial hair for one thing: the man on the left has a scruffy beard and the one on the right has a rather distinctive handlebar moustache. And come to think of it, their alliance is not a merger of corporate interests—designed to send stock prices soaring and workers wondering about their "redundancy." In fact, the men say, this merger will be good for workers and lousy for stock prices.

The man on the left is João Pedro Stédile, co-founder of Brazil's Landless Peasants Movement. The man on the right is José Bové, the French cheese farmer who came to world attention after he "strategically dismantled" a McDonald's restaurant to protest a U.S. attack on France's ban on hormone-treated beef. And this isn't Wall Street; it's the World Social Forum in Porto Alegre, Brazil.

To read the papers, these men should not be sharing a platform, let alone embracing for the cameras. Third World farmers are supposed to be at war with their European counterparts over unequal subsidies. But here in Porto Alegre, they have joined forces in a battle much broader than any intergovernmental trade skirmish. The small farmers both men represent are attempting to fight the consolidation of agriculture into the hands of a few multinationals, through genetic engineering of crops; patenting of seeds; and industrial-scale, export-led agricultural policies. They say that their enemy is not farmers in other countries, but a system of trade that is facilitating this concentration and taking the power to regulate food production away from national governments.

"Today the battle is not in one country but in every country," Bové tells a crowd of several thousand. They break into chants of "Ole, Ole, Bové, Bové, Bové" and, in a matter of hours, hundreds are wearing badges declaring, "Somos Todos José Bové" ("We are all José Bové").

This type of cross-border alliance—a globalization of movements—is the real story of the World Social Forum, which ended January 30, 2001, and attracted more than 10,000 delegates. After thirteen months of international protests against global trade institutions, the forum was a chance to share ideas about social and economic alternatives. It is a new kind of intellectual free trade: a Tobin tax swapped for a "participatory budget", national referenda on all trade agreements exchanged for local lending alternatives to the International Monetary Fund, farming co-operative models traded for community policing.

But there is one idea with more currency than any other, expressed from podiums and on flyers handed out in hallways: "Less talk, more action." It's as if talk itself has been devalued by overproduction—and little wonder. At the same time in Davos, Switzerland, the richest CEOs in the world sound remarkably like their critics: We need to make globalization work for everyone, they say, to close the income gap, end global warming.

Oddly, at the Brazil forum, designed to help talk our way into a new future, it seems as if talking has become part of the problem. How many times can the same story of inequality be told, the same outrage expressed, before that expression becomes a paralyzing, rather than catalyzing, force?

Which brings us back to the two men shaking hands. The reason the police are after José Bové (and why he is being treated like a cheese-making Che Guevara) is that he took a break from all the talk. While in Brazil, Bové travelled with local landless activists to a nearby Monsanto test site, where three hectares of genetically modified soybeans were destroyed. Unlike in Europe, where similar direct-action has occurred, the protest did not end there. The Landless Peasants Movement has occupied the land and members are planting their own crops, pledging to turn the farm into a model of sustainable agriculture.

At the first World Social Forum, the most talked-about alternative turns out to be an alternative to talking: acting. It may just be the most powerful alternative of all.

"ANOTHER WORLD IS POSSIBLE"

By Ben Ehrenreich (2003)

Porto Alegre, Brazil—If two words could conceivably sum up the mood at the 2003 World Social Forum, they would be urgency and jubilance— urgency as the war in Iraq creeps closer, and jubilance over Luiz Inacio Lula da Silva's victory in the Brazilian elections, which was taken by many as a sign that, for the moment in Latin America, at least, the new global Left has neoliberalism on the run.

Under the slogan "Another World Is Possible," the forum, an attempt to allow the so-called antiglobalization movement a chance to strategically globalize itself, was held for the third year running in Porto Alegre.

In past years, the forum's tone has been more defensive, the movement's self-image embattled. The first forum was preoccupied with the increasingly militarized response of European and North American governments to street protests. Last year's forum, despite the shock of the September 11 attacks, took place equally in the shadow of the proposed Free Trade Area of the Americas. This year that threat still loomed, but speaker after speaker referred to "the failure of neoliberalism" and "the end of the illusion of neoliberalism," even neoliberalism's "defeat," as a fait accompli.

When the cheers died down though, the grim prospect of war in Iraq was everywhere in evidence. Billboards placed by the Brazilian Communist Party, condemning imperialism and demanding peace, rose above Porto Alegre's highways. A small Iraqi delegation wandered from event to event, waving Iraqi flags and eliciting more puzzlement than applause. Posters of Bush with a Hitlerian mustache were taped to nearly every free wall at the forum and captioned, "Bush out! Iraqi oil belongs to the Iraqis!" Even the facade of a local shopping mall was adorned with a giant blue banner reading "PAZ."

Within the halls of the World Social Forum, speaker after speaker opened with comments on the urgency of the current crisis. "We meet at a very critical time in history," the London-based Pakistani writer Tariq Ali told a crowded stadium audience. "We are on the eve of a new war."

Gone, it seems, are the not-so-distant days when the diminishing importance of the nation-state was on most everyone's lips in the global justice movement, when something called "corporate globalization"—as much a European offspring as an American one—appeared to have displaced imperialism as the common enemy of the Left.

But the raw arrogance of the Bush administration's foreign policy, its refusal to make even a Clintonian show at diplomatic politesse, has rendered "empire" synonymous with the United States. At the same time, the

Bush administration has allowed the global justice movement, within the United States and abroad (as many as 1 million activists marched against the war in November at the European Social Forum in Italy), to transition fairly smoothly into a worldwide antiwar movement.

"Bush campaigned with a unity-not-divisiveness slogan," said Steve Cobble, an American delegate from Washington's Institute for Policy Studies. "He's clearly united the whole world against our war in Iraq"—and against the United States more generally.

The most urgent problem was no longer a vast and often invisible tangle of predatory corporations, national governments, and compliant international institutions, but the single enemy of American aggression, be it military or economic. "If we are going to fight for a better world, then our struggle cannot be separated from a struggle against the United States of America," said Achin Vanaik, a delegate from India.

"There is not on the one hand social and economic problems, and on the other hand political and military problems," said Egyptian scholar Samir Amin. "One cannot defeat the International Monetary Fund and the other institutions that obey the United States without defeating the military strategies of the United States. The social struggles against the United States must be articulated at all levels. As long as the aggressive, fascist strategy of the United States is not defeated, an alternative globalization will not be possible."

"PEOPLE VS. EMPIRE"

By Arundhati Roy (2005)

Radical change cannot and will not be negotiated by governments; it can only be enforced by people. By the public. A public that can link hands across national borders. A public that disagrees with the very concept of empire. A public that has set itself against the governments and institutions that support and service Empire.

Empire has a range of calling cards. It uses different weapons to break open different markets. There's no country on God's earth that isn't caught in the crosshairs of the U.S. cruise missile and the International Monetary Fund checkbook. For poor people in many countries, Empire does not always appear in the form of cruise missiles and tanks, as it has in Iraq or Afghanistan or Vietnam. It appears in their lives in very local avatars— losing their jobs, being sent unpayable electricity bills, having their water supply cut, being evicted from their homes and uprooted from their land.

It is a process of relentless impoverishment with which the poor are histori-cally familiar. What Empire does is further entrench and exacerbate already existing inequalities.

Until quite recently, it was sometimes difficult for people to see them-selves as victims of Empire. But now, local struggles have begun to see their role with increasing clarity. However grand it might sound, the fact is, they are confronting Empire in their own, very different ways. Differently in Iraq, in South Africa, in India, in Argentina, and differently, for that matter, on the streets of Europe and the United States. This is the beginning of real globalization. The globalization of dissent.

Meanwhile, the rift between rich and poor is being driven deeper, and the battle to control the world's resources intensifies. Economic colonialism through formal military aggression is staging a comeback.

Iraq today is a tragic illustration of this process. The illegal invasion. The brutal occupation in the name of liberation. The rewriting of laws to allow the shameless appropriation of the country's wealth and resources by corporations allied to the occupation. And now the charade of a sovereign "Iraqi government."

The Iraqi resistance is fighting on the frontlines of the battle against Empire. And therefore that battle is our battle. Before we prescribe how a pristine Iraqi resistance must conduct a secular, feminist, democratic, non-violent battle, we should shore up our end of the resistance by forcing the U.S. government and its allies to withdraw from Iraq.

RESISTANCE ACROSS BORDERS

To many mass movements in developing countries that had long been fight-ing lonely, isolated battles, Seattle was the first delightful sign that people in imperialist countries shared their anger and their vision of another kind of world. As resistance movements have begun to reach out across national borders and pose a real threat, governments have developed their own strat-egies for dealing with them, ranging from co-optation to repression.

The disturbing thing nowadays is that resistance as spectacle has cut loose from its origins in genuine civil disobedience and is becoming more symbolic than real. Colorful demonstrations and weekend marches are fun and vital, but alone they are not powerful enough to stop wars. Wars will be stopped only when soldiers refuse to fight, when workers refuse to load weapons onto ships and aircraft, when people boycott the economic out-posts of Empire that are strung across the globe.

"Freedom of movement"

By Michelle Chen (2009)

What if lawmakers had the guts to create comprehensive labor legislation for immigrants, enshrining their rights in accordance with international law? What if our legal system recognized immigrants' freedom of movement?

We should know better, of course, than to expect anything approaching that from Capitol Hill, where the hobbling immigration debate is dictated by business interests and xenophobia.

So, it's a good thing such a law has already been drafted for them. Years ago, in response to the growing intersection between human rights and labor migration, the United Nations developed the International Convention on the Protection of the Rights of All Migrant Workers and Members of Their Families. Recognizing that border-crossing is an economic right and necessity, the Convention's provisions include freedom from discrimination in the workplace and public services, equal protection before the law, and protection from "arbitrary expulsion," violence and intimidation by groups or individuals.

Yet in another stunning display of American exceptionalism, the United States has not joined the dozens of other countries that have ratified these common-sense principles. Washington prefers to relegate immigration issues to the domestic policy arena, which allows it to capitalize freely on a two-tier labor force.

Many immigrants' rights advocates are leveraging international law on their own. The American Civil Liberties Union, for instance, recently invoked United Nations policies in advocating for hundreds of Indian guest workers imported as cheap forced labor in the Hurricane Katrina recovery effort. U.S.-based activists have worked with the Inter-American Commission on Human Rights to investigate detention facilities in Texas and Arizona, as well as law enforcement policies toward undocumented immigrants. In July 2009, the Commission's Rapporteurship on the Rights of Migrant Workers and their Families reported that "many men, women and children detained in those facilities are held in unacceptable conditions."

And advocates for domestic workers in New York City link the struggles of home-based laborers, the vast majority of them immigrant women of color, to global economic dynamics and the country's legacy of racial oppression. To offset the lack of federal protections, Domestic Workers United is pushing for stronger state-level regulations, like livable wage standards, protection from trafficking, and integration into New York's human rights laws.

Meanwhile, the leaders of the United States, Canada, and Mexico discussed trade agreements and border enforcement at the summit in Guadalajara this week. As usual, officials focused on the movement of goods, not people.

Yet the engines of global capital are greased by the flow of labor across borders. A byproduct of economic "integration" has been economic apartheid in immigrant communities. While the political establishment works to advance the rights of corporations to trade freely, the rights of migrants to basic human dignity are brushed off the agenda.

"THIS LAND IS OUR LAND"

By Micah Uetricht (2010)

Chicago, Illinois–In late April, shortly after Arizona Governor Jan Brewer (R) signed into law one of the most stringent bills against undocumented immigrants in American history, twenty-four religious and community leaders sat down in front of a van containing immigrants being deported to their home countries as it exited a detention center in the Chicago suburb of Broadview. Chanting, "Illinois is not Arizona," the group condemned SB 1070 and demanded a moratorium on raids and deportations.

Sitting in the street a few feet from the idling van was Father Brendan Curran from Pilsen, a Mexican American neighborhood in Chicago. He estimates that half his congregation is undocumented, including the father of a high schooler with leukemia. "He risks being deported at the most important moment of his daughter's life," Curran said before his arrest. "There are thousands more like them. Families are being torn apart. We must stop these deportations."

The action was an escalation for the movement nationally, as civil disobedience has not been a widely used tactic by immigrant-rights advocates in the past.

Tania Unzueta, a twenty-six-year-old undocumented student who moved to Chicago from Mexico City with her parents at the age of ten, snapped photos of the arrestees as they were detained.

Six weeks earlier, Unzueta and other immigrant youth led a march in Chicago behind a banner that read "Undocumented and Unafraid" and then "came out" to the world as lacking legal status in the United States. She explains the difficulties of life without legal status. "You have to keep a huge part of your life secret because it's 'criminal.' It's very liberating to say, 'I'm undocumented, I didn't do anything wrong, and I shouldn't be punished.'"

Days after the Broadview arrests, on May 1, Representative Luis Gutierrez (D) of Chicago was arrested with thirty-four others in front of the White House while hundreds of thousands rallied for comprehensive immigration reform around the country. Activists promised to continue ratcheting up the pressure on lawmakers until a satisfactory federal reform bill is passed.

Pushed by Arizona Republicans, SB 1070 allows police officers to inquire about a person's citizenship if they have reasonable suspicion that a person lacks proper status—a mandate, opponents say, for racial profiling. After the law's signing, several states began considering similar bills.

The new law, which makes the failure to carry immigration documents a crime, has jump-started the immigration reform movement. With President Barack Obama castigating the state's actions, saying the law could "undermine basic notions of fairness that we cherish as Americans," his administration has now set its sights on enacting immigration reform this year.

Following the law's passage, activists called for a boycott of Arizona, causing several large organizations to pull their conventions out of the state. Protests of the bill have been widespread; condemnation of SB 1070 has been particularly strong in Chicago, the site of the 2006 immigrant-rights marches that sparked massive organizing efforts throughout the country.

The country's polarized mood is reminiscent of 2006, when Representative Jim Sensenbrenner (R-Wisc.) introduced a similarly tough anti-immigration bill in the House. Immigrants organized quickly and massively, flooding small towns and city streets around the country. The bill was defeated in the Senate, but the political will for comprehensive immigration reform was absent.

With a friendlier president in office and a Democratic majority in Congress, activists are hopeful for reform, but they aren't counting on Democrats. Many protesters saved their harshest words for the Democratic politicians they helped elect. "Legalization or no re-election" was a recurring chant in Broadview and at Chicago's May Day march.

Jenny Dale, coordinator for the Chicago New Sanctuary Coalition and an organizer of the Broadview action, said Democrats are nervous about upcoming elections. "And they should be," says Dale. "Activists are saying, 'The stalling needs to stop. We put you into power. Now you need to deliver.'"

"ALL OVER THE WORLD, MIGRANTS DEMAND THE RIGHT TO STAY AT HOME"

By David Bacon (2013)

U.S. exceptionalism—the idea that this country is somehow unique and different—has no basis in fact when it comes to migration, which is a global phenomenon. The big questions are why are the number of migrants increasing so rapidly and what should be done about it.

As people around the world try to come to terms with this reality, it is clear that Congress and the Obama administration are at one pole of an international debate. At this pole the Tea Party and Democrats find common ground. They may disagree on legalization for the undocumented, but they agree on the other basic elements of what is called "comprehensive immigration reform." Both support trade policies benefiting corporations, while turning a blind eye to the havoc and displacement they cause. And their shared "solution" is to channel displaced people into labor programs, while coming down hard on those who migrate outside the approved framework. The government spends more today on border and immigration enforcement than on all other federal law enforcement agencies combined.

In addition, authorities annually audit the records of more than 2,000 employers, ordering them to fire hundreds of thousands of workers who lack legal immigration status. And while firings of those without papers increase, so does the number of workers brought to the United States by employers with visas that tie their ability to stay to their jobs—"guest workers."

Less discussed, but just as much a part of migration policy, is the impact of global economic policies in developing countries that are the source of the migration. When the North American Free Trade Agreement (NAFTA) was enacted in 1993, 4.6 million Mexicans lived in the United State. By 2008, 11 percent of Mexico's population lived here—12.7 million people.

Again, the United States is not alone. France today, with about 66 million inhabitants, has 8.3 million migrants, up from 5.9 million twenty years ago. Italy went from 1.4 to 4.5 million in the same period. In the United States, France, Italy, and other developed countries, migrant workers are an essential part of the economy, laboring in the lowest paid and least secure jobs.

Despite this growth in migration, however, there is almost no discussion in developed countries of the reasons for it and the high cost of migration to migrants' countries of origin. Trade agreements like NAFTA and structural adjustment policies require countries like Mexico and the Philippines to cut the social budget for education, health care, and other services in order to make debt payments, while opening their economies to foreign corporations. Those countries then become increasingly dependent on the money sent home by migrants working abroad. In 2012, worldwide remittances reached $401 billion, 5.3 percent higher than 2011.

Countries dependent on remittances become labor reserves, exporting people to make up for the lack of sustainable economic development that could give them a future at home. This is called "circular" migration, since migrants aren't supposed to settle in their destination countries—just work there, send money home, and eventually return.

More than Just Labor

Periodically, under the aegis of the UN, diplomats and government representatives meet to discuss migration and development at what is known as the High-Level Dialogue on Migration and Development. In July 2013, the UN Secretary General Ban Ki-moon reported on previous sessions of the High-Level Dialogue. His report reflects the desire by many countries to treat remittances as a source of economic development and assumes that migrants should serve as an international labor supply.

While diplomats engaged in gentlemanly exchanges at the October 2013 High Level Dialogue, however, migrant organizations, unions, and other grassroots groups marched across the Brooklyn Bridge and through the streets of Manhattan, criticizing this global perspective.

The Peoples' Global Action on Migration (PGA), a coalition of civil society groups from different countries advocating for migrant rights, broke with the view of migrants as a labor supply, shared by the High-Level Dialogue and the U.S. Congress.

According to Monami Maulik, executive director of New York City's DRUM-South Asian Workers Center and the Global South Asian Migrant Workers Alliance, "We challenge the focus on remittances within this neoliberal model of managed, circular migration. We call for people over profits and a focus on human rights."

DRUM became one of the most active organizations in the United States during the "war on terror," opposing the wholesale detention of people from South Asia and the Middle East and the treatment of migrants as security threats. "Criminalization," Maulik says, "is the other side of the coin of neoliberalism—a tool for repression and control to force migrant labor to accept abysmal conditions." She and other PGA organizations campaign against "the migration-criminalization industrial complex, to end privatized, multinational profiteering from migrant labor."

Another grassroots gathering that took place simultaneously in New York City, the International Migrants Alliance (IMA), also opposed the policy of the export of labor through guest-worker programs, often called "managed migration." With member organizations in many of the developing countries that send migrants to developed ones, the IMA declaration emphasized that "Poverty, unemployment, political conflict, and general displacement of peoples, including displacement due to environmental factors, are the major causes of migration."

Most migration, in other words, is fueled by the need to survive. The alternative, asserted by groups like the United States–Mexico Binational Front of Indigenous Organizations, is the "right to stay home"—that is, to economic development that can make migration a voluntary option instead. In Oaxaca, in southern Mexico, for instance, it calls for the government to subsidize farm prices, to produce jobs and protect labor rights, and to provide better social services. This would give young people especially an alternative to leaving home to seek work in the United States.

Some organizations in the PGA, like the Global Workers Justice Alliance, advocate reforming the existing guest-worker system, "combating worker exploitation by promoting portable justice for transnational migrants through a cross-border network of worker advocates and resources." Others, however, call guest-worker programs inherently exploitative and say they should be abolished.

Many progressive immigrant-rights groups in the United States have made common cause with the global movements of migrants. Challenging the "solutions" pushed by Congress, they call for ending guest-worker programs entirely, giving all migrants residence visas and protecting their ability to bring their families to the United States. These groups, which include the American Friends Service Committee and the Dignity Campaign, also advocate renegotiating the trade agreements that lead to the displacement of communities and the forcible migration of their inhabitants.

Such voices here in the United States and abroad deserve a greater audience. If there is no effort to examine the impact of trade agreements or to look at the danger of the growth of new international guest-worker programs, a decade from now the world we live in will be one we will hardly recognize. Poverty will deepen in developing countries, the gulf between migrants and residents will widen in developed ones, and hundreds of millions of people will be trapped in a global labor system in which migration as low-paid labor is the only way to survive.

"No papers, no fear"

By Michelle Chen (2013)

Nine young people are changing the way the country talks about immigration—not from the floor of Congress or a campaign podium, but from a detention center.

In July 2013, the undocumented youth from the United States deliberately crossed the southern border into the United States, as a protest against immigration policy as well as a symbolic act of resistance to the deportation system that has loomed over them and their families since they first entered the country.

Their carefully orchestrated protest placed the nine—Claudia Amaro, Adriana Gil Diaz, Luis Leon, Maria Peniche, Ceferino Santiago, Mario Felix, Lulu Martinez, Marco Saavedra, and Lizbeth Mateo—directly on the frontline of the immigration reform debate. Six of the nine were in Mexico prior to the action, having either been deported or left the United States to avoid enforcement authorities. But Mateo, Martinez, and Saavedra are longtime activists based in the United States and "self-deported" specifically to take part in the protest.

As their story has streaked across the news headlines, they have inspired a wave of social media activism and calls for solidarity, as well as controversy in elite political circles.

In Washington, the acts of the "Dream 9" have upset the delicate politics of the immigration debate. But with their iconic graduation caps, standing defiantly at the United States–Mexico border crossing, the Dream 9 have also become a new touchstone for the migrant rights movement, especially for the more radical strands of the movement who are less willing to seek legislative "compromise" in the halls of Congress and more focused on advocating for justice.

The "Dreamer" label was born out of the DREAM Act, a bill that would provide immigration relief to undocumented young people who are pursuing higher education or military service. (It has repeatedly failed to become law in recent years.) But since the movement has mushroomed across the country and diversified, some have taken a more militant stance on demanding an end to deportations and fighting for the legal rights of their undocumented parents and other family members.

Fueled by the slogan "No Papers, No Fear," young rebels like the Dream 9 are presenting themselves as transnational activists with grassroots connections to communities struggling not just with anti-immigrant policies but various types of oppression, including poverty, educational inequality, and struggles with gender and sexual identity.

The Dream 9's act of defiance is the latest chapter in the evolution of undocumented youth activism, which sparked national debate back in 2010 with a high-profile sit-in at the office of Senator John McCain. Taking a cue from the radical student movements of the 1960s, the muscularity of their protests sent a cultural message that contrasted starkly with the congressional lobbying and saccharine messaging that has long characterized the reform advocacy of mainstream nonprofits and liberal politicians.

While some have criticized their action as too radical, Dream 9 supporters see their imprisonment as an exposure of the irrationality of the law itself. Or, as Dream 9'er Lizabeth Mateo put it, "I know you're going to think that I'm crazy for doing this ... but to be honest, I think it's even crazier that I had to wait fifteen years to see my family."

"THE IMMIGRATION MOVEMENT'S LEFT TURN"

By Michelle Chen (2014)

Who will be the Obama administration's two-millionth deportee? The question haunts neighborhoods, schools, and workplaces from Phoenix to Philadelphia.

The unlucky distinction could go to any of the roughly 11 million undocumented people who call the United States home—a carwash worker nabbed for a broken taillight; a field laborer who has overstayed her work visa; or a youth donning a cap and gown, deliberately crossing the path of the border patrol in a show of civil disobedience.

Deportations are expected to reach the 2 million mark in early April 2014, and activists are campaigning fiercely at the gates of detention centers, border checkpoints, and congressional offices to show the White House that they will not let the Obama administration reach that milestone without a fight.

Last month in Alabama, immigrant-rights advocates organized one such action by forming a human chain outside the Etowah County Detention Center, chanting "not one more"—the rallying cry of a wave of anti-deportation actions that have swept the nation over the past year, gaining political currency as a social media campaign, a slogan at street demonstrations, and more recently, a political salvo in Washington, where more conciliatory policy demands from inside the Beltway have sputtered.

One protester at the Etowah rally, Gwendolyn Ferreti Manjarrez, declared, "I am tired of living with the fear that my family or any family can be torn apart at the seams for living our everyday life."

Such pleas reflect exhaustion and exasperation with Washington, which has maintained an immigration-reform gridlock since the Senate reform bill all but died in Congress last year.

Faced with deafening silence in Congress and constant waffling in the White House, a growing number of advocates have joined the chorus calling for a moratorium on deportations. Even prominent centrist Latino organizations like the National Council of La Raza (NCLR), which lobbied hard for "compromise" legislation last year and have condemned Obama as "deporter in chief."

Demands for a moratorium on deportations are not unprecedented: advocates are proposing an extension of the White House's Deferred Action for Childhood Arrivals (DACA) program—a temporary executive reprieve for undocumented young people issued in 2012—to undocumented adults.

President Obama has acknowledged the crisis and in recent weeks signaled that he planned to ease deportations, but he stopped short of fully halting detentions and removals. The president instead ordered the Department of Justice to review deportation policy "to see how it can conduct enforcement more humanely within the confines of the law."

But while Washington dithers, grassroots activists say the current enforcement regime doesn't need to be made more "humane"—it needs to end, full stop.

"Are open borders the solution to the refugee crisis?"

By Michelle Chen (2015)

Around the world, borders are tightening as fast as they are dissolving. Even as thousands of desperate migrants from war-torn and impoverished parts of the Global South cross into the European Union, Donald Trump is vowing to build an invincible United States–Mexico border wall. Is it time to rethink borders? Or even to envision a world without them?

Within the immigration reform debate, there's been little serious grappling with the concept of borders, why we need them, and what, in a globalized world, the porous divide between nations really means for the people who happen to live on either side and for the families that are separated.

Why can't people flow across borders as freely as goods and services do under global capitalism? The idea of open migration as the human analogue to "free trade" disturbs unions that fear this would weaken protections for U.S. workers. Avowed socialist Bernie Sanders recently complicated his generally pro-immigrant stance by voicing opposition to "open borders" as a threat to labor. Others on the Left, however, argue that free movement is a human right.

Whether you're a refugee-rights activist, a labor organizer for low-wage workers, or a politician trying to calm constituents' fears of newcomers, everyone is invested in the borders that both define and divide our identities and our communities—for better or worse. To explore "open borders," *In These Times* brought together Catherine Tactaquin, executive director of the National Network for Immigrant and Refugee Rights; Daniel Costa, director of immigration law and policy research at the Economic Policy Institute and a visiting scholar at the University of California, Merced; John Lee, a blogger on the libertarian-leaning site OpenBorders; and Prerna Lal, an attorney and clinical instructor at the University of California, Berkeley School of Law's East Bay Community Law Center who was formerly undocumented.

What would be a rational response to the current panic over immigration?

CATHERINE: First, on either side of a border, as well as in transit, we absolutely need to respect and enforce the human rights of migrants, regardless of their immigration status, nationality, or citizenship.

PRERNA: I take care of about 400 undocumented students. These students and their families all have different stories to tell and different places they come from. But there's one thing they have in common, which is that somebody loves them enough to send or bring them here. It takes a lot of courage and conviction, a lot of love, to do this. Ideally we want people with this kind of courage in our countries. Our response to the refugee crisis in Central America and Syria should be to greet people with open arms.

JOHN: The refugee crisis in Europe could have been averted if these people were free to purchase plane tickets or train tickets to wherever they wanted. They can't do that. They spend a lot of money on smugglers and other people who take advantage of them. The preexisting international border regime sees fit to restrict people's movements in utter disregard of fundamental rights.

DANIEL: Part of the reason why people like the crazy things that Trump is saying is because they see companies like Disney replacing U.S. workers with workers on temporary visas who are paid some $40,000 less to do the same job, and they become rightly suspicious of how the system is managed. One of the solutions is to make sure that new migrant workers are being paid according to U.S. wage standards, allowing U.S. workers to have a fair shot at jobs and increasing transparency in the immigration system.

What's the logic behind current immigration policies?

PRERNA: Historically, immigration policies have been driven by national interest and markets.

CATHERINE: "Managed migration" has come to dominate the international discourse. It's the catchword for letting migrants move temporarily to fulfill market-driven demands. It's all framed by the paradigm of globalization and by the trade policies that create very unequal economic relationships between developed countries and developing countries.

JOHN: Yes, and that's the wrong way to frame the issue. Immigration policy primarily plays to populist xenophobia, enabling the abuse and exploitation of immigrants. We should be asking: Why shouldn't anyone be able to apply for a visa to the United States?

Say we do dismantle the system and start from scratch. What would a border-free world mean to you, either positively or negatively?

DANIEL: It is important to note that no elected official or candidate that I know of supports open borders under any reasonable definition of the term. That should tell you something, but it doesn't mean we shouldn't be engaging with the idea of it. "Open borders" in the United States means an expansion and deregulation of the temporary foreign-worker system. It would be what employers have been lobbying for for years: the ability to hire anyone from anywhere, at any time, and without having to pay a certain wage level. Or, if it means no border restrictions at all, does that mean we abandon screening procedures and let in Islamic State members?

PRERNA: People who believe in open borders believe that arbitrary political boundaries should not dictate people's real political and human rights. Much of the European Union follows an open borders system already. If it's possible in Europe, then it should be possible in the United States. Certainly we can move toward systems where political demarcation does not mean people lose their rights or their ability to move freely.

How do we address border policy within a larger framework of global inequality?

CATHERINE: We need to have a realignment within the movement, so we have a better understanding, and certainly a better set of values, regarding the centrality and significance of border policy. What can we do to ensure that we are protecting the rights of those who are crossing international borders and making passage safe?

PRERNA: The biggest problem I see is the U.S. media scapegoating of immigrants. We could shift that blame from the immigrants to the corporations that are actually looking for and hiring low-wage workers, who then can't organize for their own rights. It's not the immigrants that need to be blamed for this. It's the big corporations.

JOHN: We have to stop the demonizing of migrants' right to pursue their dreams. We must ask ourselves why we see fit to use our rights to deprive people of the right to apply for the same job that we would apply for. We need to recognize that the way the world works is one that allows our governments to simply discriminate against people because of where they were born. Everyone has a right to a safe home. Everyone has a right to a job if they qualify for it.

CHAPTER EIGHT

The Black Freedom Struggle, at the Ballot and Beyond

INTRODUCTION

By Salim Muwakkil

When *In These Times* was born, Black America was in the midst of an aggressive movement for political power. Following the Voting Rights Act of 1965, the push for electoral representation was considered the next step in a civil rights movement seeking social and economic equity. Leaders in the black community concluded that more robust participation in the political arena would aid the modest progress being made in other areas.

Much progress was needed. When the National Urban League completed its first report on the state of Black America in 1976, the year *In These Times* launched, the data was so dismal it prompted a bit of national alarm. The *New York Times* wrote an article titled "Distress Signal" in which it noted that the report was "a profoundly depressing document." The report revealed that black Americans were still nearly twice as likely as whites to be unemployed, the median black household had only 59 cents for every dollar of income in the median white household, and African Americans were three times more likely to live in poverty than whites. As of 1975, the economic gains of the 1960s had already been erased, and increasing educational attainments had not brought employment gains (nor have they since).

To reverse this trend, major black organizations focused on electing black candidates or lobbying for the appointment of black officials. The quest to insert black faces in high places also became the consensus strategy of a group of black activists, elected officials, and government officials who met at an iconic 1972 meeting in Gary, Indiana, where the first black mayor of a major U.S. city was elected in 1967. The allies' operational slogan was "unity without uniformity."

The stubborn reality that black mayors were structurally constrained from implementing the kind of progressive policies that could make real change in beleaguered black communities soon provoked splits in the Gary consensus. The Black Nationalist factions began moving away from electoral engagement. Radical leftist factions began insisting that class was given too short shrift at the meeting. But for black organizations with a civil rights provenance, electoral victories were still seen as the most efficient route to racial equity. For them, black faces in high places became a surrogate for racial progress.

The growing estrangement ended with the groundbreaking campaign of Representative Harold Washington for mayor of Chicago in 1983. It was a crusade that attracted support from a wide array of progressive forces (and a lot of coverage in *In These Times*, including this chapter's opening piece). During the bleak days of President Ronald Reagan's presidency, Washington's campaign caught fire among a variety of black constituencies usually at odds, including nationalists and leftists, business and labor leaders, church and professional groups. Washington's reform credentials also endeared him to white reformers who detested the encrusted political machine of Mayor Richard J. Daley.

The Washington campaign seemed to embody all of the promise electoral politics could deliver, with a candidate who was uniquely knowledgeable and progressive. His unlikely victory invigorated progressives nationwide mired in the doom of Reaganism. It also provided a template for the Reverend Jesse Jackson, who launched his first presidential campaign in 1984 based on Washington's crusade-campaign composite.

Jackson's 1984 campaign was surprisingly successful in expanding his appeal beyond Black America. It explicitly addressed the class divides in the American economy and attracted support from diverse racial groups. He ran again in 1988 with much greater success, as noted in this chapter's second article, winning seven primaries and four caucuses. But even that success meant little for Black America's overall prospects. Quality of life gauges (i.e., unemployment, poverty, housing, health quality rates) have changed little for most of black Americans since these political escapades have begun. In fact, the racial wealth gap nearly tripled from 1984 to 2009.

Despite such persistent disparities, during this period the energy of the black freedom movement was siphoned almost entirely into the realm of electoral politics. There were periodic spurts of protest activity, most of which were sparked by charges of police brutality—such as the beating of Rodney King in Los Angeles in 1992. (Donnell Alexander discusses that episode and its aftermath in this chapter in "Being Black in America: The Quiet Riot Continues.")

The presidential campaign of Sen. Barack Obama upped the ante of activism in the electoral realm. When it became clear that victory was possible, black Americans mobilized their electoral prowess as never before and helped elect a black man president of the United States.

Obama's victory, which I noted in "Proud of Obama … for Now," revealed the paradox at the center of black electoral politics: He defied racist tradition to become the first black U.S. president, but he became custodian of a system that still benefits from that tradition. As I noted in the "The Post-Racial President," Obama was required to reduce America's troubled racial past to an episode in a larger narrative of progress. Obama's election also altered black America's traditional oppositional stance. The most esteemed figures in Black America were Frederick Douglass, Harriet Tubman, Dr. Martin L. King, Jr., and others who, like them, critiqued the nation's racist excesses and opposed the powers that be. Obama *is* the powers that be, at least symbolically, and his presence therefore inhibited black protesters. Ironically, his victory has also bolstered the views of whites who argue that racism is a thing of the past.

Thus, it's only fitting that the latest iteration of the black freedom movement should emerge during the final years of Obama's tenure. While there were earlier glimmers, like the mobilization in Jena, Louisiana, in 2007, it was the acquittal of vigilante George Zimmerman in the 2012 killing of Trayvon Martin that truly marked the beginning of the Black Lives Matter movement. Though police violence serves as the spark for its eruptive protests, it is fueled by a recognition of the institutional racism rooted in economic as well as socio-political repression—an all-American toxic brew of race and class. As Martha Biondi argues in this chapter's penultimate article, persistent unemployment and a mass incarceration crisis driven by the "War on Drugs," among other factors, have created among many young black (and Latino) men "a new social condition we might call disposability."

Who might change that condition? As Keeanga-Yamahtta Taylor makes clear in this chapter's incisive final piece, the black political elite isn't a safe bet. New movement activists seem to realize that "black faces in high places" alone don't deliver economic and racial equality. Black faces in the street, as civil rights activists learned more than fifty years ago, tend to speed up progress.

"WASHINGTON STILL HAS A HARD ROW TO HOE"

By David Moberg (1983)

Chicago, Illinois—"Wake up, everybody," boomed the voice from a loud-speaker mounted on the car slowly winding its way through the Robert

Taylor Homes public housing project on South State Street. "Vote for Chicago. You've got the power to make history today."

Blacks throughout this city, many of them new voters, did wake up on April 12th, 1983. With a large bloc of Hispanics, a crucial group of liberal whites, and a small slice of loyal Democrats from white ethnic neighborhoods, they made history. With the election of U.S. Representative Harold Washington as mayor over Republican Bernard Epton, Chicago voters turned back the tides of fear and racism that had been generated in the campaign and chose their first black mayor. Just as important, they also dealt a death blow to machine politics and established the beginnings of a new reform coalition that should shift the city—and possibly national politics—to the left.

Moved by hope of change and a new sense of power, the black electorate swelled—filling one of the "holes" in the voting population long regarded as a left constituency waiting for a leader.

Thomas Hooper, a twenty-nine-year-old recent junior college graduate, stood between the high-rise housing project—one of the legacies of machine policies that had made Chicago so racially segregated—and the polling place in the local school gymnasium. He simply reminded voters to be sure that the election judge initialed their ballots, since there was no need to plead for their support for Washington.

"A lot of my white friends say black people aren't very political," he said. "But they'd been double-crossed so many times, they felt there wasn't a reason. Now they feel there's a reason. This is the first time a large chunk of people thought about politics, thought it mattered. Like Washington says, it's not a race question, but a question of power and greed [of those who have been in control]. If a white person had come and said the right things, we would have voted for him as the reform candidate."

Washington not only said the right things, but knew how to break the loyalty of poor blacks to the machine. "People now are ashamed to be associated with the machine," Hooper said. "They used to be proud of it."

More than most black leaders in the city, Washington has an understanding and empathy for the problems of poor and working-class whites and an open identification with causes popular among liberal and leftist whites—as evidenced by his close ties with both the labor movement and disarmament groups. But Washington, like many of his closest advisors, came to political maturity as blacks were still fighting for an end to restrictive covenants (prohibitions on the sale of homes to blacks) and the fight for open housing, which brought Martin Luther King to the city in the mid-'60s.

Memories of racial conflict run deep in the city. At a southwest side polka party for Epton just before the election, Helen Owada, a middle-aged clerk in a large mail-order firm, worried about a possible Washington victory. "We'll have a lot of race riots," she said, although most whites in the area expected riots if Washington lost. "When I was a little girl my dad told me about how they used to pull white people off the subways in 1919." She may have gotten the story inverted—facts collapse before racial fantasies—but the long-standing fears remain.

It will take great effort for Washington to bridge these gaps of racial antagonism, cultural differences, and broad misperceptions.

Washington hopes to instill confidence through an example of fairness in appointments. Many Chicagoans cannot imagine that the machine will go. But Washington likened the machine to a mortally wounded animal that will go off into the woods and die. For decades that machine perpetuated the conditions that made race such a volatile issue in this election—concentrating blacks in public-housing ghettos, deliberately maintaining segregated schools, making no effort to maintain economic stability of neighborhoods that were integrating.

Washington is likely to usher in a new era of city politics. That is likely to be based on a coalition of blacks, Hispanics, white reformers, labor, certain business and financial interests, and those white ethnics who decide to cooperate. Washington intends to encourage neighborhood participation in government planning and will rely more on mobilization of community pressure to bring about a political majority than the traditional inside dealing. The excitement and involvement generated by Washington's victory should make that task easier.

Despite exhilaration in the black community, the expectations are measured. "Some people expect jobs, so there are going to be some disappointments and resentments after two years," volunteer Thomas Hooper said. "But people who have been around politics don't expect too much. The economy is screwed up. I'm just doing this for a new day."

"JACKSON'S ASCENT AND THE DYNAMIC OF RACISM"

By Salim Muwakkil (1988)

Chicago, Illinois—"Something profound is happening in America," said Reverend Jesse Jackson upon learning of his close second-place finish in the Illinois Democratic primary and his new front-runner status. Noting recent victories in Alaska and South Carolina and his second-place finishes in states with small black populations like Maine, Vermont, Minnesota, and Idaho, Jackson asked, "Who would have thought that after thirty contests

I would be in front?" It's almost inconceivable that a black man would be leading the race for the Democratic presidential nomination twenty-three years after the bloody march for voting rights in Selma, Alabama, he said.

Jackson's inference that racism is on the wane seems reasonable. After all, a significant number of whites ostensibly are willing to support him for president and, considering this country's racist history, that is a profound development. But racism is not just a question of history, it's also a topic of current events.

No CONTRADICTION

While Jackson attracts growing numbers of whites to his presidential campaign, black students stage more demonstrations protesting racism. For some, this is not a contradiction.

"Those ostensibly opposing trends are part of the this-a-way, that-a-way paradox of American reality," explained Martin Kilson in a recent interview. Kilson, professor of government at Harvard University, said he's not confused by reports that racism is rising and falling simultaneously. "American life is always some crazy admixture of forward and backward movement."

Kilson said the historic dimension of Jackson's candidacy is more significant than the reports of growing racism. "In many ways, Jackson's surprising campaign is evidence that America is growing up," he noted, "and the Left has to learn how to admit that." Readiness to criticize this country, he insists, should be matched by a willingness to acknowledge positive developments. "We on the Left lose credibility if we fail to give the system its due."

MIXED MESSAGES

Jackson's de-emphasis of racial politics has tripped up some of his erstwhile allies who had based their strategies on the politics of racial solidarity. In Chicago, Jackson's embrace of the Cook County Democratic slate confused many of his supporters, who—though the county ticket was also endorsed by the late Mayor Harold Washington—expected him to stand with those who had second thoughts about the late mayor's strategy.

Some of Jackson's more fervent supporters contend that his populist appeal is effectively stunting the growth of racist groups rather than provoking a backlash. "Jesse is the only candidate competing with those racist groups for the populist vote, and he's winning," said Robert Starks, a Jackson campaign adviser and professor of political science at Northeastern Illinois University in Chicago.

"By reaching out for rural whites, he's defusing a lot of the fascist racism that's right below the surface in much of agrarian America," Starks added. "And he's received very little credit for this." Starks said Jackson has directly taken on the virulent anti-Semitism that lurks in this country's heartland and "offered those who trace all of their problems to a 'Jewish conspiracy' alternative explanations for the deteriorating situation in which they find themselves."

"Advocating drug decriminalization a tough stand in black community"

By Salim Muwakkil (1990)

When Carrie Saxon Perry, the black mayor of Hartford, Connecticut, began advocating drug decriminalization, she knew it would ruffle some feathers. But even she was surprised by the acrimony of her opposition. What's more, she said, her harshest critics are blacks.

"I've been called immoral, a participant in genocide and many other things since going public with my views on decriminalization last year," Perry explained. "African American critics have spared no epithet in denouncing me." And it's no wonder. The conventional wisdom among black leaders is that any attempt to lift the taint from drug use will send the wrong message to a community already reeling from drug-induced pathologies.

"But I remain convinced that we need to try something else," Perry added. "African Americans are the primary losers in this country's failed drug policies," she said. "We're filling up the jails; we're suffering the broken families, decaying communities ... We're paying the price. I believe we should be in the forefront of those seeking more effective alternatives to the law-enforcement approaches currently in place."

The two-term mayor says she believes that problems of drug abuse are issues of economics and public health rather than of criminal justice. "After finding that more than 80 percent of all of Hartford's crime is drug-related—and most of this crime involved the economics of the drug trade—it began getting clearer and clearer that the drug plague is being fueled by huge profits," Perry explains. "Therefore, it seems logical to me that the plague can be reduced by reducing the economic rewards for spreading it."

That reasoning may seem logical to Perry, but it has so far failed to attract the support—or even the interest—of all but a few black leaders.

Until recently, in fact, Baltimore Mayor Kurt Schmoke was the only black elected official willing to even consider decriminalization as a subject fit for public discussion.

The taboo is strong. Not only are officials like Perry accused of "surrendering" to the evil drug plague and ignoring the moral dimensions of the problem, but since the drug abuse so inordinately affects the African American community, they are also accused of promoting genocide.

"I respond that what we have now is akin to genocide. And I ask them how can it get any worse than what is already happening. I've seen the drug economy change the entire value system of many black communities. At one time we would shun and ostracize wrongdoers and we managed to keep a sense of moral equilibrium.

"But because of the enormous amounts of money made available by doing wrong in the drug trade, they have become the new heroes of many poverty-stricken communities," Perry explained. "How can we expect a welfare mother, just scraping to get by to feed her children, to reject a son who comes home bulging with money made in the drug economy? We've created a subculture in which criminality is a responsible career choice."

Perry added that the current approach also serves to incarcerate people who would be better served getting medical care or vocational training. The money needed to help lift those mired in poverty is instead used to build more prisons to program them for poverty.

The Bush administration's "war on drugs" may or may not ease this country's drug problem, but one thing it will certainly do is increase the U.S. prison population. And if present trends continue, an overwhelming percentage of those prisoners will be African American men.

There already are more black men in correctional institutions in this country than there are in colleges and universities, and this monumental waste of human potential reportedly will accelerate as the war on drugs intensifies.

"BEING BLACK IN AMERICA: THE QUIET RIOT CONTINUES"

By Donnell Alexander (1992)

Los Angeles, California—The April 29 not-guilty verdict in the Rodney King trial reminded everyday, working African Americans that in order to live, we must forget.

King's assailants beat their collective rap because racism runs so deep in America that, to many Americans, a prone black man looks more like a criminal than any white cop ever could. The Ventura County jury simply followed what they knew in their hearts to be true.

Black people understood this. And because they did, things happened. The downtrodden in Los Angeles went berserk, tearing up the town and delivering self-inflicted wounds, first out of rage and then out of the desire to get theirs. In their crude, crude language, they complained that, as at least one protester put it, the social contract had been broken.

But something different happened in the neighborhoods where African Americans have jobs, hopes, and lives. In their own homes even the least political of residents threw up their arms, recounting their indignation around kitchen tables and over phone lines.

But out in the rest of America—in the workplace, the classroom, and the shopping malls—they exhibited only a stony silence. What else could they do, lest they try to explain the origin of their empathy with the arsonists, murderers, and thieves?

Some tried. Students, activists, and plain folks who refused to internalize their rage demonstrated and protested, joining with those non-blacks who, while not able to know what residents of African America do, felt an outrage that demanded expression.

When the world considers African America and the riots of 1992, it will remember the strangers who roamed the streets of Los Angeles, doling out lawlessness in a savage way, meeting violence with violence. I, however, will think about the "me" in "them."

Watching the riots on television, I asked myself this question: Given a brick, a government building, and a clear shot, what would I do? The answer, by definition, made me a rioter.

Tough Question

My friend Don called me from Houston the night the cops were acquitted and L.A. burned. We grew up together in Ohio, and nowadays we talk each other through confused times.

CNN's reactionary coverage could be heard on both sides of the phone line. We did nothing but vent our spleens. The suggested courses of action and commentary were so rash and cruel I'd never repeat them in print. Then the question came, the one I knew was coming, considering the context of the night.

"So how do you do it anyway," he asked, "hang around all those white people?"

Always a tough question, one a lot of traveling residents of African America can't answer honestly. But I tried: White people, I explained, are not inherently evil or, for that matter, even inherently racist. They just do what they're told.

About that time, CNN aired a live interview with Jesse Jackson. The anchor, a woman named Susan Rook, asked, against a backdrop of flames and looters, what he and other black leaders would do to ensure that the neighborhoods of South-Central Los Angeles would be safe again.

Don and I groaned and cursed. It seemed impossible that anyone, particularly a journalist, might have considered those streets safe at any time in the last five years. The inference—not for the first time—was that a place can only be "unsafe" when whites are bearing the brunt of the violence.

With that simpleminded yet telling question, my reasoned defense of white America was undermined in total.

"Proud of Obama ... for now"

By Salim Muwakkil (2008)

Barack Hussein Obama was elected the 44th president of the United States on November 4, 2008.

What was once a distant possibility—and an audacious hope—has become an extraordinary fact. The election of a black president was considered so unlikely that it seemed silly to even contemplate. I never thought it would happen in my lifetime.

I feel pride that this nation is making bold steps to atone for its original sin. That theme also resonates with many black civil rights activists. Some have likened Obama's election to the period during the Emancipation Proclamation, and several civil rights groups organized so-called "Emancipation Watch" gatherings to monitor election results.

The notion that this election is a symbol of racial redemption is particularly striking. African Americans have been virtually lockstep in their support for the Illinois junior senator, after the Iowa primary proved that a black candidate could attract white votes. Black elected officials who since opposed Obama faced intense public criticism. Constituent discontent even forced Representative John Lewis (D-Ga.)—a civil rights icon—to withdraw his support from primary candidate Senator Hillary Clinton (D-N.Y.) and throw his support to Obama.

This was a vivid example of how Obama's electoral aspirations have interrupted the civil rights narrative that for so long has defined black

America's trajectory. Today, the African American community seems to find more value in the racial symbolism of an Obama presidency than in adhering to previous allegiances.

Charles Johnson, author of the award-winning novel *Middle Passage* and professor of English at Washington University, writes that black Americans need another narrative. In *The American Scholar* magazine, Johnson argues in a recent cover story that "a new century calls for new stories grounded in the present, leaving behind the painful history of slavery and its consequences."

That history is one of racial victimization that begins in slavery, continues through the Jim Crow and the civil rights eras, and persists into the twenty-first century. Johnson argues that this story no longer describes the lives of African Americans that increasingly are stories of success and accomplishment, perhaps best symbolized by Obama's ascent.

Johnson makes a more sophisticated argument that government efforts to redress the wounds of slavery and Jim Crow are now antiquated. He writes, "It simply is no longer the case that the essence of black American life is racial victimization and disenfranchisement ... a destiny based on color in which the meaning of one's life is thing-hood, created even before one is born."

Even as Obama reached new voters, anti affirmative action referenda passed in Nebraska and barely lost in Colorado. Similar measures have passed in four other states.

That brings me to the contradictory feelings I have about Obama's election. For some, his triumph will stand in lieu of continuing efforts to narrow the widening gap between white and black Americans in virtually every index of social well-being. To put it simply: Black America is not doing well.

Our peculiar political calculus prevented candidate Obama from candidly addressing issues of racial justice during the campaign. Any hint of racial grievance coming from a black candidate could have provoked a white electoral backlash, and the Obama team assiduously avoided that possibility.

But Obama is no longer just a symbol of Black America's racial aspirations. The African American candidate may not have been free to speak about the incarceration epidemic among black youth, or the enormous collateral damage of the war on drugs, but President Obama must be held accountable for policies that exacerbate those problems.

The "post-racial" president

By Salim Muwakkil (2009)

With the nation's first black president in the White House, some pundits have started employing the narrative of a "post-racial" America to frame events. In this view, Barack Obama's election has leveled the playing field and obviated the struggle for racial equality. In many ways Obama has played along, scrupulously avoiding comment on racial matters since he began his presidential campaign.

Yet racism persists in the Obama era, the supposedly post-racial world. According to culture critic and author Henry Giroux, this racism is different from the historical "crude racism with its biological referents and pseudo-scientific legitimations." Instead, he writes, this new breed of racism "cynically recodes itself within the vocabulary of the civil rights movement, invoking the language of Martin Luther King, Jr., to argue that individuals should be judged by the 'content of their character' and not by the color of their skin."

Obama was atypically unequivocal in July when he criticized the Cambridge, Massachusetts, police for "acting stupidly" in the arrest of Henry Louis Gates, Jr., professor of African and African American studies at Harvard University. He also raised a few eyebrows by linking the Gates arrest to the historical problem of racial profiling.

In the Gates incident, the esteemed Harvard professor was mistaken for a burglar at his own home and later arrested for "disorderly conduct" for reportedly berating Sgt. James Crowley, the officer called to investigate.

Details were still sketchy at the time of Obama's comments, and his unexpected response to the question sparked a torrent of criticism from right-wingers who were predictably eager to express their law-and-order bona fides. It also gave them fuel to inflame the kind of racial biases that tend to improve their electoral fortunes. Nixon's "Southern Strategy" lives on.

Rush Limbaugh said Obama's comments were a case of "a black president trying to destroy a white policeman." Fox News' Glenn Beck accused the president of being racist, saying Obama's words revealed a "deep-seated hatred for white people or the white culture."

The president also angered some supporters, who thought his comments were inappropriate and distracting. Many wondered why a president whose campaign discipline was legendary would make such a startling strategic mistake.

The answer likely lies in Obama's attempts to rectify what he considers an unbalanced depiction of his position on racial issues. He seems frustrated by criticism of his posture of racial neutrality, and he hinted as much when he complained to the *Washington Post*'s Eugene Robinson about coverage of his July 16 National Association for the Advancement of Colored People speech. "I've noticed that when I talk about personal responsibility in the African American community, that gets highlighted," he said. "But then the whole other half of the speech, where I talked about government's responsibility ... that somehow doesn't make news."

Obama was speaking of the media's predilection for talking about race in post-racial terms, though it's a tendency he's guilty of, too. During his campaign, most of his advisors urged him to avoid the issue as too risky. Except for his excellent speech in Philadelphia—in which he contextualized the kind of black anger expressed by Reverend Jeremiah Wright, his former pastor, even while condemning it—his campaign followed that advice and remained race-averse.

The boisterous national response to his mild rebuke of the Cambridge police reveals demagogic politicians can easily tap America's cultural reservoir of racial biases. Faced with a shrinking demographic base and diverging cultural trends, many Republicans have concluded that a return to the politics of white resentment may be the party's best shot at viability.

A black president with a progressive agenda also provides the right wing with a potent symbol of opposition. Social rifts in the United States are always exacerbated by economic uncertainty, and recession breeds uncertainty.

In April 2009, the Department of Homeland Security warned that "the economic downturn and the election of the first African American president present unique drivers for right-wing radicalization and recruitment." Just a hint of racial favoritism from Obama probably would light a fuse of potent white resentment.

At the same time, black Americans are in a deep depression and may require exactly the kind of race-specific, compensatory policies that are falling out of favor and likely to anger many other groups. Those pushing for black equality see, for example, that black American inmates comprise one tenth of all the world's prisoners and they refuse to accept that tragic reality.

This is Obama's dilemma: he must walk a narrow tightrope slick with cultural biases. As America's first black president, he must downplay black Americans' specific needs or he'll lose his political balance.

"From Hope to Disposability"

By Martha Biondi (2013)

We are living with the legacy of the civil rights movement's many losses and defeats. In June 2013, the U.S. Supreme Court sharply delimited the Voting Rights Act and further undercut already constrained efforts to increase black access to higher education. And then George Zimmerman was acquitted in the shooting death of unarmed Trayvon Martin, a verdict that symbolizes to many a growing disregard for black life, especially the lives of young black men.

It may seem odd to argue that there's a growing disregard for black life at a time when a black family occupies the White House. But in a tragic conjuncture, the post–civil rights era has overlapped with the postindustrial era and the rise of neoliberalism in the United States. These developments have precipitated a crisis for young black and Latino men whose lives are now characterized by a new social condition we might call disposability.

Disposability encompasses not only structural unemployment and the school-to-prison pipeline, but also high rates of shooting deaths as weaponry meets hopelessness in the day-to-day struggle for manhood and survival. Disposability also manifests in our larger society's apparent acceptance of high rates of premature death of young African Americans and Latinos. Handguns have killed more Americans since 1968 than have died in all U.S. wars combined. The majority of shooting-death victims between 1980 and 2010 were black, and today homicide is by far the leading cause of death for young black men.

The mass killings in white communities in Newtown, Connecticut, and Aurora, Colorado, have episodically galvanized national media attention and intensified pressure on Congress to stem the flow of guns, but invariably the power of the gun lobby has short-circuited federal action. At the same time, the ongoing death toll of young people of color never becomes a moral crisis for the nation.

On the 50th anniversary of the March on Washington, it's worth examining how African American communities, civil rights leaders, and activists have responded to this crisis. How have they diagnosed the problem, and what remedies do they advocate?

Communities step up

Voices on the Right often castigate black leaders for allegedly turning a blind eye to urban violence in favor of protesting interracial killings. Fox

News' Bill O'Reilly struck this note in his outrage over black protest in the aftermath of the George Zimmerman acquittal. Even activists on the Left have suggested that black leaders have paid insufficient attention to this crisis. At a National Association for the Advancement of Colored People event in February 2013, civil rights activist Harry Belafonte criticized black leaders for not being more visible in leading the fight against the proliferation of guns. "Where's the raised voice of Black America?" he asked. "Why are we mute? Where are our leaders? Our legislators? Where is the church?"

Belafonte is wrong. Civil rights leaders, elected officials, and grassroots activists have analyzed the problem and advocated comprehensive reforms. Indeed, residents of neighborhoods on the front lines of this violence have generated the most nuanced perspectives. Poor black communities are rarely depicted as resilient or as offering creative remedies to the multiple crises they face. Nor are their practices of grieving or memorializing the dead given much attention in the major media.

Many grassroots organizations have emerged to address the crisis. Project Orange Tree, founded by Chicago teenagers with the support of local hip hop artist Lupe Fiasco, has as its mission "preserving the lives of youth by raising awareness about structural violence." These young people believe that structural violence is the root of "deviant behavior." They reject criminalization as a solution to gun violence and demand comprehensive social remedies.

In New York City, community-based groups like Save Our Streets, Cease Fire East New York, Man Up!, and the Brooklyn Blizzards have successfully reduced violence. But then the city and state cut funding for those programs, choosing instead to focus resources on stop-and-frisk and other heavy-handed and racist policing tactics. Such grassroots organizations offer a range of perspectives on the causes of gun violence, from the easy availability of handguns to staggering rates of unemployment and the lure of gangs. Some groups, like the Black Star Project in Chicago, emphasize strengthening families and stressing fatherhood as a remedy.

Notably, none of these groups call for more police, incarceration, or other punitive responses. Besieged black communities have broken with the conventional "crime-fighting" response of politicians. Rather than see more cops and prisons as the solution, they increasingly fault the criminal legal system for stoking community-based violence.

Harry Belafonte's critique also misses the fact that black elected officials, clergy, and civil rights leaders have advocated restricting the flow of weaponry, increasing investments in urban education and job creation, and dismantling what some term the prison-industrial complex. (To be sure, black politicians, like their white counterparts, often call for more police during spikes in urban violence.)

The 1970s, 1980s, and 1990s saw high rates of black victims of violent crime, but instead of grieving for this loss of life and redoubling efforts to protect and nurture black youth, the state chose mass incarceration under the banner of the War on Drugs. In 1994, President Bill Clinton signed into law the Violent Crime and Law Enforcement Act, a bill that expanded mandatory minimum sentences and the death penalty, and built more prisons. Disappointingly, then-Senator Carol Moseley Braun (D-Ill.) sponsored an amendment requiring that juveniles be tried as adults when charged with certain violent offenses.

For the most part, the Congressional Black Caucus and civil rights leaders have denounced this approach to urban crime fighting. In 1994, the caucus put forward an alternative bill emphasizing drug prevention and job creation. Many ministers and civil rights organizations have led the call for gun restrictions, especially the trafficking of guns made and sold across county and state lines. This has been a long-standing theme of Chicago's Rainbow PUSH Coalition. "Guns come in, jobs go out" is a common refrain at the group's headquarters on the South Side. PUSH founder Reverend Jesse Jackson Sr. has led many marches to gun shops in the region. He cites the statistic that 1.2 percent of gun dealers sell 57 percent of the handguns used in violent crime. For Jackson and others, the culprits are the suppliers and manufacturers, who reap corporate profits at the expense of black lives.

Yet Belafonte's lament that some black leaders have been quiet in the face of gun violence has a degree of merit. But this reflects a broader American turn toward defining social problems as criminal problems. The solutions to this problem, just like the roots of this problem, are complex, and we would be wise to listen carefully to the residents and activists living on the front lines of urban warfare. Their remedies are inspired by a fierce commitment to black humanity—a stance at odds with the logic of disposability.

Moreover, any struggle against violence in the United States must at every instance also be a struggle against the endless war-making of the American empire. Making guns and killing people at home and abroad is big business, and we should never lose sight of this dual focus.

"IN BALTIMORE AND ACROSS THE COUNTRY, BLACK FACES IN
HIGH PLACES HAVEN'T HELPED AVERAGE BLACK PEOPLE"

By Keeanga-Yamahtta Taylor (2015)

The acrid plumes of smoke that hang over the city of Baltimore are a stark reminder of the recent past of the 1960s. But the riots over the death of twenty-five-year-old Freddie Gray seen in Baltimore over the past few days aren't simply a replay of events that took place fifty years ago. The inequities that ignited hundreds of American cities in the 1960s still exist and have, in fact, deepened over the last half-century. Then as now, pervasive police violence and harassment defines the humiliation and powerlessness of life for millions of working-class and poor African Americans.

But what makes the Baltimore uprising different from an earlier era is that the vicious attacks on African Americans have unfolded at a time of unprecedented black political power.

Fewer than forty miles from Baltimore, in the nation's capitol, resides the nation's first African American president. There are forty-three black members of Congress and two senators—the highest number of black Congress members in American history. And just as the West Side of Baltimore was erupting against the police killing of Freddie Gray, Loretta Lynch became the first black woman appointed as Attorney General.

This isn't only a national phenomenon; it's also reflected in local politics. In Baltimore, African Americans control virtually the entire political apparatus. Mayor Stephanie Rawlings-Blake and Police Commissioner Anthony Batts have been the most prominent faces of political power in Baltimore over the last several weeks. But Baltimore's City Council has fifteen members, and a majority, eight, are African American, including its president. The superintendent of the public schools and the entire board of the city's housing commission are African American. Across the United States, thousands of black elected officials are governing many of the nation's cities and suburbs.

In this respect, the events in Baltimore are dissimilar from what happened in Ferguson, Missouri, last summer. There, the small suburb just north of Saint Louis had a majority black population largely governed by a white suburban government, and the lack of black political power and representation became a narrative thread in popular explanations for what went wrong. Electing African Americans into political office in Ferguson thus became a focal point for many local and national activists.

But if the murder of Mike Brown and the rebellion in Ferguson was reminiscent of the old Jim Crow, then the murder of Freddie Gray and the Baltimore uprising is symbolic of the new black power.

Today, we have more black elected officials in the United States than at any point in American history. Yet for the vast majority of black people, life has changed very little. Black elected officials have largely governed in the same way as their white counterparts, reflecting all of the racism, corruption, and policies favoring the wealthy seen throughout mainstream politics.

Baltimore is a telltale example. Despite the lawlessness of the Baltimore Police Department, the mayor reserved her harshest comments for those involved in the uprising, describing them as "criminals" and "thugs." For anyone remotely aware of Rawlings-Blake's mayoral history, her lashing out at the victims of police corruption and brutality would not have been surprising.

Ignoring the long history of racism and the epidemic of police terrorism in shaping black life in Baltimore, the mayor, as has become typical of the black political elite, blamed the problems of the city on the African Americans who live there.

The major difference between life in cities like Baltimore today and fifty years ago is not only the existence of a black political stratum that governs and manages much of Black America, but also the ways this powerful black political class helps to deflect a serious interrogation of structural inequality and institutional racism. Instead, leaders from that political class resurrect old and convenient narratives that indict black families and culture as the central explanation for persistent racial inequality.

To maintain legitimacy within the Democratic Party, which most of these black politicians consider home, they toe the party line that emphasizes personal responsibility and rejects raising taxes to fund desperately needed social programs. And black elected officials either create or widen the space for whites to interrogate the moral habits of ordinary black people. When President Obama, Mayor Rawlings-Blake, and Attorney General Lynch refer to black protesters as "thugs" and "criminals," white Republicans do not have to.

The uprising in Baltimore has crystallized the deepening political and class divide in Black America. This is a new development in the black freedom struggle that historically has been united across class lines to fight racism. From the White House to City Halls across the country, the growth and maturation of the black political class has firmly placed them in a position of managing the crises that continue to unfold in black neighborhoods across the country. Black political operatives have no better solutions for ordinary African Americans than any other elected officials. In Ferguson and now in Baltimore, it's the movement in the streets that is bringing global attention to the racism and inequality that still thrives in American society—not black faces in high places.

CHAPTER NINE

Labor's Fate: New Solutions to Old Problems, Old Solutions to New Problems

INTRODUCTION

By Micah Uetricht

For nearly a half-century, labor journalists have had to deliver and rede-liver much of the same terrible news. Unions are in such dire straits that we have a hard time coming up with new suitably dire phrases. "Downward spiral." "Inexorable decline." "Vultures circling." Despair fatigue can set in after reading *In These Times*' labor coverage. Year after year, articles seem to be asking the same fundamental question: How can unions save themselves?

Not all of recent labor history is cause for anguish, however. Organizers in both traditional unions and nontraditional labor groups—the latter tend to represent contingent workers, such as taxi drivers or farmworkers, who lack collective bargaining rights—have experimented widely with new ways of building power in the workplace. Worker centers are one new kind of labor organization that has emerged. They tend to be community-based nonunion organizations supporting low-wage workers, and have been suc-cesssful enough to find themselves in capital's crosshairs, as I note in "Big Business Aims to Crush Worker Centers." And many unions have grown comfortable with forming broader alliances: not only with new sorts of labor groups, but also with campus-based and community groups. *In These Times* has covered these stories from the start.

The Service Employees International Union (SEIU) Justice for Janitors organizing campaign ("Cleaning House"), which began in the 1980s and con-tinued for decades, mixed tactics old and new to pressure employers. (Old tactics included strikes, mass marches, and civil disobedience; new ones included strategic corporate analysis and pressure, and extensive public-relations battles.) It ultimately organized tens of thousands of workers, though the results of contract negotiations have been mixed. The Coalition of Immokalee Workers ("Doing It For Themselves") has pioneered a new model of organizing with immigrant tomato pickers in Florida: the organization campaigns directly against some of the country's largest fast-food companies, like McDonald's, without a union. Some nontraditional labor groups, such as the New York Taxi Workers Alliance, have been so successful that during the last ten years the American Federation of Labor and Congress of Industrial Organizations (AFL-CIO) has established formal partnerships with them. United Students Against Sweatshops ("Too Cruel for School") has developed an innovative model in which North American students fight alongside garment workers in the Global South and low-wage workers on U.S. college campuses. The "student labor organization," which has local affiliates on more than 150 campuses across the United States, has repeatedly wrung victories from global clothing corporations for garment workers.

And then there's Fight for 15, a SEIU-backed campaign to both boost the minimum wage and unionize fast-food workers. Since its inception in 2012, and after numerous one-day strikes that attracted widespread media coverage, the campaign has moved low-wage workers' demand for $15 an hour from a pipe dream to the law of the land in fourteen cities and states around the country, with more wage boosts on the way. Although fast-food workers' goal of forming unions remains elusive, the legitimacy their actions have brought to workers' most powerful weapon, the strike, could evince a long-term shift in working-class militancy.

But Fight for 15 shows both the peril and the promise of new models ("Is Fight for 15 for Real?"). Some question whether the campaign has opted for camera- and social media-friendly actions that don't actually shut down production or organize a majority (or sometimes even a sizeable minority) of workers.

Many organizers seem to have looked at the state of the U.S. economy and unions and decided that building power through slow but steady organizing and leadership development among workers—who can then go organize other workers, who can then organize still *other* workers—isn't feasible. It takes time and resources, both in short supply. Besides which, building rank-and-file leadership doesn't generate much in the way of news coverage.

But not all in labor have opted for shortcuts. After a reform leadership took power in the union, more than 150,000 Teamsters took on UPS in 1997, striking successfully for wage increases and job security ("Face-Off at UPS"). The Chicago Teachers Union has been one of the few bright spots for labor in the twenty-first century ("Democratic to the CORE"). Its organizing model relied not on capturing headlines (though its actions certainly have done that) but rather on democratic, militant, bottom-up unionism. In the union's 2012 strike and 2016 one-day strike, that approach paid off.

Organizers trying to save their unions should take notice of this old-fashioned solution to their problems, as Shaun Richman does in this chapter's closing piece.

The core problems that U.S. workers face today are as old as capitalism itself—and the oldest solution to their woes can't be discarded. Whether in 2017 or 1917, the *sine qua non* of successful worker organizing is rank-and-file engagement. Without that, *In These Times* will keep delivering the same old bad news.

"CLEANING HOUSE"

By Zach Nauth (1995)

Washington, D.C.—On Pennsylvania Avenue, across the street from the offices of one of Washington's biggest landlords, dozens of helmeted police officers, their clubs drawn, corraled 200 peaceful, chanting demonstrators. A heavy plate-glass door shattered as the police chased a woman into it. Another demonstrator twisted and writhed as six officers dragged him toward a fleet of paddy wagons parked nearby.

Middle-aged men in suits and women in dresses looked around uneasily as the police carried off one demonstrator after another, many still brandishing signs and chanting slogans. Well-compensated bureaucrats and office workers from labor's conservative center, the American Federation of Labor and Congress of Industrial Organizations (AFL-CIO) headquarters a few blocks away, stood shoulder-to-shoulder with their counterparts on labor's most militant wing: janitors from El Salvador and Pittsburgh, union organizers from Guatemala and Milwaukee.

What brought these unlikely comrades together in mid-March 1995 for a five-hour ordeal of handcuffs and jail time? The march and the rush-hour sit-down action were the work of "Justice for Janitors," an innovative organizing campaign of the Service Employees International Union (SEIU). The protest, part of an eight-year campaign to organize Washington's janitors, targeted prominent building owner Oliver Carr, who has been reaping multimillion-dollar tax breaks in the midst of the District of Columbia's budget crisis. Carr also hires nonunion cleaning contractors, who in turn employ hundreds of the city's poorest residents to do dirty, difficult work at minimum wages with part-time hours and no benefits.

As the city wrestled with its fiscal crisis, the janitors' union staged a weeklong mobilization, during which it tested new direct-action strategies and schooled 200 organizers in Justice for Janitors' in-your-face tactics.

Co-sponsors included the Hotel Employees and Restaurant Employees Union (HERE) and the AFL-CIO Organizing Institute. The sponsors hope the week's activities will set an example that the AFL-CIO organizers and other mainstream Washington offices cannot ignore.

The missionary zeal of the Justice for Janitors organizers is understandable: founded a decade ago, it is now the most successful organizing campaign among service-industry workers in the private sector. And, remarkably, it has succeeded among a workforce that other unions have failed to reach—part-time, low-income workers, predominantly African Americans and Spanish-speaking immigrants, who hold jobs at the bottom of the U.S. economy. As organized labor continues its seemingly inexorable slide into irrelevance, the "J for J" model—which has won new contracts and registered impressive membership gains—looks increasingly attractive.

Justice for Janitors uses strategies—like the sit-down strike—made famous during labor's golden age in the '30s, and combines them with the nonviolent tactics of the civil rights movement. J for J molds them into a simple formula: the disruption of business as usual, plus moral authority, equals change. But this approach often runs into legal obstacles. For example, the time-honored tactic of warehouse workers refusing to handle the goods of a company whose employees were on strike, has—like many other successful union strategies—been outlawed by Congress, the courts, and the National Labor Relations Board (NLRB). So, J for J has been forced to be creative.

The campaign rejects the standard organizing method most unions now use: site-by-site NLRB-supervised elections. Stephen Lerner, the former director of organizing for SEIU's Building Services Division, who now works with the Organizing Institute and other labor groups, says, "The boss was right—our strategy was stupid: 'Join the union, lose your job.'" Indeed, one in four companies facing an organizing drive unlawfully fires employees. Even when unions win NLRB elections—and they win only 50 percent—employers often avoid negotiating first contracts. Justice for Janitors organizers liken the NLRB to a black hole that sucks in the union's time, stalls momentum, and eventually bores workers to death. Worse, they claim, many members feel that the often lengthy proceedings that accompany an NLRB election only underscore the union's weakness. Consequently, when Justice for Janitors organizes a workplace, it insists the company agrees to simultaneously recognize the union and negotiate a contract.

Other unions prefer the NLRB strategy because it's more predictable: set an election and win or lose on that date. But J for J organizers dig in for the long haul, with a high-profile, multifaceted pressure campaign. Their tactics include street theater, quickie unfair labor-practice strikes (which even nonunion employees are allowed to hold), corporate campaigns, regulatory challenges, community coalitions, boycotts, disruption of production through direct action, and nonviolent civil disobedience. The latter strategy is key: the union's principal tactic is to "physically interfere with the ability of companies to operate, produce and deliver goods and services ... unless they settle disputes that stem from antiworker action," Lerner has written in a strategy paper. Another key is to build the union as a vehicle for social justice that takes on issues of common concern to workers, their families, and the community. Workers can then be motivated by more than narrow self-interest.

The union's gains have been impressive. In its ten-year existence—a period of general decline for the labor movement—the Justice for Janitors campaign has organized an estimated 35,000 net new members. It now claims a total membership of 205,000, representing a fifth of all custodians working for private companies in the United States.

"Face-off at UPS"

By Jane Slaughter (1997)

Angela Schenburn starts her day at a United Parcel Service (UPS) center in Madison Heights, Michigan, at 3:40 a.m. as a preloader, packing boxes and Jiffy-bags into the trucks. Then she dons the regulation brown shirt and delivers packages. Schenburn logs more than forty hours at UPS each week, but because she's working two different part-time jobs, she's paid a part-time rate. She's a typical example of a national trend toward part-time jobs, a trend that has made UPS a target of the Teamsters union.

Contracts for 185,000 Teamsters at UPS—128,000 of them part-timers—expired July 31. The union is demanding that UPS convert a portion of these part-time jobs to full-time. The members voted by a 95-percent margin to strike, the union announced on July 15. Despite a record $1.15 billion profit last year, the company wants more part-timers and more outsourcing.

Eighty-three percent of the new jobs created since 1993 have been part-time, but the starting rate for part-timers, $8 to $9 an hour, hasn't budged since 1982. Full-timers now make around $20 an hour. In contract talks, the company has offered a 90-cent increase phased in over seven years for all current workers but no increase at all in the starting wage for part-timers.

Schenburn, thirty-eight, says the stereotype of UPS part-timers as "college boys" no longer holds. "The work force has changed from young kids to fathers, husbands, wives," she says. "You join a company like UPS because you're willing to work hard for these wages if you can get a chance for a future. You can't support a family on $8 an hour, even if you were full-time."

Veteran driver Gary Clark of Pontiac, Michigan, notes that full-timers have good reason to support the part-timers' demands. "The more you surround yourself with people working at eight bucks an hour, you're cutting your own throat," Clark says. "It gives the company an incentive to get rid of you."

Who will win the face-off? Teamsters for a Democratic Union organizer Bob Machado believes that because of its neck-and-neck rivalry with FedEx, UPS is "incredibly vulnerable." The company knows it can't recruit and train 180,000 scabs, he says. On the other hand, the Teamsters' strike fund is too small to last long.

Schenburn is ready to strike. "Most people have another job anyway," she says. "You have to have two jobs just to survive. Most people would rather strike, and maybe we'll make it so we only have to have one job to survive."

Editor's note: The Teamsters strike ended after sixteen days, when UPS, having lost more than $600 million, agreed to a new five-year contract. It increased wages for part-time and full-time workers, protected the union pension plan, and increased job security by stipulating that UPS would cease most subcontracting.

"Too cruel for school"

By David Moberg (2002)

On campuses across the country, a groundswell of student organizing focused on workers rights has become the dominant stream of campus politics after a period when identity politics held center stage. Born out of critiques of globalization, the new labor-oriented student movement has turned its global outrage inward, focusing on workers in the United States and, especially, at the universities themselves.

The new interest in labor issues started with campaigns against sweatshops, especially providers of university-logo clothing. But the anti-sweatshop movement, while still growing and gaining sophistication, has also turned toward support for exploited workers in the United States, from New Era cap makers on strike to farm workers picketing Taco Bell. Students are also a growing force behind unionization on campus, such as food service workers at Sodexho and living-wage campaigns for university employees or contractors—given a big boost by a sit-in last spring at Harvard. Increasingly, students who work at universities—especially graduate teaching and research assistants, but even undergraduate resident assistants—are also organizing themselves.

"There's been this explosion of student interest in labor issues," says Andrea Calver, the full-time liaison to the student movement on the staff of the Hotel Employees and Restaurant Employees Union, which won a contract for Pitzer College food service workers in California last year with student support.

This academic year has seen "the biggest influx in a long time" of groups joining the United Students Against Sweatshops (USAS), says field coordinator Amber Gallup. About 40 new affiliates have boosted the organization's total to 109, but there are another 250 college chapters that are less formally linked to USAS.

The number of campus living-wage movements has tripled this year too, and a national tour of Harvard janitors and students, organized by the Service Employees International Union (SEIU), has sparked interest on roughly eighty campuses. Inspired by the organizing and legal victories of New York University teaching and research assistants, who negotiated their first contract in February 2002, graduate student workers at Columbia, Brown, Yale, Harvard, and other universities are at varied stages in their fights for union recognition. Teaching assistant organizing has also encouraged nascent organizing among nontenured adjunct professors.

Most progressive campus activists see themselves as advocates of social justice who have focused on labor organizing as a vehicle. "I just got interested in doing labor work because it's what took hold of me initially," says Tom Cogswell, a USAS organizer from Central Michigan University. "I could just as easily have got involved in doing environmental issues. The basic issue is there's no representation in the government and no respect for individual liberties and gross inequalities and institutionalized racism. I generally work for labor rights, but I see a larger issue at hand."

University campuses have become one of the most important fronts for revitalization of the labor movement. Although some unions have worked closely with students, training and recruiting many leaders, and American Federation of Labor and Congress of Industrial Organizations (AFL-CIO) President John Sweeney has repeatedly joined campus protests, the challenge to the labor movement will be not simply to bring more of these new workers and supporters into the heart of the labor movement, but to transform itself to incorporate the new movement's broad mandate for social justice. As Gallup says of the students, "They want to be organizers, not just foot soldiers."

"Doing it for themselves"

By Mischa Gaus (2007)

The Florida tomato pickers of the Coalition of Immokalee Workers (CIW) rolled into Chicago in blustery April, ready to stand before McDonald's corporate headquarters and press their demands that the fast-food behemoth take responsibility for the miserable way its tomatoes are farmed.

It proved unnecessary. As more than 1,000 tomato pickers and their allies wound their way to Chicago, McDonald's unexpectedly agreed to all of the coalition's demands. The groundbreaking settlement will almost double salaries for farm workers, reveal where the company buys its tomatoes, and create a monitoring plan expandable to other corporate buyers. McDonald's capitulated two years into the campaign, and on the eve of the coalition's call to boycott the company. It followed a similar deal the coalition signed in 2005 with Taco Bell's corporate parent after a four-year boycott.

The 3,500 members of CIW are mostly Mexican, Guatemalan, and Haitian immigrants, many of whom left indigenous communities to work the fields of swampy southwest Florida. They have become a force far beyond their numbers. (And their agreements are good news for the roughly 6,000 transient tomato pickers of Immokalee, all of whom receive the higher wage if they pick fast-food tomatoes, regardless of whether they're CIW members.) In expanding its agreements to another fast-food giant, CIW proved the durability of its strategy—the creation of private regulations to remedy the ills of a neoliberal economic order that is unwilling or unable to negotiate political settlements.

In achieving those agreements, CIW has crafted a new pattern for civil society's tango with corporations, this time with activists in the lead. Two interlocking dynamics made possible CIW's détente with the largest fast-food chain on the globe. McDonald's is seeking to burnish its brand image after absorbing decades of assaults on every segment of its business.

The CIW, on the other hand, found in McDonald's a fulcrum to shift the fast-food industry by creating a code of conduct authored by farm workers and watched over by independent monitors. The idea is borrowed from the antisweatshop movement that eight years ago launched a similar strategy in establishing the Worker Rights Consortium, which tracks and investigates overseas garment factories producing university apparel.

This approach combines a monitoring plan outside corporate control, with the necessary transparency to verify progress, and a wage boost for the people at the point of production. Immokalee's farm workers are testing just how much leverage activists can have over companies that claim to champion social responsibility and whether corporate image vulnerability can be exploited to spread the tomato pickers' remarkable advances.

LESSONS LEARNED

The CIW began in 1993 by targeting individual tomato growers who refused to budge after years of pressure. It's a lesson not soon forgotten, says Julia Perkins, a CIW staff member. The proven way to change conditions in the fields, she says, is focusing on the only force individual growers respond to—the brand straddling the top of a supply chain. With the grocery market consolidating, the CIW won't lack for easily identifiable targets.

"We know Whole Foods buys these tomatoes," says Sean Sellers, co-coordinator of the Student Farmworker Alliance, a CIW sister group. "We know Walmart and Costco do, too."

The coalition has the ear of those astride the market. When asked in February 2007 whether they would support the coalition's demands, Burger King declined, offering the tomato pickers work in its restaurants instead. Irritated, the coalition pointed out their members already had jobs. The country's second largest burger chain shrugged, dispatching its spokesmen to say they simply couldn't dictate terms to their suppliers.

After McDonald's folded, however, the directives from fast-food corner offices became more measured. In mid-April, a Burger King spokesman said the company was "always ready to talk ... and see what we can work out."

"DEMOCRATIC TO THE CORE"

By Micah Uetricht and Jasson Perez (2012)

During September's Chicago Teachers Union (CTU) strike, local and national media rushed to frame the fight as a clash of oversized personalities: the stubborn, foul-mouthed Mayor Rahm Emanuel against the brash chemistry-teacher-turned-union-president Karen Lewis. Even progressive media hyped Lewis as the driver of the union's victory, praising her personal toughness as more than a match for Emanuel. It was classic "Great Man" historicism, tracing the strike's origins to leaders' personal traits.

Few accounts mentioned the constituencies behind these leaders. For Emanuel, this includes anti-union charter-school advocates, who donated $12 million toward his election. In Lewis's case, it was the dictates of her

30,000 members. Indeed, the CTU is one of the most vibrantly democratic union locals in the United States.

Since a 2010 upheaval within the CTU, rank-and-file teachers have made up the union's leadership, and members make many of its day-to-day decisions. Public actions are typically planned and executed by members themselves, not paid staff. And the CTU took the incredible step of extending its September strike an extra two days to ensure that members had a chance to examine and debate the proposed contract. As Lewis puts it, "We put the power into the hands of the rank and file, where it belongs."

In recent decades, as the American labor movement has declined in membership and power, several unions have undergone a sea change, with new leaders proposing bold visions for how to revitalize labor. But rarely have those visions been as closely tied to a commitment to member-led democracy as in the CTU.

SHIFTS IN LEADERSHIP

Unlike many unions, in which officials cling to power for decades, the CTU has a long history of leadership turnover. Even when leaders did not run the union democratically, the CTU's structure allowed for reform caucuses to develop. The United Progressive Caucus (UPC), which was rooted in racial justice caucuses in the 1970s but failed to push back against corporate education reform, held power for three decades. Proactive Chicago Teachers (PACT), a reform caucus pledging to recapture a past union militancy, briefly unseated the UPC in 2001—the same year that current Secretary of Education Arne Duncan became Chief Executive Officer of Chicago Public Schools (CPS), pushing an agenda of closing public schools and opening charters.

Leadership changed hands three times in nine years—an incredible frequency compared to most American unions. Then, in 2010, teachers elected the Caucus of Rank and File Educators (CORE), a reform caucus with deep roots in community-level education equality fights. CORE had learned from PACT's failures. Upon her election as CTU president, Lewis stated that CORE would "change this into a democratic union responsive to its members." CORE immediately began restructuring the union. Leadership broadened the rights and responsibilities of members in the governing House of Delegates. Fourteen member-led committees, from political action to media, were tasked with central roles in the union's day-to-day functioning. A new training program prepared delegates and members for union organizing and governance. At schools, committees of teachers, parents, and students were organized to facilitate activism independent of union leadership. Quickly, educators began to take control of their union. "We turned our members into organizers, then we cut them loose," says CTU staffer Matt Luskin.

That commitment to bottom-up engagement was on full display during the 2012 strike. Members spontaneously planned and executed actions such as protests against Democratic aldermen hostile to the strike, often without even a nudge from staff.

Kim Walls, a science teacher at Robert Fulton Elementary, had never been active before CORE members approached her in 2010. She attended the union's summer organizing program, where she first heard about tax increment financing (TIFs), a city policy that diverts resources away from public institutions such as schools to corporations.

On September 14, the union and the Grassroots Collaborative coalition planned a rally against TIFs downtown, focusing on billionaire hotel heiress and CPS board member Penny Pritzker. Her company, Hyatt Hotels, had received $5.2 million in TIF funds to build a new hotel in Hyde Park, where Walls lives.

Walls recalls Luskin telephoning her days before the action. "I said, 'Matthew, I'm not going downtown. There's a Hyatt right here.'" She told Luskin she would organize her own protest against Hyatt in Hyde Park. "He just said, 'Go for it.'"

So Walls called Hyde Park–area teachers and told them to "call their people" to come out to the action. When the day came, 300 teachers and supporters marched on the hotel—with little to no support needed from union staff.

Two extra days

After the strike's first week, many Chicagoans assumed that teachers would return to class Monday. Emanuel had lost the public relations battle: polls showed strong majorities, especially among CPS parents and Chicagoans of color, backing teachers. The union had the upper hand in bargaining, and the draft agreement CTU leaders brought to the House of Delegates meeting that Sunday, which CPS had signed off on, was rumored to be strong.

Which is why many in the local media were stunned when delegates voted to stay on strike for at least two more days—not because the proposed agreement was unfavorable, but because members wanted more time to examine it. Instead of forcing membership to decide on a contract that they had not read and did not fully understand, delegates extended the strike to ensure that members "wouldn't feel like anything was being shoved down our throats," as delegate and first-grade teacher Yolanda Thompson put it.

Favorable coverage in the mainstream press evaporated. Nevertheless, on Monday morning, teachers arrived at picket lines outside their schools at 6:30 a.m., eager to review the proposal but lacking a formal process. Becca Barnes, a ninth-grade history teacher on the South Side, says teachers at her school made photocopies of the contract, stood against a fence, and spent an hour reading through line by line, circling key sections and commenting in the margins—as though they were grading papers. As they began picketing, the contract was still on their minds. So Barnes and her fellow teachers— about one hundred of them—decided, right there on the picket line, to walk to a nearby park and read it together.

So, sitting together at a park, they read through every line, passionately debating the victories and concessions hashed out at the bargaining table. "It was very emotional," says Barnes. "Some people were sick of striking. Others said, 'This isn't good enough. This one line is reason enough for me to stay out.'"

Similar scenes took place throughout Chicago. For the first time, teachers were studying every word of their contract, the principal document governing their work lives, sometimes emotionally and contentiously, but together. The union voted to ratify the contract October 3, with 79 percent of membership in favor.

One CTU staffer, Norrine Gutekanst, says she was "a bit concerned" when delegates extended the strike, thinking "public opinion would turn against us." "It was inconvenient," she says, "[but] because this leadership is committed to bottom-up democracy, we just felt like we had to do this, and that it would result in a much stronger union."

Proponents of the CTU's bottom-up organizing style say there is no other way to win. "Top-down just does not work. It's the style of the bosses," says Kenzo Shibata, a CORE member who taught English for ten years before heading social media for the union.

Kim Walls sees her union activism, begun in earnest only three years ago, as a starting point. She and her colleagues have been emboldened through their organizing and are considering finding a teacher to run for city council. She says she texted a CTU staffer about their plans. "He responded, 'Great. Let me know when the meeting is.'"

"Even without unions, Walmart warehouse employees win change"

By David Moberg (2013)

In an era in which anti-union laws and a hamstrung National Labor Relations Board make forming a union difficult, some organizers have advanced the theory that workers without a union can still act like a union—collectively protesting conditions, seeking government intervention or even striking. When they do, the theory goes, they will often win. And if workers realize they have such power, they are more likely to have the stamina to persevere in formally establishing a union. Then they can infuse the larger labor movement with their new energy.

That theory is now looking more and more practicable as workers at businesses from car washes to Walmart win improvements, and sometimes unions, by taking action even when the path to a union is not clear. Workers at Walmart-controlled warehouses in southern California and Illinois have played a leading role in this latest mini-upsurge, using a mix of strikes, protests, and lawsuits to demand improvements. Over the past few weeks, they saw another of the incremental victories that may add up to a sea change. Seventy-five nonunion workers at a giant warehouse in Mira Loma, California, serving Walmart won big pay and benefit increases, as well as potentially more stable employment.

Before they began protesting conditions and pay at the California distribution center, most of the workers earned only about $8.50 an hour (just above California's $8 minimum wage), with no benefits. Like many in the warehouse sector, they were employed by subcontractors—in this case, Rogers-Premier Unloading Services and Impact Logistics, two companies that were retained by Schneider Logistics, which was in turn hired by Walmart.

Interestingly, the road to winning the raises began with a lawsuit that focused on winning unpaid back wages, not higher pay. Two years ago, the workers—supported by Warehouse Workers United (WWU), a worker center backed by the Change To Win union federation—filed suit charging Schneider and the subcontractors with failing to pay millions of dollars that the companies owed by law and forcing their employees to work in abusively hot conditions. Later, the federal judge hearing the case added Walmart as a defendant, striking a blow at the common legal subterfuge that big companies like Walmart use: hiring layers of contractors to avoid legal responsibility for workers who ultimately work for them and under conditions set by them.

Over the past two years, workers at the Mira Loma warehouse have also participated in protests and pilgrimages, strikes and shareholder actions.

These actions both built solidarity and nurtured the workers' will to act. And they delivered a message to managers about the workers' determination to gain better treatment that reinforced the demand for legal relief.

In February 2012, Schneider brought the roughly seventy workers for Rogers-Premier under its control as their direct employer and gave them raises and benefits. Now, according to WWU, Schneider has become the direct employer of about seventy-five Impact workers, which the worker center believes to be all or nearly all of the subcontractor's employees. For the workers, the change brought an increase in pay to around $13.50 an hour, health insurance, and paid days off for sickness and vacation. "It means it will be easier to take care of my family," Mira Loma warehouse worker Reynaldo Ríos Ibañez told Warehouse Workers United.

For the broader movement, WWU spokesperson Elizabeth Brennan argues, Schneider's shift proves that Walmart and the warehouses can pay close to a living wage without hardship. "Improving the quality of warehouse jobs and paying a living wage are possible," she says. It also makes it clearer that warehouse workers are not seasonal temps but year-round employees.

Despite these advances, Brennan says that "union recognition is a long way off" for Walmart warehouse workers. But in theory, that will come more easily now as the larger wave of strikes and protests by low-wage workers helps the warehouse workers understand that the economic problems they face are not their fault but due to a more basic problem: Their employers do not pay them enough, Brennan says.

Warehouse workers also are learning that they can bring change when they act together, including fighting back against employer retaliation. That lesson holds true of both the Mira Loma actions and the broader warehouse movement: "Every time warehouse workers have spoken up, filed complaints, or gone on strike," Brennan says, "they've won improvements."

"IS FIGHT FOR 15 FOR REAL?"

By Micah Uetricht (2013)

In August, fast-food workers in fifty-eight cities walked off the job—a dramatic escalation of a campaign for a $15-per-hour wage that has tapped into a latent anger among low-wage workers, whose economic precariousness at a time of record corporate profits has led to strikes, a tactic long thought out of style.

As Occupy Wall Street did in 2011, strikers have focused the national narrative on the appalling inequality of twenty-first century America and the evaporation of well-paying jobs with benefits. But as the campaign—backed by the Service Employees International Union (SEIU)—has advanced, some in labor have worried that the strikes focus entirely on shifting the narrative around low-wage work while giving long-term organizing among low-wage workers themselves short shrift.

To discuss the campaign, *In These Times* turned to Peter Olney, organizing director of the International Longshore and Warehouse Union, and a former SEIU organizer; Jane McAlevey, former SEIU national deputy director of strategic campaigns and SEIU Nevada executive director, who chronicled her experiences in *Raising Expectations (and Raising Hell): My Decade Fighting for the Labor Movement*; and Trish Kahle, a worker at Whole Foods and a member of the SEIU-backed Workers Organizing Committee of Chicago, a new union that is leading the Fight for 15 campaign. Representatives of SEIU were invited to participate in this discussion, but declined.

What has the campaign accomplished so far?

TRISH: We had been trying to organize at Whole Foods for at least five months in Chicago, but no unions thought it was worth investing in a campaign. Fight for 15 gave us resources to actually organize at work. After the April 24th, 2013 strike, the organizers at our store and many other stores got raises—I got a $1.50 raise and other people got small promotions. We also got management to agree to a new attendance policy. And now we actually have a water cooler and a place where we can take breaks. Fight for 15 is giving people an idea of how organizing works.

JANE: Any time we're talking about inequality nationally, it's a good thing. Many people have long argued that the labor movement needs to act on behalf of the entire working class. SEIU is doing that here.

Some say Fight for 15 is little more than a public relations campaign—do you agree?

TRISH: Among organizers, the campaign's purpose is debated. For example, on August 29, staff were making sure as many cities struck as possible, regardless of the level of organization—rather than actually organizing and exerting more power in certain workplaces. At the same time, the "minority strike" has brought a lot of organizing into the open. That has to translate into deepening the organizing and developing rank-and-file leaders.

PETER: At the Bay Area August 29 rally, there was a huge turnout of supporters, but a negligible number of fast-food workers. An organizer told me that seventy-two workers were present at a meeting to authorize a strike in forty fast-food outlets and that about forty workers walked. The action got tremendous press, but I'm concerned about actual participation by workers and what kind of organization is built in the long run.

TRISH: The organization is extremely uneven—across the country and even in Chicago. At places like Whole Foods, Subway, and Dunkin Donuts, there is a high level of worker organization.

Chicago Dunkin Donuts workers' air conditioning went off during a heat wave, and they phoned the union office and said, "We are going on strike. We put a padlock on the door. We need you to come down and support us." That shows a level of worker-driven activity that is not present at every workplace. And so the question for me is how we actually get to that level. I'm not sure the public relations tactic that relies on the goodwill of politicians and community organizations is the best or most direct way.

In Chicago, half of our staff is in research, communications, and outreach, and half is dedicated to turf organizing. We would want to see that shift toward more organizing in the stores.

JANE: Nationally, some of the bigger unions are trending toward advocacy work, and to me that is the wrong direction. In the last fifteen years, a lot of money has been donated to public relations and research. But we need money and resources devoted to teaching workers about how to use their own power—city by city, shop by shop—to win real gains.

What specific challenges does organizing the fast-food sector pose?

PETER: Unlike SEIU's previous victories with janitors—where the union already had a mighty fortress of organized commercial janitor locals in New York, Chicago, and San Francisco as a base to organize from—and with homecare workers—where you had public financing and could mobilize public power—in Walmart, or the fast-food industry, you're starting with a blank slate and doing pure private-sector organizing.

That will require a long-term commitment of resources, and particularly a commitment of creative and bright organizers like Trish who are willing to dedicate their lives to building power from the bottom up and creating networks across a city and a region.

Final thoughts?

PETER: Workers are walking out on strike and going back to work with impunity, at least initially. But then what we're seeing on the Walmart campaign, and certainly we'll see it in the fast-food campaign, is firings six months later for absenteeism or some other trumped-up infraction. How can we defend these workers? And how do we prevent a chilling effect on the rest of the workforce if we don't have the organization necessary to defend the fired workers?

JANE: Anything that encourages direct action is good. It'd be good if other unions were at least attempting new stuff like SEIU is currently doing. If organizers in every city, every region, every part of the country put their heads together, there could be a strategy to work together with the existing rank-and-file membership and go for power.

TRISH: What Fight for 15 has taught us is that if we fight we can win. We already started making gains at work. We've united when no one thought we could. So if any low-wage workers see this, I would encourage them to join us. The more united we are, the stronger we are. This is a historic moment, and I think when people look back, they're going to say we did something amazing that no one believed we could do.

"Big Business Aims to Crush Worker Centers"

By Micah Uetricht (2013)

Worker centers and other nonunion labor organizations have grown immensely over the past two decades, with some in the labor movement hoping their growth will help revive a moribund labor movement. It was perhaps inevitable, then, that the same forces working for decades to destroy unions are now launching an attack on worker centers.

The Center for Union Facts (CUF), an anti-union advocacy organization funded by corporations, took out a full-page ad in the *Wall Street Journal* in July claiming that worker centers—traditionally understood as nonunion community organizations supporting and organizing low-wage, often immigrant workers, such as the New York Taxi Workers Alliance or the Restaurant Opportunities Center United—are little more than front groups for unions. "Big labor unions are trying to disguise themselves as 'worker centers' to push their organizing and political agendas," the text reads.

The ad followed two articles in the paper, one detailing the work of such organizations alongside unions in the car wash industry in New York City, the other noting a letter by two Republican members of the House of Representatives encouraging Secretary of Labor Thomas Perez to issue a ruling on whether such groups are subject to the same financial disclosure requirements as unions.

It's probably no coincidence that the attacks on "alt-labor groups"—as labor journalist Josh Eidelson dubbed them—have stepped up just as such groups are receiving a surge of attention. Organizations like worker centers have been growing since the 1990s, but the recent strikes against fast-food and retail companies under the Fight for 15 campaign and Walmart under OUR Walmart have put nonunion labor organizing on the map—and in the crosshairs of labor's enemies. The American Federation of Labor and Congress of Industrial Organizations (AFL-CIO) has become increasingly willing to aid development of such organizations, extending a union charter to the New York Taxi Workers Alliance and signing partnership agreements with the National Domestic Workers Alliance, the National Guestworker Alliance, and the National Day Laborer Organizing Network.

Worker centers and alt-labor groups interact with unions in widely different ways. Some, like Working America, are direct projects of unions or labor federations; others, like Voces de la Frontera (VDLF) in Milwaukee, are independent of unions but sometimes work closely with them; others view unions with near-open hostility. This range seems to escape the CUF, whose ad lumps all worker centers into the same broad category as fronts for unions.

Janice Fine, an associate professor in the School of Management and Labor Relations at Rutgers, says the accusation leveled in CUF's ad that worker centers are actually stealth unions is "ahistorical." "Only a very tiny percentage grew from [unions]," she says, describing the "completely different DNA" of organizations that grew from ethnic institutions, nonprofits, legal services, and religious institutions.

Mark Brenner, director of Labor Notes, a labor reform organization that has pushed for increased transparency within unions, notes that like any nonprofit, worker centers already must file 990s, the annual required tax report for nonprofits. The real motivation to reclassify worker centers as unions is to allow bosses to attack worker centers with the same ferocity they currently use to attack unions, he says.

Restaurant Opportunities Centers United (ROC), a restaurant workers organization with ten affiliates in major cities around the country, faced similar attacks from restaurant owners targeted with lawsuits for wage theft and discrimination in New York City. The Fireman Hospitality Group, owners of eight high-end New York restaurants, responded with a countersuit alleging, among other things, that ROC "act[ed] as a front for a local union."

The National Labor Relations Board eventually ruled in ROC's favor. But Teófilo Reyes, the organization's program coordinator, says he is not surprised similar attacks are being leveled at organizations like his.

"Worker centers are doing effective work, so corporate interests are looking to stop them," Reyes says. "They want to maintain the status quo of low wages and expanding inequality."

"A CO-OP STATE OF MIND"

By Ajowa Nzinga Ifateyo (2014)

In 2006, Daniela Salazar, then a twenty-two-year-old mother of two, was making about $7.25 an hour doing restaurant work and housecleaning. For three hours every month, she also stood on the street in Brooklyn with twelve other women passing out flyers, rain or shine (and sometimes snow).

They were promoting a cleaning company of a new kind: one that would not only provide them with jobs and more money to support their families, but would also make them business owners.

That company was a worker cooperative called Sí Se Puede—"Yes, We Can" in Spanish. The women started the co-op with the help of the SCO Family of Services' Center for Family Life, a social-service agency and advocacy group for families. They marketed their business in this low-tech way for months, slowly building up a clientele until they could afford a website.

Eight years later, Sí Se Puede has sixty-four member-owners. It grossed over a million dollars in 2013. The worker co-op may soon have another source of income: a line of cleaning products. Salazar's pay at Sí Se Puede has climbed to $20 to $23 an hour, letting her work fewer hours a week and spend more time with her family, which has grown to include three children.

Back when she was leafleting on corners, Salazar never imagined that the business would enjoy such success.

"In the beginning, it was very hard to grow," she says laughing. "We look back, and we are amazed."

The worker cooperative model, in which a business is owned and controlled by its members, is rarely taught in U.S. business schools, but it is gaining a reputation as a way for social service agencies and city councils to provide jobs for workers marooned by the current economy.

"There just aren't enough jobs for all the people who need and want them," says Jessica Gordon Nembhard, associate professor of community justice and social economic development at New York's John Jay College, and author of *Collective Courage: A History of African American Cooperative Economic Thought and Practice.* "Worker cooperatives address that niche."

Social and economic justice activists also favor worker cooperatives as a way of enabling workers to participate democratically in their workplace. Co-ops are seen as a key component of what is called the "solidarity economy." That term encompasses democratic, environmentally conscious, and socially responsible companies, along with alternative exchanges such as trade and bartering—any economic system that emphasizes concern for people and economic justice over pure profit.

"Worker cooperatives are one of the best solidarity economy structures for solving the problem of participation and ownership," says Gordon Nembhard. "When you own a business, you end up with a good stable job that you have control over and an asset that can appreciate over time and give you some stability."

Today, according to the U.S. Federation of Worker Cooperatives, the United States has more than 300 worker cooperatives in fields ranging from engineering, architecture, and computer technology to taxi driving, house cleaning, and construction. Some co-ops are small enough that all members participate in day-to-day decisions, while larger co-ops may be managed through boards and committees. The 2,300 members of the Bronx-based Cooperative Home Care Associates elect a governing board, which then appoints a manager. In San Francisco, the 220-member Rainbow Grocery is managed by volunteer committees of workers and an elected steering committee.

California leads the country in worker cooperatives with fifty-six, according to data from the University of Wisconsin's Center for Cooperatives and the University of Iowa's Department of Economics. New York State has the second-most with forty, and Massachusetts comes in third with twenty-five. Chicago has nine worker cooperatives, the most well-known of which is the New Era Windows Cooperative (formerly Republic Windows and Doors), formed after fired workers occupied their factory in 2008. Worker cooperatives are blossoming, in particular, among immigrants who struggle to find employment because they are undocumented, have difficulty speaking English, or lack particular job skills.

Despite the long history of worker co-ops in the United States, only recently have municipalities considered cooperatives as a solution to a sluggish economy in which jobs are scarce and well-paying jobs even scarcer. Richmond, California, emerged as a pioneer of co-op development four years ago when Mayor Gayle McLaughlin, a Green Party member, was looking for ways to create jobs for low-income residents. She had Richmond allocate $50,000 for a consultant to lead the creation of three cooperatives, which in turn inspired an anonymous donation of $50,000 for a worker co-op loan fund.

"Co-ops tend to be more difficult to get started than conventional businesses," says Marilyn Langlois, the coordinator of the Richmond Worker Cooperative Revolving Loan Fund, which provides loans of up to $20,000 for worker cooperative development and maintenance. "But once they're up and running, they tend to be very sustainable."

Indeed, it's not easy to create a co-op within a system that, for centuries, has celebrated profits over people and individualism over the good of the whole. All businesses need a business plan, a source of reliable funding, and professionals like lawyers and accountants, but worker cooperatives face the additional challenge of learning how to operate democratically. They must figure out how to make decisions (by consensus, voting, or some other process), and then decide such questions as the rights and responsibilities of member-owners, how much money will go to workers as profits and how much will go back into operations or reserves, how to cut ties with cooperative members who do not work out, and how to handle grievances.

Not to mention that the founders of worker cooperatives are often women, immigrants, low-income people, and people of color, who face additional challenges. They may have internalized racism, sexism, and classism and need coaching and confidence boosting to believe that business ownership is not only for the white, wealthy, and male.

Studies show that all of the extra work pays off. Once workers run their own businesses, they put more into them—they stay on jobs longer and are more productive and happy. People who start worker cooperatives also gain education and organizing skills, "which means that they then also contribute to an educated civic society," Gordon Nembhard says.

"BRINGING BACK THE STRIKE MAY BE OUR ONLY HOPE"

By Shaun Richman (2016)

On December 14, 2015, Chicago Teachers Union (CTU) Vice President Jesse Sharkey announced the results of the union's strike authorization vote. For the second time in three years, the union's membership voted overwhelmingly to strike if necessary. "Our ability to withhold our labor is our power," declared CTU President Karen Lewis on the eve of voting.

That axiom, that strikes are where unions derive their power, is pretty out of favor these days. A wave of disastrous strikes and lockouts beginning in the Reagan era that helped de-unionize much of American industry has left the surviving labor movement skittish about the prospect of full-scale walkouts. But bright spots like Fight for 15, Bargaining for the Common Good, and the Chicago teachers strike have shown that workers can win strikes—if one defines victory as workers walking away from the ordeal feeling more powerful.

In his book *Only One Thing Can Save Us,* labor lawyer Thomas Geoghegan expresses a preference for one-day strikes, which he has seen used effectively by the hotel employees union. In such a strike, a union signals its intent to return to work after twenty-four hours, allowing strikers to impact the employer's business but protecting them from permanent replacement.

My own union work so far has been in hotels, home health care, and education. I have worked on only a small number of work stoppages, most of a limited duration. In my experience, employers are working from such an ossified playbook that unions can get a lot of mileage out of doing the last thing that the boss and his lawyers expect.

For example, hotel employees can cost the company more money by not striking on the day the company expects, thus costing them the expense of paying and lodging scabs as well as the continued payroll costs of the union members who stayed on the job an extra day.

I don't prescribe a perfect form of strike. American workers will not learn to strike again from articles like this or books like Geoghegan's, which are really more for labor nerds and bookish organizers—they will only learn to strike by watching contemporary examples of workers striking. Since it's hard to raise chickens without eggs, even one-day "publicity strikes" have an educational value.

POSSIBLE PATHS FORWARD

Our challenge is to inspire even nonunion workers to think about their power and how to exercise it using the tools we have on hand: a union movement with miniscule density in only a handful of service- and public-sector industries largely led by staff who have precious little personal experience with leading job actions. We should be clear about how deep this deficit is.

One of the most promising labor projects of the moment is Bargaining for the Common Good. This is an effort by public-sector unions in Washington, Oregon, California, Minnesota, Wisconsin, Illinois, and Ohio to align their bargaining demands with each other and with community demands around progressive taxation, affordable housing, youth incarceration, and government transparency.

Another promising project is the Fight for 15. Some have dismissed the series of rolling one-day strikes for increases in the minimum wage and organizing rights as mere public relations stunts. But there is something deeply radical and significant at play here. Workers who don't even technically have a union are proving their value—and their power—to their bosses by withholding their labor.

A few years ago, it would have been inconceivable to most union strategists that the lowest paid and most vulnerable workers would be willing to risk it all as these fast-food workers have done. But, then, one is reminded of the old Dylan lyric: "When you got nothing, you got nothing to lose."

CHAPTER TEN

After the Crash: Searching for Alternatives

Introduction

By Frances Fox Piven

Protest movements tend to cluster in what are sometimes called "movement eras." The reasons are obvious. The disturbances, especially economic disturbances, that provoke one group to rise in anger and defiance affect others whose circumstances may be similar. These other groups may raise a different banner because their identities are different. Of course, it is also true that protest movements in one sector of a society can encourage protest in another.

In the aftermath of the recent economic crash, all sorts of groups and campaigns have emerged to challenge the status quo. We've seen a growing willingness to use more confrontational tactics among labor and racial justice activists and a renewed interest in socialism. In 2011, protests in the Wisconsin capitol by students and workers were soon followed by the youthful Occupy protests that spread rapidly from city to city. (We meet Occupy activists from across the country in this chapter's "An Occupy Road Trip" and "Voices From the Occupation.") Anti-foreclosure campaigns, profiled in "No Vacancies" and "Anti-Foreclosure Activists Put BlackRock in a Hard Place" in this chapter, gained steam around this time, while undocumented immigrant youth rights activists were also ramping up their tactics. The Fight for $15 campaign for higher wages began in 2012, with the Black Lives Matter movement—covered in the final three pieces—emerging the following year.

The importance of movement eras in shaping American history can hardly be exaggerated. From the revolutionary era when artisans and farmers took up arms against the British, to the abolitionist era when ardent white abolitionists in the North were joined by runaway slaves in the South, to the Populist era when insurgent farmers rose against the railroad and the banks, to the mass strikes of the 1930s, to the civil rights movement, moments of mass defiance do more than bring problems otherwise suppressed into the political limelight. They also threaten institutional disorder, compelling elites to address those issues.

Something like this is happening now. Why? As in the past, it is the broken promises of America's ruling elites, spectacular inequalities, pervasive insecurity and democratic processes turned into a circus of money and propaganda while elemental rights are blocked or twisted.

I say "broken promises" because it captures the core of the theories that dominate the study of social movements. Most of the time most people conform to the rules that govern social life. They conform because that is the condition for enjoying the routines of daily life, for the comforts of family and community, for a modicum of respect and well-being. When those comforts and rewards shrink or disappear and the ruling groups in a society are thought to be at fault, people are likely to rise up, especially if they believe they can have some effect on those who are responsible.

No wonder that in these eras some of the early expressions of discontent occur in electoral politics, the institutional arena that seems to promise that ordinary people can have an effect on the conditions that rule their lives. In our own era, we have seen socialist Kshama Sawant win a city council seat in Seattle ("Can Socialists Win Elections in the U.S.?" explains why). Bill de Blasio became mayor of New York City, the very capital of capitalism, campaigning on the theme of a tale of two cities: a city of the rich, and a city of the poor. And an avowed socialist, Bernie Sanders, was a serious contender for a major party nomination in 2016. (Joseph M. Schwartz describes Sanders' socialism and his campaign's appeal in "Bringing Socialism Back.")

There is truth, of course, in the old idea that electoral politics is the swamp in which dissidents drown, at least eventually. But a more hopeful truth lies in the complex interplay between movements and electoral politics. Movements can bring conflict and therefore interest and enthusiasm into electoral politics, and successes in that institutionalized realm can then energize movements.

Which brings me to the key question: Just what do protest movements do that gives them a political impact? The signposts by which we recognize a movement are familiar: the noise and clamor, the marches and crowds. These are the instruments of movements trying to communicate their issues to a broad audience, issues that have been ignored or submerged by official politics. Our contemporary movements have been brilliant and successful communicators. Their occupations and slogans and street actions have shifted the dominant American political discourse. Except on the extreme Right, politicians now have to at least pay deference to the issues of extreme inequality and police brutality.

But the big and victorious movements of our history have done more than communicate. They have mobilized the most fundamental source of power of ordinary people: the power to refuse to cooperate with the institutionalized routines upon which social life depends. The paradigmatic expression of this power is of course the strike, when workers refuse to play their normal role in economic production. But domestic workers and precarious workers and students and city dwellers and debtors can also assert their power. If factory workers walk out, the factory comes to a halt; but if nannies stay home, so do the parents whose children they mind; if urbanites block highways, traffic stops; if debtors refuse, lenders are at risk—and so is a financial system anchored to massive debt.

We've seen the disruptive potential of masses of defiant people before. It produced the big reforms of American history, from electoral representative government to the end of chattel slavery to curbs on monopoly, to legal protection of unions, to legislated civil rights for African Americans. To be sure, reforms can be and have been whittled away once movements subsided. But sadly, there are no permanent victories in political life. This is why we have to rise again. This is why the new movement era is so important.

"TAKE THE FIGHT TO THE STREETS"

By Stephen Lerner (2011)

A new activism is emerging in the United States and abroad, where people, in unexpected places, are standing up to challenge the rich and powerful. From recent uprisings in Egypt; to young people and workers in Europe marching and striking against shortsighted austerity plans; to the battle of nurses, teachers, firefighters, and community members in Wisconsin and the sit-ins and occupations of banks starting around the country, a movement is starting to grow.

After being battered and on the defensive, we have an opportunity in the United States to go on the offensive to transform the economy and politics of our country and create shared prosperity for all. Corporations have $1.6 trillion in cash reserves and are making record profits. After trillions in bailouts, they are even bigger and more dominant than before the economic crash.

In an ironic twist of history, the same people responsible for the global financial and economic meltdown are using a crisis of their own making to amass wealth and power in concentrations not seen since the beginning of the twentieth century. We are experiencing a corporate counterrevolution—the goal of which is to reverse the arc of the last one hundred years—to undo the historic gains that built up the middle class and secured greater equality; freedom; and economic, racial, and social justice.

REDEFINING THE PROBLEM

In order to further its goals, the Right has successfully created a narrative in which "big government, unions, and public employees are bankrupting the country and killing jobs." We need to shift that narrative to "Wall Street, multinational corporations, and the super-rich are bankrupting governments and communities, shipping away jobs, foreclosing our homes, destroying the middle class, and threatening our children's future."

Until we break this corporate stranglehold, we will have no money to solve state budget crises. In state after state, Democrats will make massive cuts to services and public-employee jobs like their Republican counterparts—they just won't demand an end to collective bargaining on top of it. And absent a strategy of escalating and dramatic actions that expose the wrongdoing of corporations and the uber-rich that got us into this mess, we are trapped in a strategy that depends on politicians to rein in the very corporations they are in thrall to.

Creating massive insecurity for Wall Street, corporations, and the super-rich is a precondition for fixing the economy and country. There can be no new "social contract," no "new New Deal," no comprehensive legislation that allows workers to organize and no limits to corporate power as long as corporate CEOs feel insulated from the suffering they cause.

They know far better than we do that their hold on power is dependent on our acquiescence to their false premises and pseudo free market ideology. Therefore we must directly challenge them in the streets so that they have more to lose by ignoring the public interest than by accepting real change.

Conditions have never been riper for a campaign to protect and grow the middle class. Escalating actions and civil disobedience are already springing up at banks, in politician's offices, at corporate franchises, and at home evictions around the country. In Los Angeles, dozens of homeowners from the Alliance of Californians for Community Empowerment were recently arrested sitting in at JP Morgan's offices to protest unfair foreclosures. In Washington, D.C., National People's Action occupied the Bank of America opposite the Treasury Department. In Detroit, the United Automobile Workers recently occupied a Bank of America branch by conducting a teach-in on the economy in the bank lobby. In Albany, New York, community groups and students occupied the capitol to protest budget cuts. In

Philadelphia, a sheriff's sale of a home was physically blocked. In Rochester, New York, Take Back the Land organized a two-week-long eviction defense that resulted in multiple arrests of local activists. This is just the beginning of what is possible.

"AN OCCUPY ROAD TRIP"

By Arun Gupta (2011)

A trope about mass movements is that they spring up from nowhere. That appears to be the case with the Occupy Wall Street movement, which went from an idea to a social force that reshaped the national debate in barely a month.

It may appear to be rootless, but the occupation of the Wisconsin state capitol in February 2011 and smaller successful episodes—like the Republic Windows and Doors sit-in in Chicago in December 2008, university students taking over part of a New School university building in the same month, and the three week "Bloombergville" encampment in New York City this past June—all influenced or shaped the Occupy Wall Street movement, which sprouted out of Manhattan's Zuccotti Park on September 17.

With its anarchist social norms and emphasis on economic issues and horizontal decision-making, the Occupy movement is also the heir to the "alter-globalization" movement that came to prominence during the 1999 World Trade Organization ministerial meetings in Seattle.

The Occupy movement was most profoundly influenced by the wave of democratic uprisings and public occupations that have stretched from Egypt, Tunisia, Bahrain, and Syria to Spain, Greece, Chile, and Puerto Rico over the last year.

This movement began as an anticapitalist revolt, and at Liberty Park the anticapitalism current is strong. In other large occupations I have visited, such as Chicago, Detroit, Philadelphia, and Pittsburgh, anticapitalism is also a recurring theme. But in each one there is also a mix of broad, even contradictory politics. Many occupiers told me they still see a central role for capitalism and that the main problem is the "system no longer works" and that the "American Dream is dead."

Many occupiers decline to offer specific demands, and that has helped this movement succeed by focusing outrage at the concentration of power and wealth among the 1 percent. The vagueness about demands allows everyone to see their particular issue as equivalent to everyone else's, thus creating a broad movement that even extends to the Right despite the anticapitalist

orientation. In various cities, from D.C. to Detroit, I have encountered occupiers who call themselves Republicans or conservatives or sound exactly
like Tea Party members in espousing values of self-reliance, hard work,
community, and locally based solutions, and declaring their opposition to
centralized power and government.

Nonetheless, outside the major cities, concrete demands percolate to the
surface. In Toledo, Ohio, a city rich in abandoned housing, Candice Milligan,
a thirty-year-old trans woman who lost her job as an auto mechanic two
years ago, says jobs and home foreclosures are important issues.

In Youngstown, Ohio, Chuck Kettering Sr., fifty-six, calls himself "the
poster boy for the rust belt." He says that the North American Free Trade
Agreement was "one of the biggest blows to our local economy." In 1973, he
started working for U.S. Steel, laboring in the blast furnace area at two different plants that shuttered. That was followed by auto-parts maker Delphi,
which he left in 2008 after his pay was due to be slashed from $28 an hour
to $16.

Karen Joseph, a fifty-nine-year-old Youngstown native, mentions the
new national health care law as a major concern, explaining that her family
spends about $800 a month on health insurance, one-third of their income.
Joseph is one of many who say good-paying jobs need to return; she has
been unsuccessfully trying to find work for the last five years.

At Occupy Detroit, Jerry Edwards, fifty-eight, says he started working
as a teenager in factories, including fourteen years at the Ford Saline plant
in Ypsilanti making dashboard panels. Leaning on a cane and with limited
work prospects because of kidney damage he suffered as a child, Edwards's
story is not unusual, but through the Occupy movement he now has a space
to tell it—and to be heard.

While visiting ten occupations in the Northeast and through the Great
Lakes in October, I have met homeless veterans, Latina mothers, gay activists,
African American youth, retired professors, anarchists, nurses, unemployed
union members, students, families, socialists, Native Americans, conservatives, and full-time workers representing dozens of different occupations.
We should thank the ruling elite: they have made class relevant again. What
is so powerful about this moment is that so many different groups of people
have banded together under the banner of the "99 percent."

At Liberty Park, Los Angeles Kaufman, a long-time activist and parent
of two children, says, "What this movement has done in a short period of
time is astonishing. It's sparked a national conversation about the concentration of wealth, and has the plutocrats quaking in their boots and Obama
nervous. Who needs demands when you can do that?"

"VOICES FROM THE OCCUPATION"

By Jeremy Gantz (2011)

The Occupy protesters have been ridiculed by the press, celebrated by the Left, and reviled by the Right—but rarely allowed to speak for themselves. After the initial New York protest morphed into a national movement in October, reporters struggled to understand the spectacle and pundits stepped in to pontificate and prognosticate. They were right about one thing: united in anger, the mostly young protesters have lost faith in America's political and economic system—but they don't always agree on how to repair it.

In October, *In These Times* held a call with protesters around the country, hoping to illuminate their intentions, ideals, and ultimate goals. Joining the discussion were Caitlin Manning, a filmmaker involved with Occupy Oakland; Jesse Myerson, a member of Occupy Wall Street's Media and Labor Outreach committees; Sam Jewler, who quit an internship to dedicate his time to Occupy DC; and Natalie Wahlberg, an unemployed college instructor on Occupy Chicago's Press Committee.

How do you respond to someone who says Occupy protesters don't really represent the 99 percent, that they're marginal and far more radical than most people?

CAITLIN: I have problems with the 99 percent rhetoric. On the one hand, it's true that the 1 percent who are running the country have a lot of power. On the other hand, among the 99 percent, there are divisions. It has been said many times that the cops are part of the 99 percent. But we at Occupy Oakland took a firm stand at the very beginning that cops—as long as they're cops—are not our friends and are not part of our movement. The Tea Party is part of the 99 percent, but they're not part of the movement.

JESSE: I take the opposite view. A sense pervades a lot of the population of Liberty Park in New York that the 99 percent isn't the claim that "everyone stands with us," but the claim that "we stand with everyone." Austerity budgets, demanded by the Wall Street fat cats who crashed the economy, threaten the jobs and pensions of cops as well. Christian fundamentalists and Tea Party folks would recoil at the gender queers we have down here with us, but they're losing their jobs as well. There is a moral beauty and a quiet nobility in standing with people who don't stand with you. They too are victimized by the same system that incentivizes abuse and exploitation.

How are Occupy committees trying to increase participation to reflect the full range of struggles that Americans engage in?

JESSE: In addition to labor unions, in New York we've been reaching out to the populations most affected by cuts to valuable social services. That includes people living in poverty, the unemployed, and not-for-profit organizations that work on foreclosure resistance. We're trying to make sure that the people who are left behind most are leading us and that we're responding to their needs.

SAM: We've got a lot of homeless people in our occupation. They've been particularly helpful with teaching us how to survive the colder weather.

CAITLIN: In Occupy Oakland, homeless people have really become very active in the camp. A lot of them have experience in food preparation, like at churches, so they've brought a lot of expertise to us. And in Oakland there's a very long history of black militancy—a lot of those people who are involved now in various grassroots communities have been working with us.

Many Occupy sites are increasingly defined by the struggle for public space, by conflicts with police. How crucial is a stable protest site for building a sense of community and the movement more broadly?

NATALIE: It is essential to have a permanent place where we can have and grow a community. There's a lot of press about our interactions with the police, but we choose to use that as a platform to get the Occupy Chicago message out.

SAM: These places are not just "places"; these are our communities that we've built. A lot of people are sleeping there every single night, so it's more than just a base from which we protest.

CAITLIN: Yeah, it's a model of the new society that we're all struggling to develop in these encampments. Incredible transformations happen, like one guy was telling me the other day about how he used to be homophobic but because of all the queer people and trans people involved, he totally changed his mind.

Why is it important that these protests are structured so horizontally, with various committees rather than clear leaders? What is the downside of the highly egalitarian General Assemblies?

JESSE: The downside in New York is that it becomes inefficient, almost crippling. Which is fine. That's the thing about democracy—it takes forever and it requires a lot of diligence. If what you wanted was efficiency, you'd turn to totalitarianism. The Occupy Movement is trying to show that our country's democracy is a facade, behind which there's this ugly plutocracy where the wealthy control the government. Setting up this alternative, radical democracy draws a stark contrast to the type of democracy offered by the 1 percent.

CAITLIN: In Oakland the General Assembly process has been evolving. There have been moments of clusterfuck, but a facilitation committee meets everyday and says, "OK, this didn't work. We have to modify our process."

NATALIE: Even though our democracy is painful and slow, people want to be involved. I think that just speaks to the empowerment they feel of being part of a movement that actually listens to them—part of a society that they have a stake in.

"The violent silence of a new beginning"

By Slavoj Žižek (2011)

What to do after the Wall Street occupation, after the protests that started far away (in the Middle East, Greece, Spain, United Kingdom) reached the center, and now, reinforced, roll back around the world? One of the great dangers the protesters face is that they will fall in love with themselves, with the nice time they are having in the "occupied" places. In a San Francisco echo of the Wall Street occupation on October 16, a guy invited the crowd to participate as if it was a hippy-style happening in the 1960s: "They are asking us what is our program. We have no program. We are here to have a good time."

Carnivals come cheap—the test of their worth is what remains the day after, and how they change our normal daily life. The protesters should fall in love with hard and patient work—they are the beginning, not the end. Their basic message should be: the taboo is broken. We do not live in the best possible world. We are obliged to think about alternatives.

The Western Left has come full circle: after abandoning the so-called "class struggle essentialism" for the plurality of antiracist, feminist, gay rights, etc., struggles, "capitalism" is now re-emerging as the name of THE problem. So the first lesson to be learned is, Do not blame people and their attitudes. The problem is not corruption or greed, the problem is the system that pushes you to be corrupt. The solution is not found in the slogan "Main Street, not Wall Street," but to change the system in which Main Street cannot function without Wall Street.

There is a long road ahead, and soon we will have to address the truly difficult questions—questions not about what we do not want, but rather about what we DO want. What social organization can replace the existing capitalism? What type of new leaders do we need? What new institutions, including those of control, should we shape? The twentieth century alternatives obviously did not work.

It is thrilling to enjoy the pleasures of the "horizontal organization" of protesting crowds with egalitarian solidarity and open-ended free debates, but as we do so we should bear in mind the words of Gilbert Keith Chesterton: "Merely having an open mind is nothing; the object of opening the mind, as of opening the mouth, is to shut it again on something solid."

This holds also for politics in times of uncertainty: The open-ended debates will have to coalesce not only in some new Master-Signifiers, but also in concrete answers to the old question: "What is to be done?"

At the same time it is important to simultaneously remain subtracted from the pragmatic field of negotiations and "realist" proposals. Everything we say now can be taken (recuperated) from us—everything except our silence. This silence, this rejection of dialogue, of all forms of clinching, is ominous and threatening to the establishment, as it should be.

Wall Street protests are a beginning, and one has to begin like that. A formal gesture of rejection is more important than positive content, because only such a gesture opens up the space for a new content. So we should not be terrorized by the perennial question: "But what do they want?" After all, this is the archetypal question addressed by a male master to a hysterical woman: "You whine and you complain, but do you know at all what you really want?" In the psychoanalytic sense, the protests effectively are a hysterical act, provoking the master, undermining his authority. And the question "But what do you want?" aims precisely to preclude the true answer—its real purpose is: "Tell it in my terms or shut up!"

"No vacancies: squatters move in"

By Rebecca Burns (2012)

After three years of staying in her sister's living room, Tene Smith decided to move her family into a home that had sat vacant on Chicago's South Side for more than two years.

With the help of Liberate the South Side, a Chicago-based organization that targets vacant homes for re-occupation and spent months renovating the house, Smith and her three children moved in during a public ceremony attended by community members and the media in January 2012. "I was fearful when I first made this commitment," she said, "but as the days passed I had a sense of independence that had eluded me for a long time."

The term "squatter" conjures images of the predominantly young, urban hipsters who in decades past claimed vacant property in areas such as New York City's Lower East Side. But with five times as many vacant homes as homeless people in the United States today, a new wave of squatters—just as likely to be hard-hit families like Smith's as young activists making a political statement—is moving into vacant foreclosed properties in cities like Chicago, New York, and Minneapolis.

Today's housing movement has yet to approach the pace of its predecessors—historians Richard Boyer and Herbert Morais estimate that in 1932, unemployed workers' councils moved 77,000 evicted families back into their homes in New York City alone. But buoyed by the support of the Occupy movement, housing rights groups have stepped up their efforts.

With more than 1 billion people worldwide now living in informal settlements, journalist Robert Neuwirth argues that squatters' communities are among the primary creators of housing in the developing world. Now, in the context of a global foreclosure crisis, a squatters' movement is emerging across the developed world to claim otherwise vacant buildings as homes.

In Spain, established squatters' networks have converged with the M-15 movement of "indignados." The collaboration between experienced squatters and M-15 activists has produced, among other things, highly functional "squatting offices" in major cities that coordinate information on empty buildings and offer consultations to people who wish to squat.

In Ireland, squatters linked to the Occupy movement have begun taking over the thousands of properties that speculators handed to the National Assets Management Agency, a national bank created to buy up bad property development loans after the housing market crash.

Though many U.S. states have "squatter's laws" stipulating that occupants who have been in a property for more than thirty days can only be evicted through a formal legal process, the ambiguity surrounding the situation can be dangerous for families living in vacant homes.

After Tene Smith and her family had been occupying their new home for more than a month, its long-absent owner, who had fallen into foreclosure in 2007, re-emerged. Smith decided to leave, acknowledging that "our fight was with the bank and not the homeowner."

Housing groups have in the past two years won a string of less ambiguous victories by pressuring banks to reduce the principal of mortgage holders in foreclosure. For the first time, politicians are calling for a large-scale principal write-down. But Max Rameau, an organizer with the housing rights group Take Back the Land, says it would be a shame if the movement were to stop there. "If the government puts out a principal reduction offer, and the movement jumps on it and … does nothing for the low-income people of color who suffered the most under this crisis, that will be a real sellout," he says.

Rameau, who has been moving people into vacant homes and doing eviction defenses with Take Back the Land since 2007, says that principal reduction only helps homeowners who are employed and does nothing for the public housing residents facing a crisis that is "objectively worse" than the foreclosure crisis.

Though the mortgage crisis has created political space for a movement to emerge, Rameau says that the ultimate goal is to create more affordable housing and to give communities control over how it is managed. "Our real objective is not to target banks," he concludes. "Our real objective is to fulfill the human right to housing."

"ANTI-FORECLOSURE ACTIVISTS PUT BLACKROCK IN A HARD PLACE"

By Sarah Jaffe (2013)

The pink granite on the floor and walls of BlackRock's New York City head-quarters at 52nd Street and Park Avenue provided excellent acoustics for the protest chants that echoed through it Wednesday afternoon. Members of New York Communities for Change (NYCC) and the Home Defenders League took the investment management company to task for suing Richmond, California, after the city pledged to use eminent domain to save its residents from foreclosures.

"A lot of these companies try to hide under cover of darkness," Skipp Roseboro, one of the NYCC members at the action, said. "We're trying to call attention to their actions."

NYCC members made up a good part of the thirty or so people who walked in a picket line through BlackRock's lobby, waving NYCC flags and holding signs that declared "The big banks took our homes away through predatory lending. Now, we're taking them back."

Jean Sassine of Queens Village held a letter from the Home Defenders League to BlackRock CEO Laurence Fink, whose $75.8 million salary makes him the highest paid financial services CEO in the country. He admitted before a crowd at a public event earlier this month that if something was not done about "wage compression" and foreclosures, "we're going to have a greater 'have' and 'have-not' society."

"Mr. Fink knows that keeping neighborhoods together should be a priority but has decided to fight the city of Richmond," Sassine declared in the lobby of BlackRock, his words echoing off the granite and from the mouths of his colleagues in the "people's mic" style of crowd repetition. "He has decided to make BlackRock a leader in doing the wrong thing."

The protest was just one of several actions taking place across the country on Wednesday, coordinated by the Home Defenders League in solidarity with Richmond and its underwater homeowners. The city of Richmond has put forth a plan to seize 624 homes under its right of eminent domain—which requires the city to pay market value for the homes. Because this market value is less than the mortgages on the homes, which banks have refused to write down, this action would allow the city to sell the homes back to the homeowner at a lower rate, thereby lowering their mortgage payments and preventing foreclosure.

The banks and financial entities in question—BlackRock, PIMCO, and Wells Fargo among them—have dug in their heels and sued the city rather than accept the offered price. Fink argues that preventing foreclosures is not an appropriate public purpose for eminent domain. Instead, he suggests that cities use the privilege in ways that were "for the better of the whole than the few," as when Los Angeles tore down a neighborhood to build Dodger Stadium in the 1950s.

Embattled homeowners like Sassine can't hope to match the resources BlackRock and the rest of the finance industry can bring to bear, so they're hoping a bit of public shaming will help. "BlackRock is not a commercial bank. They don't have storefronts that regular people visit," he said, so it's harder for everyday people to understand their role in the ongoing mortgage crisis. (BlackRock doesn't issue loans—instead, the company is an investor in financial products backed with Richmond mortgages.)

Sassine got involved with NYCC because his own Queens Village home is in foreclosure. He works in the film industry, which means his employment is often temporary to begin with, and money has been tight since the financial crisis. "We got into trouble when I got laid off at the same time as my wife needed surgery," he said. "We had to choose between paying the mortgage and health insurance."

"Can socialists win elections in the U.S.?"

By Bhaskar Sunkara and Micah Uetricht (2013)

"Indian-origin Kshama Sawant is first elected socialist in U.S.," read a headline from *The Times of India*, the world's most widely circulated English-language daily. This was testament to the attention Sawant's campaign for

Seattle City Council has generated—and to how much of America's socialist heritage has been forgotten.

Sawant isn't even the thousandth elected socialist in the United States, much less the first. At its peak a century ago, the Socialist Party of America polled at 6 percent nationally, had two representatives in Congress, and boasted hundreds of state and local legislators.

But for more than a generation, socialism has been virtually invisible on the American scene. Its return in several high-profile local city council races—Sawant's in Seattle, Ty Moore's in Minneapolis, and Seamus Whelan's in Boston—has been surprising.

Sawant's victory and Moore's close race have been labeled by some progressives as Cinderella tales of sorts: scrappy first-time politicians backed by a marginal socialist party (Socialist Alternative) battling against the Democratic Party. There's something appealing about the narrative. Yet the reality on the ground was different.

Sawant and Moore had the backing of the local housing and immigrant-rights movements, as well as labor. Sawant drew official endorsements from four different union locals, including her own, the American Federation of Teachers Local 1789. Moore attracted the support of the Service Employees International Union (SEIU) Minnesota State Council.

Both candidates out-fundraised their opponents and had access to labor and community activists willing to put in long hours to support their campaigns, creating a vastly superior ground game to the Democrats. Sawant also had the curious support of prominent liberal media outlets—most notably Seattle's alt-weekly *The Stranger*, which endorsed her campaign early on and covered it closely. *The Stranger* news editor Dominic Holden says that while the paper, and most Seattleites, don't share Sawant's politics, they saw in Sawant someone who would take on the "toady, aging city council that is increasingly out of touch with the people who live here."

The centerpiece of Sawant's campaign was a push for a $15-per-hour minimum wage, echoing the ongoing national push by fast-food workers. She also raised the idea of rent control in a city where housing costs are sky-rocketing. Both the minimum wage and affordable housing became central not only to Sawant's race, but to Seattle's other 2013 campaigns as well.

"People said, 'Okay, maybe I'm not a socialist, but I support these demands, and I like that this person seems like a serious fighter for these demands,'" Sawant says.

Though Sawant has secured a seat in City Hall, she sees electoral victories as offering limited gains. "This can't be our endgame," she says. "We can't accept that pushing the Democrats to the left is as far as we can go. We are looking for a much, much bigger change in society. But it's a process, and you have to bring people with you on the things you agree with, while being honest about your disagreements."

"Bringing socialism back"

By Joseph M. Schwartz (2015)

Socialism. For most of recent U.S. history, the word was only used in mainstream discourse as invective, hurled by the Right against anyone who advocated that the government do anything but shrink, as antitax advocate Grover Norquist once put it, "to the size where I can drag it into the bathroom and drown it in the bathtub."

How is it, then, that Senator Bernie Sanders (I-Vt.), a democratic socialist, has repeatedly drawn crowds in the thousands or tens of thousands in cities and towns throughout the nation? In a country that's supposed to be terrified of socialism, how did a socialist become a serious presidential contender?

Young people who came to political consciousness after the Cold War are less hostile to socialism than their elders, who associate the term with authoritarian Communist regimes. A *New York Times*/CBS News survey taken shortly before Sanders's November 19, 2015, Georgetown University speech on democratic socialism found that 56 percent of Democratic primary voters felt positively about socialism versus only 29 percent who felt negatively. Most of those polled probably do not envision socialism to be democratic ownership of the means of production, but they do associate capitalism with inequality, massive student debt, and a stagnant labor market. They envision socialism to be a more egalitarian and just society.

More broadly, a bipartisan consensus has developed that the rich and corporations are too powerful. More than forty years of ruling class attacks on working people has revived interest in a political tradition historically associated with the assertion of working class power—socialism.

What is democratic socialism?

So what do we mean by "democratic socialism"? Democratic socialists want to deepen democracy by extending it from the political sphere into the economic and cultural realms. We believe in the idea that "what touches all should be governed by all." The decisions by top-level corporate CEOs and managers, for example, have serious effects on their employees, consumers, and the general public—why don't those employees, consumers, and the public have a say in how those decisions get made?

Democratic socialists believe that human beings should democratically control the wealth that we create in common. The Mark Zuckerbergs and Bill Gateses of the world did not create Facebook and Microsoft; tens of thousands of programmers, technical workers, and administrative employees did—and they should have a democratic voice in how those firms are run.

To be able to participate democratically, we all need equal access to those social, cultural, and educational goods that enable us to develop our human potential. Thus, democratic socialists also believe that all human beings should be guaranteed access, as a basic social right, to high-quality education, health care, housing, income security, job training, and more.

And to achieve people's equal moral worth, democratic socialists also fight against oppression based on race, gender, sexuality, nationality, and more. We do not reduce all forms of oppression to the economic; economic democracy is important, but we also need strong legal and cultural guarantees against other forms of undemocratic domination and exclusion.

For Sanders, "democratic socialism" is a byword for what is needed to unseat the oligarchs who rule this new Gilded Age. In his much-anticipated Georgetown speech, Sanders defined democratic socialism as "a government which works for all of the American people, not just powerful special interests." Aligning himself with the liberal social-welfare policies of Franklin D. Roosevelt and Lyndon B. Johnson, Sanders called for restoring progressive income and strict corporate taxation to fund Medicare for All, paid parental leave, publicly financed child care, and tuition-free public higher education.

In truth, Sanders is campaigning more as a social democrat than as a democratic socialist. While social democrats and democratic socialists share a number of political goals, they also differ on some key questions of what an ideal society would look like and how we can get there. Democratic socialists ultimately want to abolish capitalism; most traditional social democrats favor a government-regulated capitalist economy that includes strong labor rights, full employment policies, and progressive taxation that funds a robust welfare state.

EMBRACING THE "S" WORD

Sanders has generated a national conversation about democratic socialist values and social democratic policies. He understands that to win such programs will take the revival of mass movements for low-wage justice, immigrant rights, environmental sustainability, and racial equality. To build an independent Left that operates electorally both inside and outside the Democratic Party, the Sanders campaign—and socialists—must bring together white progressives with activists of color and progressive trade unionists. The ultimate logic of such a politics is the socialist demand for workers' rights and greater democratic control over investment.

If Sanders's call for a political revolution is to be sustained, then his campaign must give rise to a stronger organization of long-distance runners for democracy—a vibrant U.S. democratic socialist movement.

"FROM HASHTAG TO STRATEGY: THE GROWING PAINS OF BLACK LIVES MATTER"

By Bill Fletcher, Jr. (2015)

In the last several months, the Black Lives Matter (BLM) movement has made headlines by engaging often aggressively—with Democratic presidential candidates. Each action brought with it pointed questions and often, tactical criticisms.

Meanwhile, several national and local organizations have come to be identified with the movement. Questions are emerging: How should we approach electoral politics? Should struggles for reforms be connected to a longer-term struggle for social transformation? Can U.S. capitalism accommodate the movement's demands?

Today, we lack a strong, conscious, self-identified Left, both nationally and within Black America. Despite the overall strength of the Black Lives Matter movement, the weakness of the Black Left has contributed to a downplaying of ideology, strategy, and the centrality of the black working class in the movement.

In These Times organized a panel to examine the challenges faced by BLM. Alicia Garza is a co-founder of the Black Lives Matter Network and helped conceive the slogan in 2013; Jamala Rogers is a founding member of the St. Louis–based Organization for Black Struggle and a long-time community organizer; R.L. Stephens is the founder of Orchestrated Pulse and an organizer in Minneapolis who was present at the Baltimore protests following the death of Freddie Gray.

Let's set some context: What exactly is Black Lives Matter?

ALICIA: I like this question because it's often confused. The Black Lives Matter Network was founded in 2013 after Trayvon Martin's killer was acquitted. Then there is the broader movement that is emerging to fight for black lives and has taken on the moniker of BLM … The movement has many ideologies and approaches, but is unified by the desire to make black lives matter.

Folks use BLM because it gives them a platform. At the Black Lives Matter Network, we aren't concerned with policing who is and who isn't part of the movement. If someone says they are part of the BLM movement, that's true—if they're working to make sure that black lives do matter. But we don't control the movement.

JAMALA: I don't think most people on the ground think BLM is overshadowing their work. The reason that the moniker or hashtag BLM took off is because it resonated in such a way with the Mike Brown case—that was like the straw that broke the camel's back. But it wasn't just that. It was not just centered on police violence—it was other kinds of issues, too.

R.L.: There's an organization called Black Lives Matter, but then there's the cultural moment and the political space that the hashtag and the organization have opened up to create a lot of movement opportunities. My question has always been, how are those movement opportunities being managed both by the BLM organization as well as all these other political actors who are trying to seize this momentum?

I've noticed a growing divide between rhetoric from the dominant voices within the Black Lives Matter Network and what I've heard from black people on the ground. Many see BLM rhetoric, tactics, and strategy as irrelevant to their lives and struggles. There's not actually a substantive connection there: people don't feel meaningfully engaged and advocated for by those entities. I'm seeing a lot of representational tactics, but I'm not seeing real power built at the ground level for marginalized people.

Another problem has to do with the substance of the demands. A primary demand of BLM, the organization and its affiliates, has been to ask politicians to say "Black Lives Matter." BLM activists recently met with Hillary Clinton, and one of them, after being asked directly by her for their demands, said essentially, "We as black people won't tell you what to do, so you shouldn't tell us what to do." That was staggering to me.

ALICIA: We have been clear that our strategy is to push the Democrats to acknowledge black people's concerns. This may not be your tactic—that's okay. It's not just about candidates saying "Black Lives Matter," though it is about exposing where candidates stand in relation to black people.

JAMALA: Whenever you pressure somebody in power, you need demands. But many newer people who are joining this movement don't know how that's done. That's okay. It's an opportunity for us to say, "Here's how it could have been done differently." But I'm not going to say, "You shouldn't have done that."

I see people critiquing tactics. But if somebody is doing something toward a collective goal—political education or campaigning for an elected official—that's fine. That's part of building a movement.

"Black Lives Matter Puts Prosecutors on Trial"

By Jennifer Ball (2016)

An unexpected winner emerged in the March 15, 2016 primaries: the movement for black lives. In major upsets, voters in the Chicago and Cleveland areas ousted two sitting prosecutors accused of bungling police-shooting cases. Young black activists staged formidable campaigns to oust the incumbents, providing concrete evidence of the movement's impact. By signaling that officials who fail to hold police accountable will pay a political price, the victories could also change the calculus of upcoming local elections.

According to a 2009 study, prosecutors win re-election as much as 95 percent of the time. Until now, even those criticized for their records on police prosecutions have generally emerged unscathed. Daniel Donovan, the former district attorney for Staten Island who failed to secure an indictment of police involved in the 2014 chokehold death of Eric Garner, went on to win a special election to the U.S. House in May 2015.

Not so for Cook County State's Attorney Anita Alvarez or Cuyahoga County Prosecutor Tim McGinty, whom voters sent packing by decisive margins. McGinty was pilloried last year for dissuading a grand jury from indicting the Cleveland police officers involved in the fatal 2014 shooting of twelve-year-old Tamir Rice, who was killed while playing with a toy pellet gun. Alvarez waited thirteen months to press charges against the Chicago police officer who shot Laquan McDonald sixteen times. Critics believe she might never have done so if a video of McDonald's killing had not been released under court order.

While recognizing the importance of getting hostile prosecutors out of office, many activists say they can be most effective by remaining independent from electoral campaigns. Assata's Daughters, a grassroots collective of black women, was one of several Chicago groups that staged rallies, banner drops, and teach-ins as part of the effort to defeat Alvarez. The campaign "set the precedent for how young black people can organize against elected officials without endorsing other candidates," says member Tess Raser. She emphasizes that the group will continue to hold Alvarez's progressive successor, Kim Foxx, accountable. "We recognize that no head prosecutor is going to save us, that no politician will be what saves us."

"THE RADICALISM OF BLACK LIVES MATTERS"

By Martha Biondi (2016)

Already, the Black Lives Matter (BLM) movement and the violence it exposes feel like a fixture of our media and social landscape, the images jarring and unrelenting: Tamir Rice, a boy playing with a toy gun, shot by charging police; police chasing middle-aged Walter Scott and shooting him in the back; the cold-blooded execution of Laquan McDonald on a Chicago street; and most recently, the close-range shooting of Alton Sterling in Baton Rouge and the point-blank killing of Philando Castile in Falcon Heights, Minnesota, as he reached for his wallet, next to his girlfriend, before the eyes of her child. At the same time, the determined, angry, mournful protests nationwide—on interstate highways, on college campuses, in city streets— have become highly visible as the first sustained grassroots challenge to American policing in U.S. history.

Despite the media's reductive framing, the movement is far from single-issue. If Bernie Sanders's presidential campaign sought to revitalize an electoral Left, BLM—along with the immigrant-rights struggle and the Fight for $15—is reminding us of the power of mass action, moral outrage, youth leadership, civil disobedience, boisterous demonstrations, sophisticated use of media, and spirited ideological debate in building a Left consciousness and a movement.

A closer look at BLM advocacy reveals a more comprehensive approach to social change than the media typically allows. Again and again, BLM has challenged the abandonment of black communities underlying this wave of police violence.

What unites the broad tent of BLM organizations and voices is a frustration with the lack of accountability for police who use excessive force and with the state's typical response: a task force or commission report that garners laudatory headlines and leads nowhere. Instead, this generation envisions more far-reaching change, including, even, a world without police. The insistent radicalism of the movement's demands and tactics place it at the vanguard of a re-energized Left.

A REAWAKENING

In late July, groups under the broad umbrella of the BLM movement, including Black Youth Project 100 (BYP 100), BLM DC, Million Hoodies, and the #LetUsBreathe Collective, organized a series of nationwide protests that illustrate the movement's radical ethos. Most targeted offices of police unions, which have shielded police from accountability after they use deadly force. The occupation of these offices, in acts of civil disobedience, led to a spate of arrests.

In Chicago, activists focused on shutting down the Homan Square police complex, a notorious "black site" where, according to the *Guardian*, thousands of people have been secretly detained and interrogated, and some tortured.

Notwithstanding a circle of stoic, heavily-armed police, the event was suffused with determination, black affirmation, and righteous anger. As protesters put their bodies on the line to block entrances to Homan Square, a buoyant crowd of young people chanted, "We don't need no cops" and "We shut shit down." Followed by a "mic check" that led to rounds of "we are here because we love queer black people"; "we are here because black people deserve to be free"; "the whole damn system is guilty as hell"; and "I believe that we will win!"

This defiant black-led youth movement is the first of its kind since the black freedom struggle of the 1960s. It's important, however, to see it not only within the history of black struggle, but within the history—and future—of the Left. Many may associate the U.S. Left and socialist traditions with white male leadership, a focus on class, and a disregard of race, gender, and sexuality, but this is inaccurate and incomplete. Black, Latino, and Asian American activists of all genders have participated in Old and New Left traditions for over a century, waging struggles to press anti-imperial, antiracist, and feminist consciousness to the forefront of movements for social change. Major leaders of the civil rights movement identified as socialists, most famously Martin Luther King, Jr. Yet for many young activists of color, the word "socialist" still has a white male ring to it, and the Sanders campaign's initial fumbling with BLM unfortunately revived this older association.

For leftists to assume, based on BLM's critiques of Sanders, that the movement is a phenomenon apart from the Left, without a class lens and with nothing to teach it, would be a grave mistake. The movement has exposed, for example, how the neoliberal order uses policing to shift the burden of taxation from those with the most to those with the least. Police nationwide ticket the poor to bring in revenue in low-tax jurisdictions. Officer Darren Wilson's killing of Michael Brown in Ferguson and the resulting outpouring of protest led to the exposure of the financial entrapment of poor black drivers and pedestrians. The Department of Justice concluded that every branch of government in Ferguson was guilty of racial discrimination for targeting African Americans with fines and fees.

Protests over police killings have also revealed the lengths to which police go to thwart poor people's efforts to survive on the margins. Police approached Eric Garner in Staten Island while he was selling loose cigarettes; they approached Alton Sterling while he was selling CDs on a sidewalk. Both men were just trying to eke out a living.

THE NEW GENERATION

BLM reflects its generation's experiences with a punitive state. A distrust of public institutions has generated an anti-statist thrust among many activists. Some in the movement do endorse more traditional reforms, but calls to "de-escalate," "defund" and "disarm" pervade BLM discourse, along with even more radical calls for police and prison abolition.

This distrust contrasts with earlier generations of leftists who have tended to see government as a redistributive and progressive force, whether in delivering pensions, clean water, the National Endowment for the Arts, or Medicare. However, for a generation raised in an era of social welfare cuts, regressive taxation, endless war-making, militarized police, and robust prison expansion, an expansive state has been shown to be a menace.

The worldview of BLM's young activists has also been shaped by black, ethnic, gender, and queer studies, as well as their coming-of-age in the era of mass incarceration, neoliberalism, endless wars, and globalization. For them, acknowledging the diversity of black experiences—as much as the quest for black unity—has been a touchstone of their political education. They are attuned to the particular vulnerability of trans folk, for example, to violent policing. Moreover, they are committed to holding up the experiences and perspectives of black women, including queer black women, who are the movement's visionaries and strategists. To some, the term "intersectionality" may seem academic, but BLM leaders have put intersectionality into practice. They've embraced a capacious progressive politics supporting prison abolition, gender justice, immigrant rights, and critiques of capitalism.

A MORE PERFECT UNION

Just as the phrase "Black Power" once inspired white fear, anger and rebuke, "Black Lives Matter" has been criticized and misunderstood from its inception. Former New York City Mayor Rudolph Giuliani and Donald Trump have blamed it for racial discord and violence against police. Such vitriolic rhetoric gives cover to many police departments for their heavy-handed response to BLM marches and demonstrations. In Baton Rouge, after the slaying of Alton Sterling, police forcefully broke up protests and arrested scores of protesters.

At the same time, however, polls show that BLM has won support and respect from many white Americans, even if, as *New York Times* columnist Nicholas Kristof recently concluded, "White America, however well-meaning, is astonishingly oblivious to pervasive inequity."

BLM is helping force a more honest discussion about race in America. The movement against police violence has reactivated an antiracist struggle in American cities, a healthy departure from the fog of "post-racialism" in the early Obama era. Moreover, BLM organizations participate in coalitions with other movements and attract significant multiracial youth support for their actions nationwide. At the recent convention of the American Federation of Teachers in Minneapolis, hundreds of teachers marched behind a large "Teachers4BlackLives" banner to protest the police killing of Philando Castile. The movement is pushing educators, legislators, and activists in allied movements to more forcefully engage the impact of race and racism in U.S. society.

Despite the many challenges ahead and the continuing power of police and politicians to block accountability, BLM has accomplished what no progressive movement has in a long time: it has activated sustained grassroots organizing across the country and provoked a concerted response from those in power. As the crises of neoliberalism continue to unfold and popular dissatisfaction with the major parties persists, we can be sure that BLM will continue to challenge and inspire us with its radical vision.

Contributors

Donnell Alexander is an award-winning writer, editor, film producer, and radio producer.

David Bacon is a writer, photographer, and former union organizer. He is the author of several books, including *The Right to Stay Home: How U.S. Policy Drives Mexican Migration*.

Dean Baker is a contributing editor at *In These Times*. He is the co-founder of Center for Economic and Policy Research and the author of several books, including *Getting Back to Full Employment: A Better Bargain for Working People*.

Jennifer Ball is a former *In These Times* intern and graduate of the Medill School of Journalism, Media, Integrated Marketing Communications at Northwestern University.

Dennis Bernstein is a host of Flashpoints on the Pacifica radio network and the author of *Special Ed: Voices from a Hidden Classroom*.

Martha Biondi is a professor of African American Studies and History at Northwestern University and author, most recently, of *The Black Revolution on Campus*.

Connie Blitt creates short documentary videos and social media campaigns for progressive nonprofits.

Rebecca Burns is an *In These Times* associate editor. She covers labor, housing, and higher education. Her writing has also appeared in *Al Jazeera America*, *Jacobin*, *Truthout*, *AlterNet*, and *Waging Nonviolence*.

Robert B. Carson was a professor of business and economics at SUNY Oneonta. He died in 2015.

Michelle Chen is a contributing editor at *In These Times* and *Dissent* and an editorial fellow at CultureStrike. She is also a co-producer of Asia Pacific Forum on Pacifica's WBAI and *Dissent*'s Belabored podcast.

Noam Chomsky is Institute Professor and Professor of Linguistics (Emeritus) at the Massachusetts Institute of Technology and the author of dozens of books on U.S. foreign policy.

Peter Cole is a Professor of History at Western Illinois University. He is the author of *Wobblies on the Waterfront: Interracial Unionism in Progressive Era Philadelphia*.

Adam Doster is an associate editor at Houstonia, where he writes and edits features. He has written for several publications, including *The Atlantic*, *Sports Illustrated*, *Fast Company*, and the *New York Times*.

Richard B. Du Boff is professor emeritus of economics at Bryn Mawr College and the author of *Accumulation and Power: An Economic History of the United States* (1989), *America's Vietnam Policy: The Strategy of Deception* (1966), and numerous articles in *In These Times*, *Commonweal*, *Challenge*, *Monthly Review*, and other publications

Barbara Ehrenreich is a founding sponsor and a contributing editor at *In These Times*. She is a longtime writer and activist whose many books include *Nickel and Dimed: On (Not) Getting By in America* and, most recently, *Living with a Wild God*. She is the founder of the Economic Hardship Reporting Project.

Ben Ehrenreich is a novelist and freelance journalist. His most recent book is *The Way to the Spring: Life and Death in Palestine*.

Adam Fifield's work has appeared in the *New York Times*, *Washington Post*, *Christian Science Monitor*, and *Philadelphia Inquirer*, where he was a staff writer. He is the author of *A Blessing Over Ashes*. From 2007 to 2013, he served as the deputy director of editorial and creative services at the U.S. Fund for UNICEF.

Leon Fink is Distinguished Professor of History at the University of Illinois at Chicago and editor of the journal *Labor: Studies in Working-Class History of the Americas*.

Bill Fletcher, Jr. is a racial justice, labor, and international activist and author of several books, including *"They're Bankrupting Us!": And 20 Other Myths About Unions*.

Stephen Franklin is a former labor reporter for the *Chicago Tribune* and the author of *Three Strikes: Labor's Heartland Losses and What They Mean for Working Americans* (2002).

David Futrelle is a writer living in Chicago. He blogs at WeHuntedThe Mammoth.com.

Jeremy Gantz, an *In These Times* contributing editor and an executive editor at Imagination Publishing, was on the magazine's staff from 2008 to 2012. He studied U.S. history at Carleton College and journalism at Northwestern University, and was a Fulbright scholar in Sri Lanka.

Mischa Gaus, a former *In These Times* contributing editor, was editor of *Labor Notes*, the largest independent union publication in the United States. He is now staff director for United Food & Commercial Workers Local 2013 in New York City.

Thomas Geoghegan is a Chicago-based labor lawyer. He is the author of more than half a dozen books, including *Which Side Are You On?: Trying*

To Be for Labor When It's Flat on Its Back and, most recently, *Only One Thing Can Save Us: Why America Needs a New Kind of Labor Movement.*

Juan González is co-host of Democracy Now! with Amy Goodman. He was a columnist for *In These Times* and for the *New York Daily News*, and he is the author of several books including *Harvest of Empire: A History of Latinos in America.*

Laura Gottesdiener is a news producer at Democracy Now! The author of *A Dream Foreclosed: Black America and the Fight for a Place to Call Home,* she has written for *Rolling Stone, Mother Jones,* and various other publications.

Alexander Gourse is a student at Stanford Law School. He has a Ph.D. in U.S. history from Northwestern University.

David Graeber, a professor of anthropology at the London School of Economics, is the author, most recently, of *The Utopia of Rules: On Technology, Stupidity, and the Secret Joys of Bureaucracy.* He is also an activist.

Arun Gupta is a founding editor of the *Indypendent* magazine and was a founding editor of the *Occupy Wall Street Journal.* He is the author of the forthcoming *Bacon as Weapon of Mass Destruction: A Junk-Food Loving Chef's Inquiry into Taste.*

Christopher Hayes is a former senior editor of *In These Times.* He hosts the Emmy Award-winning "All In with Chris Hayes" on MSNBC. He is also editor-at-large of *The Nation.*

Beau Hodai is a former *In These Times* staff writer. He is the founder of DBA Press, an online news publication and source materials archive.

Ajowa Nzinga Ifateyo is a member of the Grassroots Economic Organizing collective and has been a staff writer for the *Los Angeles Times, Morning Call,* and *Miami Herald* newspapers. Cooperatives are her passion.

Sarah Jaffe is a former staff writer at *In These Times.* She is the author of *Necessary Trouble: Americans in Revolt* and a fellow at the Nation Institute. Her writings have been published in the *New York Times, The Atlantic, The Nation,* and many other publications. She is co-host of *Dissent* magazine's Belabored podcast.

John Judis is a founding editor of *In These Times.* He is the author of numerous books including *The Emerging Democratic Majority* (with Ruy Teixeira) and *Genesis: Truman, American Jews, and the Origins of the Arab/Israeli Conflict.*

Richard Kazis is a senior consultant at MDRC, Brookings Institute, and Charles A. Dana Center.

Naomi Klein, a former *In These Times* columnist, is an award-winning journalist and author of *This Changes Everything: Capitalism vs. The*

Climate, *The Shock Doctrine: The Rise of Disaster Capitalism*, and *No Logo*. She writes a regular column for *The Nation*, which is syndicated internationally.

David M. Kotz is the Professor of Economics at University of Massachusetts-Amherst and Distinguished Professor of Economics at Shanghai University of Finance and Economics.

Stephen Lerner is a labor strategist. He is a former organizer with Service Employees International Union and was an architect of the Justice for Janitors campaign.

Nelson Lichtenstein is a professor of history at the University of California, Santa Barbara, and directs the Center for the Study of Work, Labor, and Democracy. He is the author or editor of more than a dozen books, including *Walter Reuther: The Most Dangerous Man in Detroit* and *State of the Union: A Century of American Labor*.

Kari Lydersen is a contributing editor at *In These Times*. She is a Chicago-based journalist and the author of five books, including *Mayor 1%: Rahm Emanuel and the Rise of Chicago's 99 Percent*. She is co-director of the Social Justice News Nexus, a reporting fellowship at Northwestern University's Medill School of Journalism.

Manning Marable (1950–2011) was the founding director of the Institute for Research in African American Studies at Columbia University. He was the author of many books, including *How Capitalism Underdeveloped Black America* and *Malcolm X: A Life of Reinvention*.

Daniel Marschall, who was an *In These Times* staff writer in the 1970s, is executive director of the AFL-CIO Working for America Institute. A lecturer in sociology at George Washington University, he is the author of *The Company We Keep: Occupational Community in the High-Tech Network Society*.

David Moberg is a senior editor of *In These Times* and has been on the staff of the magazine since it began publishing in 1976. He has a Ph.D. in anthropology from the University of Chicago.

Salim Muwakkil is a senior editor of *In These Times*, where he has worked since 1983. He is the host of "The Salim Muwakkil Show" on WVON, Chicago's historic black radio station.

Ralph Nader is a consumer advocate, lawyer, and author. His most recent book is *Breaking Through Power: It's Easier Than We Think* (City Lights Open Media).

Zack Nauth is an administrator at SEIU Healthcare IL Benefit Funds.

W. P. Norton is an independent journalist whose publishing credits include *The Progressive* magazine, the *Capital Times*, and the *Moscow Tribune*, where he covered post-Soviet Russia from 1993 to 1995.

Jasson Perez is a former national co-chair of the Black Youth Project 100 and a former organizer for Service Employees International Union Local 73.

Rick Perlstein is the author of *The Invisible Bridge: The Fall of Nixon and the Rise of Reagan*, *Nixonland: The Rise of a President and the Fracturing of America*, and *Before the Storm: Barry Goldwater and the Unmaking of the American Consensus*. His essays and book reviews have been published in *The New Yorker*, the *New York Times*, the *Washington Post*, *The Nation*, the *Village Voice*, and elsewhere. He lives in Chicago.

Frances Fox Piven is Distinguished Professor of political science and sociology at the Graduate Center of the City University of New York. She is the author or co-author of numerous books, including *Poor People's Movements: Why They Succeed, How They Fail*; *Regulating the Poor: The Functions of Public Welfare*; and *Why Americans Don't Vote and Why Politicians Like It That Way*.

Shaun Richman is a contributing writer at *In These Times*. He is a former organizing director at the American Federation of Teachers.

Arundhati Roy is the author of the novel *The God of Small Things*, for which she received the 1997 Booker Prize. The novel has been translated into forty languages worldwide. She has written several nonfiction books, including *Field Notes on Democracy: Listening to Grasshoppers* and *Walking with the Comrades*. She lives in New Delhi.

Bernie Sanders is the junior senator from the state of Vermont and was a Democratic candidate for president in 2016. He was a regular contributor to *In These Times* for many years.

Joseph M. Schwartz is a professor of political science at Temple University. He is a vice-chair of Democratic Socialists of America and the author, most recently, of *The Future of Democratic Equality: Reconstructing Social Solidarity in a Fragmented U.S.*

David Sirota is a former senior editor at *In These Times*. He is the senior editor for investigations at International Business Times and the author of several books including *Back to Our Future: How the 1980s Explains the World We Live in Now—Our Culture, Our Politics, Our Everything*.

Jane Slaughter is a Detroit-based labor journalist and the former editor and director of *Labor Notes*. She is the author of *Concessions and How to Beat Them*.

Joseph Sorrentino is a writer and photographer who has been documenting the lives of agricultural workers on both sides of the U.S./Mexico border for twelve years.

Bhaskar Sunkara is the editor and publisher of *Jacobin* magazine.

Keeanga-Yamahtta Taylor is an assistant professor in the department of

African American Studies at Princeton University. She writes on black politics, social movements, and racial inequality in the United States, and she is the author of *From #BlackLivesMatter to Black Liberation*.

Doug Turetsky joined New York City's Independent Budget Office in January 2001 as communications director, and was appointed chief of staff in 2004. He has also written numerous articles on New York City and related subjects for local and national publications.

Micah Uetricht is a former editor at *In These Times*. He is an associate editor at *Jacobin* and the author of *Strike for America: Chicago Teachers Against Austerity*. He is currently at work on a biography of the late labor dissident Jerry Tucker.

Ian Urbina is a reporter for the *New York Times* and has degrees in history from Georgetown and the University of Chicago. His work ranges from domestic and foreign policy to commentary on everyday life.

Nicholas von Hoffman, a veteran newspaper, radio and TV reporter, and columnist, is the author of several books, including *Radical: A Portrait of Saul Alinsky*.

James Weinstein (1926–2005) was the founding editor and publisher of *In These Times*. A historian, he was the author of four books, the most celebrated of which was *The Corporate Ideal in the Liberal State: 1900–1918*.

Jeffrey A. Winters is a professor of political science at Northwestern University.

Spencer Woodman is a journalist based in New York. He has written on labor for *The Nation* and the *Guardian*.

Slavoj Žižek is a contributing editor at *In These Times*. He is a Slovenian philosopher and psychoanalyst and the international director at the Birkbeck Institute for the Humanities at the University of London. His many books include *Living in the End Times* and *First as Tragedy, Then as Farce*.

Index

1 percent, 1, 43, 45, 46, 86, 215, 217, 219
9/11. *See* September 11
99 percent, 216, 217
2008 crash, 3, 8, 25, 50, 51

ABC, 42, 83–4
Abriel, John A., 102
Abu Dhabi, 100
Abzug, Bella, 35
Acuff, Stewart, 69
Addams, Jane, 142
Adult Protective Services (APS), 137, 138
Afghanistan, 148, 157
African Americans, 2, 3, 54, 74, 112, 115, 116, 124, 129, 171–88, 213, 232
    leaders, 31, 36
Airbnb, 115
Alabama, 11, 166, 176
Alaska, 152, 175
Alexander, Donnell, 172
Ali, Tariq, 156
Alvarez, Anita, 229
Amazon.com, 124
American Bankers Association (ABA), 83
American Civil Liberties Union (ACLU), 102, 103, 159
American Council for Capital Formation (ACCF), 32, 33
American Federation of Labor and Congress of Industrial Organizations (AFL-CIO), 13, 18, 32, 54, 55, 58, 67–9, 70, 73, 190, 191, 195. *See also* Kirkland, Lane

Organizing Institute, 152
American Federation of State, County and Municipal Employees (AFSCME), 69–71, 78
American Federation of Teachers (AFT), 77–8, 224, 233. *See also* Weingarten, Randi
American Friends Service Committee, 164
American Legislative Exchange Council (ALEC), 107–10
American Medical Association, 18
American Motors Corporation (AMC), 15
American Revolution (1776), 68
The American Scholar, 181
Americans for Fairness in Lending (AFFIL), 93, 94
American University, 126
Ameriquest, 90
Amin, Samir, 157
Anderson, Mark, 18
Anderson, Phil, 85, 86
Andersen Consulting, 104
Angus, Candace, 91, 92, 93
Appalachian Mountains, 129
Apple, 115
Arab American, 106
Arab Uprising, 149
Argentina, 74, 158
Arise Chicago Worker Center, 136
Aristotle, 43, 48
Arizona, 159, 160–61
    Phoenix, 166
    SB 1070, 160–61

Army Corps of Engineers, 39–40
Arthur Andersen, 87
Assata's Daughters, 229
Atlantic Ocean, 141
AT&T, 109

Bacon, David, 148, 149
Badger, Rick, 78
Bahrain, 215
Baltimore, 178, 187–8, 227
Bangladesh, 9, 20, 21
Ban Ki-moon, 162
Bank of America, 74, 81, 214
Bapat, Sheila, 136
Bargaining for the Common Good,
    209–10
Barnes, Becca, 200
Bastille Day, 81
Batts, Anthony, 187
Baxter, Russell, 11
Bechtel, 106
Beck, Glenn, 182
Belafonte, Harry, 185–6
Benetton, 20, 21
Bentonville, Arkansas, 72
Berkeley School of Law's East Bay
    Community Law Center, 168
Bernard, Elaine, 75
Bernstein, Dennis, 99
Bernstein, Jared, 112
Bicchieri, Leone José, 131
Binational Front of Indigenous
    Organizations, 164
Biondi, Martha, 173
Black America, 171–88, 227–33
Black Lives Matter, 3, 55, 149, 173, 211,
    227–33
Black Power, 187, 233
BlackRock, 222–3
Black Star Project, 185
Black Youth Project 100 (BYP 100),
    231
Blain, Mike, 125
Blitt, Connie, 99
Bloomberg, Michael, 49, 85
Booth, Paul, 69
Boston, 35, 224
Bové, José, 154–5

Boyer, Richard, 221
Brazil, 74, 78, 86, 154
    Communist Party, 156
    Porto Alegre, 154–5, 156–7
Brenner, Mark, 206
Bretton Woods Agreement (1944), 25
Brewer, Jan, 160
British Petroleum, 113
Brooklyn Blizzards, 185
Brown, Mike, 187, 228, 231–2. See also
    Ferguson, Missouri
Brown, Robert, 128, 129
Brown, Wilford, 11
Brown University, 195
Brunei, 25
Buffalo Beast, 107
Buffet, Warren, 2
Bureau of Labor Statistics, 94, 116,
    132, 133
Burger King, 197
Bush, George H. W., 17, 28, 83, 113,
    178
Bush, George W. See Bush
    administration
Bush administration, 25, 39–42, 46,
    47, 88–8, 99, 105–7, 156–7
Business Roundtable, 32, 46
Butcher, Willard C., 81
Byrne Edsall, Thomas, 35

California, 27, 31, 58, 74, 93, 96, 136,
    152, 195, 201, 208, 210
    Bay Area, 203
    Oakland, 152, 217–19
    Proposition 13 referendum
    (1978), 27, 31
    Richmond, 208, 222, 223
    San Diego, 152, 153
    San Francisco, 136, 208, 219
    Ventura County, 179
    See also Los Angeles
Calver, Andrea, 195
Cambridge University, 150
Campbell Works, 10
Campen, Jim, 93, 94
Campodonico, Ed, 123
Canada, 17, 20, 44, 122–3, 159–60
    Jonquiere, 72

Quebec, 72, 153, 154
Quebec City, 153
Capital One, 91
Capitol Hill. *See* U.S. Congress
Carlton Group, 32
Carlton Hotel, 32
Carr, Oliver, 191
Carrefour, 20
Carrier Corporation, 9
Carter, Jimmy. *See* Carter
    administration
Carter administration, 1, 10, 12, 14, 29,
    30, 31, 34, 35, 61, 95
Castile, Philando, 230, 233
Cayman Islands, 87
CBS News, 225
Cease Fire East New York, 185
Center for Constitutional Rights
    (CCR), 121
Center for Union Facts (CUF), 205,
    206
Center on Budget and Policy
    Priorities, 112
Central America, 103, 168
Central American Free Trade
    Agreement, 7–8, 70–71
Central Americans, 101
Central Michigan University, 195
Chamber of Commerce, 32
Chandler, Marc, 86
Change to Win (CTW), 55, 70, 71, 201
Chaplin, Ralph, 142
Charlottesville, Virginia, 128
Chase Manhattan, 81, 84
Chemical Bank, 84
Chen, Michelle, 9
Cheney, Dick, 105–6
Chesterton, Gilbert Keith, 220
Chiapas, 150–51
Chicago, 16, 17, 32, 74, 91, 100, 105, 120,
    142, 172, 185, 197, 208, 229
    African-Americans, 173–7
    Broadview, 160–61
    cab companies, 117–18
    domestic workers, 136–7
    immigrants, 160–61
    Michigan, Lake, 7
    Park Manor, 90

Pilsen, 160
police, 229, 231
privatization, 112–14
protests, 35, 75, 215, 221
South Side, 7, 9, 186, 200, 220
Chicago Coalition for the Homeless,
    124
Chicago Housing Authority, 114
Chicago New Sanctuary Coalition,
    161
Chicago Public Library, 9
Chicago Teachers Union (CTU), 190,
    197–200, 209–10
Chicago Theological Seminary, 45
Chicago Workers Collaborative
    (CWC), 131
The Children's Place, 20, 21
Chile, 215
China, 8, 25
Chinese workers, 95
Chomsky, Noam, 149
Chrysler Corporation, 7, 15–17, 62
Citigroup, 48
Citizens for Tax Justice, 31
Citizens Trade Campaign, 18
(American) Civil War, 1, 12
Clausen, A. W., 81
Clawson, Dan, 75
Cleveland, Grover, 29
Clinton, Bill. *See* Clinton
    administration
Clinton, Hillary, 25, 29, 180, 228
Clinton administration, 17–19, 22, 25,
    66, 84, 88–9, 95, 113–14, 186
CNN, 24, 137, 154, 179–80
Coalition of Immokalee Workers
    (CIW), 189, 196–7
Coalition on the Academic
    Workforce, 138
Coalition Provisional Authority, 106
Cobble, Steve, 157
Cogswell, Tom, 195
Cold War, 54, 225
Colorado, 181
    Denver, 59, 60
    Loveland, 71
Columbia University, 195
Comcast, 109

Communication Workers of America, 104, 124
Conant, Carl, 60, 61
Congressional Black Caucus, 186
Congress of Industrial Organizations (CIO), 25, 64
Congress on Racial Equality (CORE), 190, 197–9
Connecticut
    Hartford, 177
    Newtown, 184
Consumer Protection Act, 80
Continental Illinois, 81
Cook County, 176, 229. See also Chicago
Coolidge, Calvin, 29
Cooperative Home Care Associates, 208
Cornell University, 75
Corrections Corporation of America, 99, 101–3, 109
    CCA Laredo Service Processing Center, 101
Costa, Daniel, 168–70
Costco, 197
Council 40, 78
Council of Economic Advisers, 132–3
Courtney, Marcus, 124–5
Cowell, Susan, 121
Crowley, James, 182
Curran, Father Brendan, 160
Cuyahoga County, 229

Dale, Jenny, 161
Daley, Richard J., 114, 172
Daley, Richard M., 113, 114
Daley, William, 17
Daniels, Mitch, 40
Davos, Switzerland, 155
Debs, Eugene, 142
Decker, Annie, 152
Declaration of Independence, 34
Deferred Action for Childhood Arrivals (DACA), 167
Delaware, 92
Delaware American Civil Liberties Union, 126
Delphi, 216

Democracy for America, 73
Democratic National Convention, 23
Democratic Party, 17, 29–31, 35, 75, 113, 188, 224, 227
Demos, 94, 133
Denmark, 100
Denver Post, 41
Depository Institutions Deregulation and Monetary Control Act (1980), 81
Detroit, 106, 214, 215, 216
Deutsche Banks Securities, 86
Dhaka, Bangladesh, 20
Dignity Campaign, 164
Disney, 168
District of Columbia. See Washington, D.C.
Dodd-Frank Wall Street Reform, 80
Dodger Stadium, 223
Domestic Workers United, 159
Donovan, Daniel, 229
Douglass, Frederick, 173
Dream 9, 165–6
DREAM Act, 149, 165
Dreamer movement, 55
DRUM-South Asian Workers Center, 163
Du Boff, Richard, 28
Duncan, Arne, 198
Dunkin Donuts, 204
Duquesne University, 137
Dylan, Bob, 210

East Asia, 120
Eatwell, John, 150
Economic Policy Institute, 19, 168
Economic Recovery Tax Act (1981), 32n2
Edwards, Jerry, 216
Egypt, 78, 213, 215
Ehrenreich, Barbara, 138
Ehrenreich, John, 138, 148
Eidelson, Josh, 205
Electronic Data Systems, 104
El Salvador, 191
Emancipation Proclamation, 180
Emanuel, Rahm, 112–13, 197
English Channel, 141

Enron, 79, 87–8
environmental protection, 18, 19
Epton, Bernard, 174–5
Equal Rights Amendment, 28, 56
Etowah County Detention Center, 166
Europe, 13, 25, 99–100, 121–2, 123,
    141–2, 213
    protests, 155, 156, 158
    refugees, 168, 169
European Social Forum, 157
European Union, 142, 167, 169
Exxon Mobil, 109
Exxon Valdez oil spill, 83

Facebook, 226
Fair Labor Standards Act (1938), 136
Fairley, Kimberla, 106
fair trade, 152
Federal Aviation Administration
    (FAA), 60
Federal Deposit Insurance
    Corporation (FDIC), 81
Federal Reserve. See U.S. Federal
    Reserve
FedEx, 53, 194
Ferguson, Missouri, 187–8, 231–2. See
    also Brown, Mike
Ferreti Manjarrez, Gwendolyn, 166
Fiasco, Lupe, 185
Fifield, Adam, 99
Fight for 15, 55, 190, 202–6, 209, 210
Financial Times, 41, 151
Fine, Janice, 206
Fink, Laurence, 222
Fink, Leon, 9
Fireman Hospitality Group, 206
Florida, 126, 189–90, 196
Footman, Alexander, 127
Ford, 53, 216
Fortune, Stan, 72–3
Fox Entertainment Group, 127
Fox News, 50, 182, 184–5
Fox Piven, Frances, 28
Fox Searchlight, 127
Foxx, Kim, 230
France, 20, 74, 154, 162
Francis, Pope, 100
Franklin, Benjamin, 142

Freedman, Henry, 104–5
Freelancers Union, 117
Freeland, Gene, 104
Free Trade Area of the Americas
    (FTAA), 153, 156
French Revolution, 81, 141
Friedan, Betty, 35
Friedman, Milton, 28, 45–6, 47, 123
Futrelle, David, 28

Gallup, Amber, 195
Gallup, 29
Galt, John, 51
Gandhi, Mahatma, 142
The Gap, 153
Garcia, José, 94
Garment Industry Development
    Corporation, 121
Garner, Eric, 229, 232
Garza, Alicia, 227
Gates, Bill, 43, 226
General Accounting Office, 83
General Motors, 62
Geoghegan, Thomas, 28, 209–10
Georgetown University, 225, 226
Georgia (US), 30, 133
Gerard, Leo, 78
Germany, 20, 44, 113
Gibson, William, 115
Giroux, Henry, 182
Giuliani, Rudolph, 233
Glass-Steagall Act (1934), 85, 95
Glatt, Eric, 127
Global South, 21, 24, 148, 167, 190
Global South Asian Migrant Workers
    Alliance, 163
Global Workers Justice Alliance, 164
Glock, 133
GNP (gross national product), 119
Goldman, Debbie, 104
Goldwater, Barry, 113
Gomez, Alfredo, 134
Gonzales, John, 101
Google news, 141
GOP. See Republican Party
Gordon Nembhard, Jessica, 207–9
Gorobegko, Donald, 9
Göteborg University, 141

Graeber, David, 149
Graff, Julia, 126
Gray, Freddie, 187–8, 227
Great Depression, 66, 74, 79, 80, 81, 85
Great Lakes, 216
Great Recession, 55, 74, 80, 112
Greece, 43, 215, 219
Green Bay Packers, 68
Green Party, 208
Greenspan, Alan, 46, 51
GSV Advisors, 113
GSV Capital, 113
Guardian, 231
Guatemala, 67, 191
Guevara, Che, 155
Guinen, Mary Beth, 56
Guizot, François, 43
Gulf Coast, 39
Gutekanst, Norrine, 200
Gutierrez, Luis, 161
Guyette, Jim, 65

Halliburton, 105–7
Halliburton KBR Small Business Liaison, 106
Hammer, R. K., 93
Harrison, Bennett, 67
Harrison, Gary, 65–6
Hartmarx, 74
Hartz, Louis, 37
Harvard janitors, 195
Harvard Trade Union Program, 75
Harvard University, 80, 122, 176, 182, 194, 195
Hassanien, Sal, 106, 107
Hatton, Erin, 132–3
Hawaii, 136
Hayes, Christopher, 2, 55, 99
Hearst, 127
Henwood, Doug, 86
High-level Dialogue on Migration and Development, 163
Hillberg, George, 64
Hispanics, 31, 91, 120–21, 174, 175. *See also* Latinas/Latinos
Hodai, Beau, 99
Holden, Dominic, 224

Home Defenders League, 222, 223
Homestead Resort, 83–4
Hong Kong, 85, 86
Hooper, Thomas, 174, 175
Hormel (Geo. A. Hormel & Co.), 54, 64, 66
Horowitz, Sara, 117
Hotel and Restaurant Employees (HERE), 192, 195, 209–10
House Banking Committee, 83–4
House Ways and Means Committee. *See* U.S. House Committee on Ways and Means
Houston, Jeannie, 106
Houston Chronicle, 40
Hughes, Patrick, 101
Hurd, Richard, 75
Hyatt hotel chain, 199
Hyde Park, 199

Iacocca, Lee, 15, 16, 17. *See also* Chrysler Corporation
Ibañez, Reynaldo Ríos, 202
Idaho, 175
Illinois, 22, 74, 160, 180, 201, 210
Galesburg, 7, 22, 23
Immigration and Naturalization Service (INS), 101–3, 154
Immigration Reform and Control Act (1986), 121
Impact Logistics, 201
India, 150–51, 157, 158
Indiana, 23, 55, 77
Gary, 171–2
Indianapolis, 9
Indonesia, 86
Industrial Workers of the World, 142
Institute for Policy Studies, 157
Inter-American Commission on Human Rights, 159
Inter-American Development Bank, 18
International Convention on the Protection of the Rights of All Migrant Workers and Members of Their Families, 159
International Ladies' Garment Workers' Union (ILGWU), 121

International Longshore and
    Warehouse Union, 203
International Migrants Alliance
    (IMA), 163–4
International Monetary Fund (IMF),
    25, 155, 157
International Trade Commission, 12
International Trade Organization
    (ITO), 25
In the Public Interest (ITPI), 111, 112
Iowa, 180
Iraq, 55, 99, 105–7, 156–7, 158, 171–2
Iraq war, 55, 105–7, 148, 156–7
Ireland, 221
Irving, Duane, 10
Islamic State, 169
Italy, 157, 162

Jackson, Rev. Jesse, 74, 172, 175–7, 180,
    186
Jakubek, Ania, 136–7
Japan, 14
Jeep, 15
Jefferson, Thomas, 44
Jesus Christ, 27
Jewler, Sam, 217
Jim Crow, 2, 181, 187
Jiménez, Antonio, 135
Joe Fresh, 20, 21
John Jay College, 207
Johnson, Charles, 181
Johnson, Lyndon B., 226
Jontz, Jim, 18
Joseph, Karen, 216
Journal of Economic Perspectives, 113
JP Morgan, 214
Judis, John, 8, 27
Justice for Janitors, 189, 191–3

Kahle, Trish, 203
Kamenetz, Anya, 125
Kamiya, Marla, 121
Kansas, 107
Kasich, John, 77, 117
Katrina, Hurricane, 28, 39, 41–2, 159
Katula, Mike, 11–12
Kaufman, Henry, 82
Kaufman, Los Angeles, 216

Kauser Capital LLC, 85–6
Kelley, Maryellen R., 67
Kelly Services (formerly Kelly Girl
    Service), 132
Kemp, Jack, 31, 32
Kennedy, Robert Francis, 30
Kettering Sr., Chuck, 216
Keynes, John Maynard, 88
Kildee, Dale, 58
Kilson, Martin, 176
King, Martin Luther, 173, 174, 182, 231
King, Rodney, 172, 178
Kirkland, Lane, 32. *See also* AFL-CIO
Klein, Naomi, 148
Knewton, 113
Knox College, 23
Koch, Charles, 107
Koch, David, 107
Koch Industries, 107, 109
Kofinis, Chris, 72
Korea, 86
Kovalik, Daniel, 137
Kristof, Nicholas, 233
Kuwait, 105, 107

Labor Day, 121
Labor Notes, 206
Lahore, 141
Lake Pontchartrain, 41
Lal, Prerna, 168–70
Landless Peasants Movement, 154–5
Langlois, Marilyn, 208
Latin America, 120, 156
Latinas/Latinos, 74, 116, 173, 186, 216.
    See also Hispanics
Lee, John, 168
Lee, Thea, 19
Leeds, 141
less-than-truckload shipments (LTL),
    63
#LetUsBreathe Collective, 231
Levin, Andy, 73
Levinson, Jerome, 18
Lewis, John, 180
Lewis, Karen, 197–8, 209
Lexus, 67
Liberty Park, 215, 216, 217
Lichtenstein, Nelson, 69

Liedman, Sven-Eric, 141
Light, Paul, 111
Limbaugh, Rush, 182
Lincoln, Abraham, 37, 44
Linder, Marc, 68
Lively, William, 58
Lockheed Martin Corp., 99, 103–5
Lockheed Martin Information
    Management Systems, 104–5
Logan, Tracy, 131, 132
Loma, Mira, 201–2
Long, Fred, 58, 59
Long-Term Capital Management, 86
Los Angeles, 35, 103, 120, 172, 178–80,
    214, 223. See also California
Louisiana, 40, 41
    Baton Rouge, 230, 233
    Jena, 173
    New Orleans, 10, 28, 39–42
    See also Katrina, Hurricane
Luskin, Matt, 199
Lykes Corp., 10, 11–12
Lynch, Loretta, 187, 188

M-15 movement, 221
Machado, Bob, 194
MacNeil-Lehrer Newshour, 66
Maestri, Walter, 41
Mahoning Valley Organizing
    Collaborative, 96
Maine, 175
Malaysia, 25, 86
Mango, 20
Manning, Caitlin, 217
Manning, Robert, 92
Man Up!, 185
maquiladora factories, 18
Marable, Manning, 27
March on Washington (1963), 184
Marine Corps, 101
Marlboro, 15
Marshall, Carol, 22
Martin, Trayvon, 227–8
Martínez Sánchez, María, 135
Marx, Karl, 38
Mason-Dixon line, 69
Massachusetts, 49, 136, 208
    Cambridge, 182, 183

Master Lock, 8
Mateo, Lizbeth, 165–6
Maternal and Child Health Program,
    36
Maulik, Monami, 163
Maytag, 22–3
McAlevey, Jane, 203
McBride, Lloyd, 11
McCain, John, 166
McCray, Betty, 131, 133
McDonald, Laquan, 229, 230
McDonald's, 38, 53, 154, 190, 196–7,
    229
McGinty, Tim, 229
McGovern, George, 30
McGuigan, Tim, 101–3
McIntyre, Robert, 31
McLaughlin, Gayle, 208
Medicaid, 103, 104, 111
Medicare, 232
Medicare for All, 226
Melnick, Herbert, 58, 59
Meriwether, John W., 86
Mexican American workers, 68, 153,
    198
Mexico, 9, 17, 18, 19, 22, 23, 134, 151,
    159–60, 162–3, 165
    Mexico City, 160
    Oaxaca, 164
    Tijuana, 153
Michigan, 55
    Detroit, 106, 214, 215, 216
    Flint, 28
    Grand Rapids, 110
    Madison Heights, 193
    Pontiac, 62, 193
    Ypsilanti, 216
Microsoft, 53, 123–5, 226
MidAmerican Building Services, 112
Middle East, 163, 219
Midwest Center for Labor Research,
    16
military-industrial complex, 45–6
Milligan, Candice, 216
Million Hoodies, 231
Milton Friedman Institute, 45, 46
Milwaukee County Courthouse, 112
Minimum Wage Act, 139

Minnesota, 54, 64–6, 175, 210, 224, 230
    Minneapolis, 221, 224, 227, 233
Minnesota State Council, 224
Minor, Mandy, 126
Mississippi, 39, 132, 133
Mississippi River, 41
Missouri, 77
    Ferguson, 187–8, 231–2
    Saint Louis, 187, 227
Moberg, David, 7, 28, 54, 55
Modern Management, Inc., 58
Moneta, 128, 129
Monsanto, 155
Moore, Ty, 224
Morais, Herbert, 221
Muehlenkamp, Robert, 58, 59
Myers, Bobby, 130
Myerson, Jesse, 217

Nash Motors plant, 15
National Alliance For Fair
    Employment (NAFFE), 124
National Assets Management Agency,
    221
National Association for the
    Advancement of Colored People
    (NAACP), 183, 185
National Association of Colleges and
    Employers, 127
National Association of
    Manufacturers, 32
National Council of La Raza (NCLR),
    167
National Day Laborer Organizing
    Network, 206
National Domestic Workers Alliance,
    136, 206
National Education Association, 61
National Employment Law Project,
    130
National Endowment for the Arts, 232
National Guestworker Alliance, 139,
    206
national health insurance, 122–3
National Labor Relations Act (1935),
    67
National Labor Relations Board
    (NLRB), 1, 73, 118, 192, 201, 206

National Moratorium on Prison
    Construction (NMPC), 102
National Network for Immigrant and
    Refugee Rights, 168
National People's Action, 214
National Union of Hospital and
    Health Care Employees, 58
National Urban League, 171
Native Americans, 216
Nebraska, 181
Nelson, Erin, 23
Neuwirth, Robert, 221
New Deal, 43, 84–5, 113, 115, 214
New Era Windows Cooperative
    (formerly Republic Windows and
    Doors), 208
New Mexico, 134–6
New Mexico Center on Law &
    Poverty (NMCLP), 135
New Orleans, 10, 41, 39–42
    Katrina, Hurricane, 28, 39, 41–2,
    159
    levees, 39, 41–2
    Pontchartrain, Lake, 41
New Politics Institute, 127
New School, 215
Newsweek, 47
New York, 31, 59, 74, 159, 208
    Albany, 214
    Buffalo, 153
    Rochester, 215
    Syracuse, 50
New York City, 35, 49, 85, 120–21, 136,
    159, 163–4, 205–6, 207, 212, 221
    Bronx, 208
    Brooklyn, 207
    Brooklyn Bridge, 163
    Harlem, 129
    Lower East Side, 221
    Manhattan, 85, 104, 127, 163, 215,
    222
    Park Avenue, 85
    Queens, 67, 222, 223
    Staten Island, 229, 232
New York Communities for Change
    (NYCC), 222
New York State Department of Labor,
    120

New York Taxi Workers Alliance, 190,
205–6
New York Times, 29, 127, 137, 171, 225,
233
New York University, 111, 195
Nike, 8, 153
Nissan, 131–3
Nixon, Richard. See Nixon
administration
Nixon administration, 27, 30–31, 182.
See also Watergate
Nobel Prize, 45
Noble, Josh, 71–2
Norquist, Grover, 225
North American Free Trade
Agreement (NAFTA), 7–8, 17, 18,
19, 22–5, 69, 149, 150, 153, 162, 216
Northeastern Illinois University,
176–7
Nygaard, Ingrid, 68

Obama, Barack. See Obama
administration
Obama administration, 8, 22, 23–4,
25, 50, 55, 74, 76, 113, 162, 216
African Americans, 180–83,
188, 233
deportations, 147, 166–7
economic crisis, 94–5, 129
senator, 114, 172–3
Occupy movement, 1, 3, 55, 147, 211,
215–20, 221
Occupy Wall Street (OWS), 202–3,
215, 217–18, 219–20
O'Hare Airport, 105
Ohio, 10–12, 77–8, 117, 179, 210
Campbell, 10–12
Cleveland, 229
Mahoning River Valley, 10
Struthers, 10
Toledo, 216
Youngstown, 7, 10–12, 95–7, 216
Old Style beer, 16
Olin Wright, Erik, 38
Olney, Peter, 203
O'Neil, Maureen, 95–7
OpenBorders, 168
Opinion Research Corporation, 29

Orchestrated Pulse, 227
Oregon, 210
O'Reilly, Bill, 185
Organization for Black Struggle, 227
Orwell, George, 44
OUR Walmart, 206
Outten & Golden, 127
Owada, Helen, 174–5
Oxford English Dictionary, 141

Pacific Lumber Company, 152
Pacific Rim, 22
Paff, Ken, 63
paid holidays,
Panzer, Leonard, 85
Parish, Jefferson, 41
Parker, Mike, 39, 40, 42
Parks, Rosa, 74
Parsons, 106
Paulson, Henry, 46
PBS (Public Broadcasting System), 50
Pennsylvania, 7, 35, 137, 166, 183
Peoples' Global Action on Migration
(PGA), 163, 164
Perez, Thomas, 205
Perkins, Julia, 197
Perlstein, Rick, 100
Perot, Ross, 22, 49
Petsin, Robert, 15–16
Pfizer Pharmaceuticals, 109
Philadelphia, 35, 166, 183, 215
Philippines, 162
Phillip Morris International, 109
PIMCO, 223
Pittsburgh, 137, 191, 215
Pittsburgh-Post Gazette, 137
Pitzer College, 195
Plan for Transformation, 114
Plato, 49
Poland, 136–7
PostMates, 115
precariat, 115–17, 139
prison-industrial complex, 185
Pritzker, Penny, 112–13, 199
Proactive Chicago Teachers (PACT),
198
Professional Air Traffic Controllers'
Union (PATCO), 54, 59–60, 61

professoriat, 138
Project Orange Tree, 185
Public-Private Fair Competition Act,
   109
Puerto Rico, 215

Quazzo, Deborah H., 113

Ragan, Andy, 11
Rainbow Grocery, 208
Rainbow PUSH Coalition, 186
Rambeau, Dave, 60
Rambler, 15
Rameau, Max, 221–2
Rana Plaza, 20–21
Rand, Ayn, 51
Raser, Tess, 229–30
Rawlings-Blake, Stephanie, 187–8
RCA, 53
Rea, Patrick, 106
Reagan administration, 16, 27–9, 31–5,
   66, 83, 95, 103, 125, 172
   air traffic controllers, 54, 60–61
Refugee Legal Services, 101
Reich, Robert, 19, 20, 66, 67
Rental Assistance Demonstration
   Program, 114
Republican Party, 35, 54, 110, 233
Republic Windows and Doors, 74–6,
   215. See also New Era Windows
   Cooperative
Restaurant Opportunities Center
   United (ROC), 205, 206
Reuters, 113
Reyes, Teófilo, 206
Rice, Tamir, 229, 230
Rich, Matt, 85
Richards, Shirley, 10
Richman, Shaun, 191
Richmond Worker Cooperative
   Revolving Loan Fund, 208
Rio Grande Valley, 101
Robert Fulton Elementary, 199
Robert Taylor Homes, 173–4
Robinson, Eugene, 183
Rochester Institute of Technology,
   92
Rogers, Jamala, 227

Rogers-Premier Unloading Services,
   201–2
Rolls Royce, 113
Romney, Mitt, 48–9
Rook, Susan, 180
Roosevelt, Franklin Delano (FDR),
   44, 66, 226
Rosario, Angelica, 136
Roseboro, Skipp, 222
Rostenkowski, Dan, 27, 32, 33
Rousseau, Jean-Jacques, 43
Roy, Arundhati, 148
Royal Canadian Mounted Police, 153
Ruckelshaus, Catherine, 130
Russia, 61, 86
Rutgers University, 206

Saia, Justin, 131–2
Saint Louis, Missouri, 187, 227
Salazar, Daniela, 207
Salomon Brothers, 82
Sanders, Bernie, 3, 9, 28, 100, 167, 212,
   225–7, 230
San Francisco, 136, 208, 219
Sassine, Jean, 222, 223
Save Our Streets, 185
Savings & Loans, 79, 83, 95
Sawant, Kshama, 212, 223–5
Sawyer, Diane, 42
Saxon Perry, Carrie, 177–8
Schenburn, Angela, 193
Schmoke, Kurt, 178
Schneider Logistics, 201–2
Schor, Juliet, 122, 123
Schwartz, Joseph M., 212
SCO Family of Services' Center for
   Family Life, 207
Scott, Walter, 230
Seattle, 123–5, 151, 158, 215, 224
Seattle City Council, 224
Second World War, 11, 12, 24, 75, 119
Seeger, Pete, 50
Sellers, Sean, 197
Selma, Alabama, 176
Senate Banking Committee, 83
Sennet, Richard, 44
Sensenbrenner, Jim, 161
September 11 148, 156

Service Employees International Union (SEIU), 56–7, 59, 71, 73, 189, 190–92, 195, 203–5, 224
Sewell, Jesse, 17
Sharkey, Jesse, 209
Shenandoah Valley, 129
Shibata, Kenzo, 200
Shrum, Robert, 29
Sierra Club, 73
Silicon Valley, 36, 115
da Silva, Luiz Inacio Lula, 156
Simes, Jerry, 65
Sirota, David, 28
Sí Se Puede, 207
Small Business Administration, 105
Smith, Adam, 31
Smith, Geoff, 91
Smith, Tene, 220, 221
Socialist Alternative, 224
Socialist Party of America, 224
Social Security, 41, 126
Sodexho, 194
solidarity, 2, 60, 141–3, 148–9
Solis, Hilda, 129
Soni, Saket, 139
Soros, George, 43, 86
Soto, Matías, 134–5
South Africa, 149, 158
South Asia, 163
South Carolina, 175
South Dakota, 92
Southeast Asian workers, 95
Southeast Louisiana Flood Control, 41
South Korea, 14
Spain, 20, 215, 219, 221
    Guadalajara, 160
Sparrow, Mary, 112
Standard and Poor's, 63
Stapleton airport, 59, 60
Starks, Robert, 176–7
Star Valley Painting Contractors Inc., 128
State Public Interest Research Groups, 126
State University of New York at Buffalo, 132
Stedile, Joao Pedro, 154
Steinem, Gloria, 35

Stephens, R.L., 227
Sterling, Alton, 230, 232, 233
The Stranger (newspaper), 224
Student Farmworker Alliance, 197
Subway, 204
Suffolk University Law School, 128
Summit of the Americas, 153
Swarthout, Luke, 126
Sweden, 44, 141
Sweeney, John, 67, 70, 71, 195
Sylvia, Alicia, 72
Syria, 168, 215

Taco Bell, 194, 196
Tactaquin, Catherine, 168–70
Tafoya, Fernando, 102–3
Taft-Hartley Act (1947), 115–16
Taiwan, 13, 14
Take Back the Land, 215, 221–2
Target, 8
TaskRabbits, 115
Taylor, Keeanga-Yamahtta, 173
Teamsters, 54, 63, 190, 193–4
Teamsters for a Democratic Union, 63, 194
Teamsters United Rank and File,
Tea Party, 50, 162, 216, 217
Tennessee, 102, 131, 133–4
Tennessee Valley Authority (TVA), 113
Tex, 20
Texas, 104, 159
    Dallas, 67–8
    El Paso, 120
    Houston, 179
    Jacksonville, 72
    Laredo, 101
    Weatherford, 73
Texas Integrated Enrollment Service, 104
Texas Workforce Commission, 104
Thailand, 86
Thatcher, Margaret, 113
Third Reich, 113
Thompson, Tommy G., 16, 17
Thompson, Yolanda, 200
Thornberry, Matthew, 133
Time, 47
The Times of India, 223

Times-Picayune, 41
Time Warner Cable, 109
Tobin tax, 155
Tocqueville, Alexis de, 43
Trade Adjustment Assistance, 8
Trans-Pacific Partnership (TPP), 8, 22, 23, 25
Traub, Amy, 133
Triangle Shirtwaist Company fire, 120
Truman, Harry, 25
Trump, Donald, 9, 25, 44, 167, 233
Tubman, Harriet, 173
Tunisia, 215
Turner, Juno, 127

Uber, 115–17
United Automobile Workers (UAW), 13, 17, 53, 54, 62, 63, 214
  Locals Opposed to Concessions, 62
United Food and Commercial Workers (UFCW), 64, 65, 71–3
United Kingdom, 24, 113, 219
United Nations, 159, 162
United Progressive Caucus (UPC), 198
United Steelworkers (USW), 10, 11, 78, 137
UNITE HERE, 71
University of California, 168
University of California, Merced, 168
University of California, Santa Barbara, 69
University of Chicago, 28, 45
University of Illinois-Chicago, 136
University of Iowa, 208
University of Maryland, 127
University of Massachusetts, 75
University of South Florida, 126
University of Wisconsin, 76, 208
Unzueta, Tania, 160
UPS (United Postal Service), 190, 193–4
U.S. Army, 105
U.S. Border Patrol, 101, 153–4
U.S. Chamber of Commerce, 46
U.S. Congress, 17, 18, 22, 25, 31, 40, 43, 46, 58, 60, 85

deregulation, 83, 84–5, 92
  Katrina, Hurricane, 41
  migration, 163, 167
U.S. Constitution, 100
U.S. Customs Court, 14
U.S. Department of Commerce, 113
U.S. Department of Homeland Security, 183
U.S. Department of Justice, 99, 167, 232
U.S. Department of Labor, 129
U.S. Federal Reserve, 31, 46, 80, 86
U.S. Federation of Worker Cooperatives, 208
U.S. Government Accountability Office (GAO), 116
U.S. House Committee on Ways and Means, 13, 31, 32
U.S. House Subcommittee on Labor-Management Relations, 58
U.S. Immigration and Naturalization Service (INS),
U.S. Senate, 31, 46, 80
U.S. Steel, 7, 216
U.S. Supreme Court, 92, 126, 184
U.S. Treasury, 46, 214

Valdes, Pilar, 151
Vanaik, Achin, 157
Van Buren, Anthony M., 128–30
Verizon, 109
Vermont, 153
Vietnam, 25
Vietnam War, 30, 54, 60, 151, 157
Violent Crime and Law Enforcement Act, 186
Virginia, 83, 128–30
Vitter, David, 40
Voces de la Frontera (VDLF), 206
Vojtko, Margaret Mary, 137–8
Voltaire, 43
Voting Rights Act (1965), 171, 184

Wagner Labor Relations Act, 61–2, 73
Wahlberg, Natalie, 217
WakeUpWalMart.com, 73
Walker, Betty and Tyrone, 90

Walker, Scott, 55, 76–8, 107
Walls, Kim, 199
Wall Street, 46, 47, 50, 80, 85, 154, 214
Wall Street Journal, 93, 205
Walmart, 20, 53, 55, 72–3, 109, 148, 197, 201–6
    Tire and Lube Express, 71
Walmart: The High Cost of Low Price, 71
war against the poor, 33–4
Warehouse Workers United (WWU), 201–2
war on drugs, 3, 173, 178, 181, 186
War on Terror, 148, 163
Washington, Harold, 172, 174–5, 176
Washington Alliance of Technology Workers (WashTech), 123–5
Washington, D.C., 41, 191–3, 214, 216
    Pennsylvania Avenue, 191
Washington Post, 42, 183
Washington Software Alliance, 124
Washington State, 123–5, 139, 153, 210
    Seattle, 123–5, 151, 158, 215
Washington Times, 40
Washington University, 181
Watergate, 30, 31. See also Nixon administration
wealth defense industry (WDI), 28, 49
Weinbaum, Eve, 75
Weinberg, Hedy, 102–3
Weingarten, Randi, 77–8. See also American Federation of Teachers
Weinstein, James, 1, 3
Weiss, Ted, 59
Welfare Law Center, 104–5
Wells Fargo, 74, 223
West Coast Industrial Relations (WCIR), 58–9
West Germany, 14
West Virginia, 55, 61
Whelan, Seamus, 224
White House, 19, 34, 39, 40, 161, 184
Whole Foods, 197, 203, 204
Wilhelm, John, 71

Wilson, Darren, 231. See also Ferguson, Missouri
Wilson, Woodrow, 31
Winters, Jeffrey, 28
Wisconsin, 55, 77, 107, 112, 210, 211, 213, 215
    Kenosha, 14, 16, 17
    Madison, 76
    Milwaukee, 112, 191, 206
Wisconsin Act 10, 78
Wisconsin Farmers Union, 211
Wolin, Sheldon, 76
Women, Infants and Children Feeding Program, 36
Woods, Paul, 76–7
Woodstock Institute, 91
Woodview Hospital, 58
Worker Rights Consortium, 196
Workers Organizing Committee of Chicago, 203
Working America, 206
World Bank, 25
World Social Forum, 148, 154–5, 156–7
World Trade Organization, 148, 151, 215
Wright, Rev. Jeremiah, 183
Wynn, William, 65

Ya Basta!, 153
Yale University, 195
Yamada, David, 128
Yates Services, 131
Yellow Cab Co., 118
Yeltsin, Boris, 86
Youngstown Sheet and Tube Co. See Campbell Works
YouTube, 9

Zakaria, Fareed, 24
Zapata, Wilfredo, 120
Zapatistas, 150
Zenith, 13
Zimmerman, George, 173, 184–5
Zuccotti Park, 215
Zuckerberg, Mark, 226
Zylinska, Magdalena, 137